KU-266-790

Human Resource Management in Higher and Further Education

SRHE and Open University Press Imprint
General Editor: Heather Eggins

Current titles include:

Ronald Barnett: *Improving Higher Education*
Ronald Barnett: *Learning to Effect*
Ronald Barnett: *Limits of Competence*
Ronald Barnett: *The Idea of Higher Education*
Tony Becher: *Governments and Professional Education*
Robert Bell and Malcolm Tight: *Open Universities: A British Tradition?*
Hazel Bines and David Watson: *Developing Professional Education*
Jean Bocock and David Watson: *Managing the Curriculum*
David Boud *et al.*: *Using Experience for Learning*
Angela Brew: *Directions in Staff Development*
John Earwaker: *Helping and Supporting Students*
Roger Ellis: *Quality Assurance for University Teaching*
Gavin J. Fairbairn and Christopher Winch: *Reading, Writing and Reasoning: A Guide for Students*
Shirley Fisher: *Stress in Academic Life*
Diana Green: *What is Quality in Higher Education?*
Sinclair Goodlad: *The Quest for Quality*
Susanne Haselgrove: *The Student Experience*
Jill Johnes and Jim Taylor: *Performance Indicators in Higher Education*
Ian McNay: *Visions of Post-compulsory Education*
Robin Middlehurst: *Leading Academics*
Henry Miller: *The Management of Change in Universities*
Jennifer Nias: *The Human Nature of Learning: Selections from the Work of M. L. J. Abercrombie*
Keith Noble: *Changing Doctoral Degrees*
Gillian Pascall and Roger Cox: *Women Returning to Higher Education*
Graham Peeke: *Mission and Change*
Moira Peelo: *Helping Students with Study Problems*
Kjell Raaheim *et al.*: *Helping Students to Learn*
Tom Schuller: *The Future of Higher Education*
Michael Shattock: *The UGC and the Management of British Universities*
John Smyth: *Academic Work*
Geoffrey Squires: *First Degree*
Ted Tapper and Brian Salter: *Oxford, Cambridge and the Changing Idea of the University*
Kim Thomas: *Gender and Subject in Higher Education*
Malcolm Tight: *Higher Education: A Part-time Perspective*
David Warner and Elaine Crosthwaite: *Human Resource Management in Higher and Further Education*
David Warner and Gordon Kelly: *Managing Educational Property*
David Warner and Charles Leonard: *The Income Generation Handbook*
Sue Wheeler and Jan Birtle: *A Handbook for Personal Tutors*
Thomas G. Whiston and Roger L. Geiger: *Research and Higher Education*
Gareth Williams: *Changing Patterns of Finance in Higher Education*
John Wyatt: *Commitment to Higher Education*

Human Resource Management in Higher and Further Education

Edited by
David Warner and
Elaine Crosthwaite

The Society for Research into Higher Education
& Open University Press

Published by SRHE and
Open University Press
Celtic Court
22 Ballmoor
Buckingham
MK18 1XW

First Published 1995

Copyright © The Editors and Contributors 1995

All rights reserved. Except for the quotation of short passages for the purposes of criticism and review, no part of this publication may be reproduced, stored in a retrieval system or transmitted, in any form or by any means, electronic, mechanical, photocopying, recording or otherwise, without the prior written permission of the publisher or a licence from the Copyright Licensing Agency Limited. Details of such licences (for reprographic reproduction) may be obtained from the Copyright Licensing Agency Ltd of 90 Tottenham Court Road, London, W1P 9HE.

A catalogue record of this book is available from the British Library

ISBN 0 335 19377 3 (pb) 0 335 19378 1 (hb)

Library of Congress Cataloging-in-Publication Data
Human resource management in higher and further education / edited by
   David Warner and Elaine Crosthwaite.
      p.   cm.
   Includes bibliographical references and index.
   ISBN 0-335-19378-1 (hb) ISBN 0-335-19377-3 (pbk.)
      1. College personnel management—Great Britain.   2. Universities
   and colleges—Great Britain—Administration.   I. Warner, David,
   1947- .   II. Crosthwaite, Elaine, 1952- .
   LB2331.685.07H86   1995
   378.1'1'0941—dc20   94-33900
                                                                  CIP

Typeset by Graphicraft Typesetters Ltd, Hong Kong
Printed in Great Britain by St Edmundsbury Press Ltd
Bury St Edmunds, Suffolk

Contents

Contributors   vii

Foreword by Peter Knight   xi

Selected Abbreviations   xiii

1 Setting the Scene   I
   Elaine Crosthwaite and David Warner

2 Managing Change   7
   David House and David Watson

3 Developing a Human Resource Strategy   20
   Elizabeth Lanchbery

4 Managing Diversity   32
   Rebecca Nestor

5 The Learning Organization   44
   Jennifer Tann

6 Effective Communication   56
   Jo Andrews

7 Managing and Rewarding Performance   70
   David Bright and Bill Williamson

8 Executive Recruitment   86
   Diana Ellis

9 Essential Employment Law   94
   Geoffrey Mead

10 Making Educational Institutions Safer and Healthier   118
   Patricia Leighton

11 Developing Managers   134
   Elizabeth Walker

12 Industrial Relations Strategies and Tactics   152
Roger Ward

13 Managing Information   171
John McManus and Emily Crowley

Bibliography   184

Index   191

The Society for Research into Higher Education   199

Contributors

The views expressed in this book are those of each contributor and are not necessarily those of his or her employer.

Jo Andrews is Director of the National Employee Communication Centre which is based in the Business School at the University of Central England in Birmingham. The bulk of her work, studying the strengths and weaknesses of companies' internal communication policies, has been in the private sector. More recently she has been involved with several public sector organizations, including schools, where she has conducted staff, parent and pupil communication audits.

David Bright is a Lecturer in Employment Relations at Durham University and Co-Director of the University's Human Resource Development Unit. His research interests include reward and recognition, negotiating behaviour and HRD strategy.

Elaine Crosthwaite is the Manager of Education Quality at the Institute of Personnel and Development. She previously taught at Nottingham Trent University and Coventry University and worked as a Personnel Manager for the British Oxygen Company. Her previous publications include articles on training, equal opportunities and personnel management in higher education as well as an exam guide for the Open University and a recent book entitled *Passing Your IPM Exams*.

Emily Crowley is a consultant with KPMG Management Consulting. She has worked in the IT industry since 1986, moving from a systems house background to the training division of a multinational computer hardware corporation, developing and presenting courses in IT and management skills. Emily joined the consultancy division of a major HR software supplier in 1989, where her responsibilities included systems specification and build for major implementations within the public and private sectors.

Diana Ellis studied at the Universities of Durham, Bristol, Salamanca and St Andrews before becoming Director of an educational organization where she ran courses and marketed them in Latin America, Japan and Europe. Later she became Headmistress of a girls' independent day and boarding school after which she joined the John Lewis Partnership as a Senior Manager. At NB Selection Diana heads the Education Practice which has been specifically set up to assist Governors and Councils with the appointment of heads, principals and vice-chancellors.

David House is Deputy Director of the University of Brighton, where he has particular responsibility for resources (including human resources) and academic support services. He is a former specialist adviser to the Council for National Academic Awards on institutional management, and has published and lectured on information management and funding policies.

Peter Knight is the Vice-Chancellor of the University of Central England in Birmingham, having previously been a Deputy Director at Lancashire Polytechnic. Peter is currently a member of the Audit Committee of the Higher Education Funding Council for England and Chairman of the Polytechnics and Colleges Employers' Forum. He was appointed to the National Advisory Body for Public Sector Higher Education and the Polytechnics and Colleges Funding Council. In 1978 he was President of the National Association of Teachers in Further and Higher Education.

Elizabeth Lanchbery is now Personnel Director at Kingston University, but she was Assistant Director (Human Resources) when she was first appointed. The changes of title provide a clue to the major cultural change in the organization over the last few years in which the HR function generally and Elizabeth in particular has played a major role. Elizabeth is responsible for all aspects of HR at Kingston University including equal opportunities for students and staff. She came into higher education from the National Health Service where she had held a number of personnel and training posts at both operational and strategic levels.

Patricia Leighton is Professor and Head of the Employment Relations Research and Development Centre at Anglia Polytechnic University. She has researched and written widely on both employment law and education law. Among her publications are *Schools and Employment Law* and *The Work Environment: The Law of Health, Safety and Welfare at Work*.

John McManus is a principal consultant with KPMG Management Consulting and has worked for the last nine years on the implementation of integrated software systems with a particular emphasis on international and HRM issues. He has held management positions in both the public and private sectors and has lectured widely on the topic of HRM systems in Europe and the USA.

Geoffrey Mead is a barrister employed at Norton Rose who has previously lectured in law at the Universities of Southampton, Surrey and Thessalonika. His specialist areas are Employment Law and Discrimination Law and he has published extensively on both.

Rebecca Nestor is Equal Opportunities Officer at the University of Oxford, a position she has held since 1992. After graduating in 1985, she began her career at the Greater London Council and subsequently held various equal opportunities posts in local government.

Jennifer Tann is Professor of Innovation Studies and currently Dean of the Faculty of Education and Continuing Studies in the University of Birmingham. She was formerly Director of Continuing Education at the University of Newcastle upon Tyne and prior to that a Reader in Aston University Business School.

Elizabeth Walker joined The Staff College in 1990 where she specializes in the areas of human resource and personnel management, organizational development, strategic management, management theory, organizational skills, equal opportunities, appraisal and delegation. Prior to this appointment she worked for ten years for Fullemploy, a voluntary sector equal opportunities and vocational education and training organization. Elizabeth has had seven years' experience of freelance training and consultancy, has worked in Eastern Europe and is involved in both MCI and MBA programmes at The Staff College.

Roger Ward is the Chief Executive of the Polytechnics and Colleges Employers' Forum and the Chief Executive of the Colleges Employers' Forum. He was educated at the Universities of Lancaster and City in the UK and at the University of North Carolina in the United States. He is a Fellow of the Institute of Personnel and Development.

David Warner is a Professor and Pro-Vice-Chancellor at the University of Central England in Birmingham having previously worked in a school, an FE college and the Universities of East Anglia and Warwick. He has published extensively on many aspects of educational management and is the co-editor of *Visual and Corporate Identity* and *Managing Educational Property* (Open University Press), co-author of *The Income Generation Handbook* (Open University Press) and editor of the journal *International Education*.

David Watson is Director of the University of Brighton having previously taught at Crewe and Alsager College of Higher Education and the former Oxford Polytechnic. He is the author of *Margaret Fuller, Managing the Modular Course, Developing Professional Education* (with Hazel Bines), *Arendt* and *Managing the University Curriculum* (with Jean Bocock). Professor Watson is a former member of the Council for National Academic Awards and the Polytechnics and Colleges Funding Council. He now sits on the Higher Education Funding Council for England and chairs its Quality Assessment Committee.

Bill Williamson is Director of the Department of Adult and Continuing Education at Durham University. His research interests include the processes of adult learning, empowerment and recognition.

Foreword

Peter Knight

Human Resource Management in universities and colleges cannot be discussed without an understanding of values and cultures associated with further and higher education. Any attempt to transfer into post-school education new principles of personnel policy, without considering the environment within which those principles are going to have to be brought into effect, is likely to fail. Commercial and businesslike approaches may be a good starting point, but there will always be the need to modify and test such ideas before applying them in the unique environment of education.

The problem is made more complex by the fact that the value system is not uniform. There are different traditions and beliefs in the old universities when compared with those inherited by the new universities. Colleges of further education, while they may still have some attitudes and values comparable to those of the new universities, are still likely to be heavily influenced by the human resource policies of the local authorities which were responsible for them until April 1993. Human resource and industrial relations issues are always difficult when the environment into which they are introduced is as complex as post-school education.

It is inevitable that most human resource issues in post-school education centre around the problems associated with managing and motivating teaching staff. It is for the teaching staff of the university or college that the cultural changes are most acute. For example, in the old universities teaching staff still, correctly, perceive themselves as 'members' of the university. They are the institution that employs them. In many respects this is a highly desirable and valued attitude that should enhance all aspects of industrial relations and human resource management in those institutions. In practice it can lead to an elite perception by that group of staff and dissatisfaction from other categories of staff who perceive themselves as less valued by their employer. The collegiate nature of many of the old universities means that change, particularly if controversial, is far harder to implement because of lengthy and pseudo-democratic decision-making processes.

Despite this and other difficulties, human resource management in higher and further education is changing, principally as a result of adopting many of the policies that have been identified as good practice in other environments. When managing people it is essential that any institution identifies clearly the objectives that it is seeking to achieve, decides on a process by which change is going to be managed, and ensures that it effectively communicates with its staff about the objectives. If these steps are followed in an increasingly complex industrial relations environment in relation to changes in employment law, then an effective human resource policy will result.

There is no doubt that the comprehensive coverage of human resource issues presented in this book and written from the context of post-school education, will be of great assistance to all in further and higher education whether they are seeking to implement or resist change!

Selected Abbreviations

AC	Appeal Cases
ACAS	Advisory, Conciliation and Arbitration Service
AER	All England Law Reports
APC	Association of Principals of Colleges (changed title in 1990 to APCT)
APCT	Association of Polytechnic and College Teachers
APT	Association of Polytechnic Teachers
APT&C	Administrative, Professional, Technical and Clerical
AUA	Association of University Administrators
AUT	Association of University Teachers
CBI	Confederation of British Industry
CDP	Committee of Directors of Polytechnics
CEC	Commission of the European Communities
CEF	College Employers' Forum
CMLR	Common Market Law Reports
CMS	Certificate in Management Studies
CNAA	Council for National Academic Awards
CPIS	computerized personnel information system
CRE	Commission for Racial Equality
CV	curriculum vitae
CVCP	Committee of Vice-Chancellors and Principals
DES	Department of Education and Science (now renamed Department for Education)
DfE	Department for Education (new name of DES)
DMS	Diploma in Management Studies
EC	European Community
ECJ	European Court of Justice
EDT	effective date of termination
EEC	European Economic Community
EOC	Equal Opportunities Commission
EPCA	Employment Protection (Consolidation) Act

EU	European Union
FE	Further Education
FEFCE	Further Education Funding Council for England
FEFCW	Further Education Funding Council for Wales
FHE	Further and Higher Education
FHEI	Further and Higher Education Institution(s)
GMBATU	General Municipal Boilermakers and Allied Trades Union
HE	Higher Education
HEFCE	Higher Education Funding Council for England
HEIST	Higher Education Information Services Trust
HMI	Her Majesty's Inspectorate
HR	human resource
HRD	human resource development
HRIS	human resource information system
HRM	human resource management
HSE	Health and Safety Executive
ICR	Industrial Cases Reports
IPM	Institute of Personnel Management
IQ	intelligence quotient
IRLR	Industrial Relations Law Reports
IT	information technology
ITr	industrial tribunal
JES	job evaluation study
LEA	Local Education Authority
MBA	Master of Business Administration
MBO	management by objectives
MCI	Management Charter Initiative
MLP	maternity leave period
NAB	National Advisory Body for Public Sector Higher Education
NALGO	National Association of Local Government Officers
NATFHE	National Association of Teachers in Further and Higher Education
NHS	National Health Service
NJC	National Joint Council
NUPE	National Union of Public Employees
PC	personal computer
PCEF	Polytechnics and Colleges Employers' Forum
PCFC	Polytechnics and Colleges Funding Council
PCNNC	Polytechnics and Colleges National Negotiating Committee
PRINCE	Projects In Controlled Environments
PROMPT	public sector project management methodology (now succeeded by PRINCE)
PRP	performance-related pay
QB	Queen's Bench Reports
RADAR	Royal Association for Disability and Rehabilitation
RSI	repetitive strain injury

SCOP	Standing Conference of Principals
SiiPS	selection and implementation of information packaged software
SWOT	strengths, weaknesses, opportunities and threats
TGWU	Transport and General Workers' Union
TUC	Trades' Union Congress
TULRCA	Trade Union and Labour Relations (Consolidation) Act
TUPE	Transfer of Undertakings (Protection of Employment)
TURERA	Trade Union Reform and Employment Rights Act
UFC	Universities Funding Council (replaced by the national Higher Education Funding Councils)
UGC	Universities Grants Committee (replaced by the Universities Funding Council)
UK	United Kingdom
USA	United States of America
USDU	Universities Staff Development Unit
WRULD	work related upper limb disorder

1

Setting the Scene

Elaine Crosthwaite and David Warner

The importance of human resource management

Until relatively recently, human resource management (HRM) was not a widely used term within education. There were usually personnel or staffing departments in institutions in the university and former polytechnic sectors of higher education (HE), but much of the function in colleges of further education (FE), schools and even in the former polytechnics was carried out by personnel staff based in the relevant local authority. Furthermore, heads of department were appointed on the basis of their academic achievement or business experience, but the recruitment specification would rarely have given significance to the skills of managing people and handling change. This situation is now changing rapidly as a result primarily of recent legislation coupled with a drive towards a more 'managerialist' approach promoted from many sources, but especially the Jarratt Report (1985).

There is an undeniable need for the effective management of human resources which represents by far the most substantial element of the budget of all educational institutions. As yet comparative figures are not available, but it may be estimated that, on average, staff costs represent 65 per cent of the budget of the former polytechnics, slightly less in the old universities owing to external research income, and between 70 to 85 per cent in colleges of FE and schools.

The key legislation

The legislation which has accelerated much of this change is the Education Reform Act of 1988 and the Further and Higher Education Act of 1992. As a result of the former, some 84 HE institutions were taken out of local authority control and established as independent corporations, the majority with exempt charity status, and schools were given the right of local management and the opportunity to opt for Grant Maintained Status in certain cases. As a result of the latter, all FE and sixth form colleges were similarly made independent corporations and certain HE institutions (including all of the former polytechnics) were given the right to adopt the title of *university*. For this reason during the remainder of this chapter we will refer to those institutions which were universities prior to the 1992 Act as *old universities* and those which have gained the title subsequently as *new*.

To avoid confusion in future chapters, we must point out now that the process of gaining institutional independence involved a preparatory stage commonly known as *incorporation*. It enabled the institution concerned to get ready for formal independence by setting up in advance new bureaucratic procedures (especially in the financial and HRM areas), new committee structures and a new shadow Governing Body. Consequently, the HE institutions were incorporated in 1988, but did not become independent until 1 April 1989 and the FE colleges were incorporated in 1992 and became independent on 1 April 1993.

The principals' perspective

In 1991 a survey was undertaken by the authors of this chapter (Warner and Crosthwaite 1992a) which underlines the importance of HRM by revealing the views of some of the most senior managers of HE institutions. All of the principals of the new universities and colleges of HE were asked to rank the five most important areas of management in their institution to be selected from property, finance, HRM, income generation, marketing and quality with an opportunity to add two others. Although four of the principals stated that all of the areas were of equal importance, the uniformity of response was overwhelming. Almost all of the principals ranked financial management amongst their first two priorities, and just over half marked it top. However, HRM came a very close second to financial management and ahead of quality management, despite the fact that it appears to be on everyone's lips all of the time. The other three suggested areas of management received a low ranking in the descending order of property, marketing and income generation.

The principals were also asked which HRM issues they considered to be the most important. Again there was a uniformity of response which placed the following as the four most important: appointment of staff, staff development, internal communication and appraisal. With regard to the amount of time spent on HRM, new university principals spent an average of just under one day a week in the area, while college of HE principals did about one-and-a-half days. A couple of principals, however, claimed to spend at least half of every week on HRM!

This same research project showed that almost all new universities and the generalist colleges of HE increased the staff in their personnel units substantially around the time of gaining independence and moreover, that nearly 60 per cent of all principals indicated a need to expand further their personnel units. A similar phenomenon is currently taking place in many colleges of FE.

Human resource management or personnel management?

There has been much debate about the conceptual difference between human resource management and personnel management (see for instance Armstrong 1987; Clark 1993; Fowler 1987; Guest 1989 and 1991; Torrington 1988).

At the one extreme there are a number of authors who believe that the terms are simply interchangeable and, it has been observed that in many cases, the personnel department/unit has simply been retitled to give it a new and more contemporary image (Guest 1989). We, however, consider that there is an essential difference and for the purposes of this book we have used the following stipulative definitions:

Human Resource Management is that part of management which is concerned with the effective utilization of the human resources of an organization. It is conducted by all managers: principals/senior managers at the strategic level, personnel specialists in an advisory and auditing role, and line managers at an operational level.

Personnel Management is the function carried out in personnel departments/ units by personnel specialists and personnel practitioners ranging from Personnel Director/Manager to Personnel/Training Officer and Personnel Administrator/Assistant. Personnel may or may not include the payroll function, and it is made clear where payroll is relevant to the topic, whether the term personnel encompasses payroll or not.

We have used this distinction between HRM and personnel management because we believe, in accordance with Kessler, that HRM embraces 'a strategic approach to "people management", the integration of employees on the basis of commitment and not mere compliance with instructions; and an organic, devolved business structure as against a bureaucratic centralised one'. (Kessler 1993: 20). A study by John Storey in 1992a found little evidence of such integration in British companies, but did reveal that there has been an increased focus on the individual employee, in particular in recruitment and selection, the clear communication of objectives, training and development, and on the evaluation and rewarding of performance.

We believe that educational institutions at times display all of these underlying values of HRM. Moreover, the organization structure of educational institutions already has many of the features which business organizations are moving towards in response to competitive pressures. These include:

- Flatter organizations with people coming together in teams for specific projects.
- Teams made up of knowledge workers who may be core employees, on short-term contracts, consultants or part-time workers.
- New technology enabling staff to produce their own papers and reports, and rely less on secretarial staff.

- A decline in manual occupations and growth in managerial, professional and associate-professional occupations.
- A greater use of all forms of flexible working in order to achieve a close match between workforce provision and work requirements.
- An empowered rather than a command structure which provides an environment which encourages information exchange, innovation and individual development.
- An organization climate which is customer-driven, quality focused and increasingly competitive.
- Line managers more fully responsible for the management of performance and taking a more active part in the recruitment, assessment, reward and development of people.

The major developments which are driving change and the emerging trends in people management are described in much greater depth in the Institute of Personnel Management's Consultative Document *Managing People – The Changing Frontiers* (1993).

The importance of the personnel department

By making a distinction between HRM and personnel management we are not overlooking the important role of personnel departments/units in educational institutions. Indeed, in previous research (Warner and Crosthwaite 1993b) we have looked at them in some depth. In particular, we were concerned to examine the differences between the staffing, structure and functions of such units in old and new universities, the situation in new universities pre- and post-independence, and the similarities/differences between HE institutions and similar sized organizations in the public and private sectors.

One area of our study was concerned with identifying the key tasks which are undertaken by personnel units. Using the task/activity categories originally identified by Mackay and Torrington (1986), our research produced rankings from personnel unit heads, shown in Table 1.1, where 1 is the most important.

The ordering of the tasks is very similar in the old and the new universities with the exception of payroll administration which is not commonly undertaken in old university personnel units. The results are also similar for colleges of HE, although training does come surprisingly low. Of perhaps even more interest, however, we discovered that pre-independence no head of a new university personnel unit reported directly to the principal of his or her institution, whereas after independence just over 30 per cent of them had gained direct access, while a further 50 per cent reported to a deputy principal. Moreover, whatever their line of reporting, just over 50 per cent of new university personnel heads and almost 70 per cent of HE college personnel heads claimed to participate in the senior management team meetings of their institutions. Recent anecdotal evidence indicates that these percentages are now even higher.

Table 1.1

	A *Polys – pre- incorporation*	B *Polys – post- incorporation*	C *Colleges – post- incorporation*	D *Old Universities*
Employee relations	2	1	1	2
Recruitment/selection	1	2	1	1
Training	7	4	11	4
Discipline/grievance	3	3	7	6
Health/safety/welfare	10	10	3	10
Appraisal	14	4	9	3
Redundancy/dismissal	6	7	10	9
Job evaluation	8	9	3	5
Organization/management development	10	8	12	7
Payroll administration	5	12	3	14
Manpower planning	10	11	7	12
Changes in work organization	4	4	6	8
New technology	8	12	12	10
Fringe benefits	13	14	14	13

On the other hand, we found that it was very uncommon for the head of an old university personnel unit to report direct to the principal of his or her institution. The vast majority (almost 90 per cent) reported to the head of administration. However, this result stems more from the structure of the management of old universities rather than any reduced role for their heads of personnel as, at the time of our research, slightly more of them (54 per cent) participated in their institution's senior management team meetings than in the new universities.

The use and scope of this book

Human Resource Management in Higher and Further Education has been written by a mixed team of academics, senior managers and management consultants from the private sector. It aims to provide a comprehensive coverage of all aspects of human resource management written in such a way that a senior manager and/or personnel practitioner may want to read straight through the whole book in order to gain a full picture. At the same time, each chapter has been constructed to be free-standing and to provide a fairly in-depth treatment of the topic which it covers. The editors have therefore added a brief comment at the head of each chapter and removed inconsistencies, but we have not attempted to homogenize individual styles and approaches, nor to eliminate repetition which is necessary to understand a chapter read in isolation.

Perforce the book has been produced largely from an HE perspective because institutions in that sector are a little further down the road in developing HRM policies – owing to their head start of at least four years. Much of the content examines the effects of the seminal legislation referred to earlier from a variety of different positions, often by key players in the action. However, the issues and responses experienced by HE institutions will be equally valid for FE and sixth form colleges and very relevant to most schools.

The challenge for the newly independent institution is to develop a human resource strategy which is in line with its mission statement and institutional aims. Implementation of this strategy will demand skills in managing change and diversity, effective communication and in effecting culture change. There will be a new employee relations climate which will signal a need for different approaches according to the local situation. More sophisticated selection techniques will be required to ensure that high calibre people are employed and more attention must be given to employee development and remuneration. Legal aspects cannot be ignored, including expert knowledge of employment law and safe and healthy work practices. Systems are needed to manage the personnel information requirements of the organization and important choices are to be made on whether to carry this out in-house. These problems and opportunities are the same for all educational institutions whatever their size and nature.

HRM is an area of management where change occurs frequently, almost, it seems, on a daily basis. Of necessity, therefore, some of the detailed information and the case studies contained in this book will become dated fairly quickly, but the key principles will remain the same for a long time and should function as a stimulus for *your* new ideas and action.

2

Managing Change

David House and David Watson

Editors' introduction

Some of the ground covered in this chapter is similar to that in the following
one, but from an entirely different perspective – the macro rather than the
micro. The authors examine a number of key issues (contracts, appraisal,
teaching observation, reward systems and performance-related pay) and con-
clude that change is most successfully managed when the organization's values
and objectives are understood and shared by both managers and the managed. Fortunately, this is a result which, prima facie, educational institutions
should be able to achieve as a consequence of their very nature.

Introduction

For every set of institutional managers in further and higher education (FHE)
calling for a cultural change across the organization there is a strong body of
organized staff opinion pointing to a crisis in morale; or so it seems to the
outside observer trying to understand the dynamics of the institutions. In this
sense the phrase *managing change* itself seems crude and ideologically loaded.
It can give the impression of 'managers' 'changing' conditions either whim-
sically, or to serve their own peculiar interests. Often the impression is given
that the primary motive of change is to capture the attention of the *managed*
rather like a desperate classroom teacher making the pupils sit on their hands.
Similarly the importation of terms like *human resource management* from the
commercial–industrial sphere can be used by staff to caricature change as
deeply threatening to professional roles and the peculiar kind of corporate life
that is bound up in a college or a university. The language can be used, by
one side or the other, to defeat the meaning.

In this chapter we attempt to set out the key questions raised by any analysis of new demands upon and achievements of human resource management

in higher and further education. Our perspective is at once idealistic and realistic. There is much value to be retained in the motivation, self-image and practice of academic and other staff in our institutions. Simultaneously, there is much to be gained from a rigorous appraisal of new demands placed upon these institutions (legitimate or otherwise) and how they might be approached or met.

Corporate culture and morale

Managing change is often elided by institutional managers into changing the culture or the ethos of the organization, whether to make it more competitive or efficient under new conditions, or simply better able to deliver upon its historical commitments. There have been several crude attempts to characterize the strategic tendencies and management styles of the post-Jarratt universities, the 'higher education corporations' under the Polytechnics and Colleges Funding Council (PCFC), and most recently the 'further education corporations' of the Further Education Funding Councils (FEFC) (see Cryer and Elton 1990; Halsey 1992). The critics focus on the motives and the qualifications of what they regard as a new breed of managers, as if the Education Reform Act of 1988 and the Further and Higher Education Act of 1992 had swept away the senior and middle management cadre and replaced it overnight with government placemen and women.

Rather like corporate culture, staff morale is an easily misinterpreted concept. The interests of one side in saying that it is good and the other that it is bad are too obvious. It would be hard to find any representative of a group of more than, say, 100 employees (even one less used to the cut-and-thrust of arguments about values than the average teaching staff common-room) who would tell the employer that morale is good. The chief problem is that individuals compartmentalize attitudes towards different aspects of their life and work. The current deep anxieties among teachers in FHE are compounded partly from their feelings about external threats (chiefly declining resources) and partly from uncertainties about a new management regime. On the other hand the sectors have been noted for an innovative response to the resource challenge (with what must be regarded as staggering productivity gains), and there is plenty of in-house evidence of job satisfaction and corporate loyalty (Lindsay 1987: 12–15).

A pair of critical questions play across this debate. First, what is the model of the academic community and can it be shared? Secondly, what kinds of professional role are implied? Various stereotypes can be appealed to in constructing the academic community. Teachers like the model of the mediaeval university, as a community of scholars, taking decisions through a process of harmonious consensus-building; formerly and formally that is the meaning of *universitas*. Managers prefer the model of the commercial–industrial corporation: an undifferentiated individual in legal terms, ruthlessly disciplined, and wherein performance against institutional aims is rewarded and noncompliance (as well as poor performance) punished.

Neither of these stereotypes, of course, bears much relationship to reality. The university was always corrupted, by its unofficial leadership and the outside world. The corporation is equally regularly corrupted by the irrationality of its internal culture, and especially its capacity to resist change.

There has been, over the last five years, no shortage of externally-driven changes to resist. There have been the two major pieces of legislation referred to above, which have, *inter alia*, abolished two planning and funding bodies (the University Grants Committee – UGC and the National Advisory Body for Public Sector Higher Education – NAB) and one validating body (the Council for National Academic Awards – CNAA); established two new funding councils (the Universities Funding Council – UFC, and the Polytechnics and Colleges Funding Council – PCFC) and then abolished both; established three new funding councils to deal with the totality of higher education in England, Wales and Scotland; required changes to statutes to eliminate tenure and limit the powers of the visitor; required the funding councils to secure a process of quality assessment; and given the Secretary of State for Education significant powers to impose terms and conditions on payments of grant to the funding councils. These latter powers have been used to secure pay settlements which conform to government set norms, to force institutions to introduce observation of teaching into their appraisal processes, and to introduce performance related pay (PRP).

Successive funding councils have adopted varying approaches to distributing resources, sometimes forcing expansion through competitive bidding, at other times insisting upon stability or contraction through the imposition of penalty clauses. This concentrated framework of external regulation and of government direction to funding councils has done little to reinforce notions of individual institutions, with their diverse missions, preparing and implementing strategic plans in an autonomous way. For staff at the chalk face, it has created a real sense that there are two masters – their institutional managers and employers with their own agenda for change, and a government with its own agenda playing across a range of public life. Institutional leaders can almost feel staff looking past them towards the larger agenda on the wall beyond, and face considerable challenges in gaining and retaining the trust of those whom they lead.

The former polytechnics, even before incorporation, were perhaps closer to the commercial–industrial model than to the collegiate, working mainly with permanently appointed senior staff operating in a recognizable, if not always perfectly functioning, management structure. The temptation simply to reinforce this model has been considerable, and it has not been unknown for vice-chancellors of traditional universities to cast envious glances at the perceived power of the director of a polytechnic to impose change by diktat, unfettered by the obstructive stance of a conservative senate. An alternative approach, however, and the one we favour, is to recognize that developing best practice in all large organizations has been moving away from closed and hierarchical approaches towards open and participative structures, in which teamworking is the norm. We do not therefore see the abolition of all committees and a move to government from an Executive Suite as the necessary concomitant of incorporation. A culture in which the leaders ensure that the necessary hard questions are asked of the stakeholders (and that their answers are taken seriously, but not uncritically) is better for long-term staff morale than one which either opts for short-term popularity (accepting and adopting uncritically departmental and faculty plans and priorities) or seeks to limit the involvement of the stakeholders.

More significantly in operational terms, we can examine what has happened to professional roles – for managers and support staff as well as lecturers. Managers have had to interpret the external steers, position their departments or institutions against these requirements, and interpret for their colleagues what can or should be accommodated or resisted. The liberation promised by changes in governance like incorporation has been at least substantially qualified by a new set of external constraints (and what often seems like an even more demanding and volatile set of political masters). In this context professional formation of managers has taken on a fresh importance, evidenced by the recent rapid development of functional groups (Estates, Personnel, Finance, Fundraisers, etc.) across the binary line (Gray 1989).

The rhetoric of professionalism is relatively new for managers in higher education. For lecturers it is part and parcel of the historical inheritance. As several commentators have pointed out, however, in its historical form it has proved extraordinarily contentless: a piece of occupational code designed primarily, the cynic would suggest, to preserve demarcations (from administrators and support staff) rather than to define and validate activity and behaviour in the heartland. Oliver Fulton (1993), concluding a series of reflections on 'human resources in the universities' convened by the Standing Conference of European Rectors, points to the paradoxical truth that 'the academic profession is profoundly *unprofessional* [his emphasis], especially in its orientation to teaching.' New conditions are rendering this view obsolete, if not institutionally dangerous. Tenure is only one of a number of concepts about practice that have not been able to survive critical scrutiny (see Allison 1990).

The terms of trade

The proposition that an FHEI's most critical resource is the time of its academic staff has perhaps properly been blurred by a greater recognition of the role and value of other staff. Nevertheless, if the key tasks of teaching and research are to be approached effectively, the framework within which academic staff operate needs careful and continuous reconsideration. The serious debates so far have taken place over contracts, appraisal, the observation of teaching, and reward systems.

Contracts

The 84 institutions established as higher education corporations through the Education Reform Act 1988 arrived in the PCFC sector with a legacy of formal terms and conditions of employment – for all staff – which had their basis in local government. The *Silver Book* (NJCLA) set out formal conditions of service for lecturers in both further and higher education; administrative, technical and professional staff shared the *Purple Book* (NJCLA) with local government officers; and the *White Book* (NJCLA) grouped manual staff in polytechnics and colleges with local authority manual workers. Some rapid change was inevitable, since higher education corporations could barely accept a framework for settling salaries and conditions of service in which they had no direct negotiating role. Through the establishment of a Polytechnics and Colleges Employers' Forum (PCEF), the institutions sought first to define the general nature of the changes sought, and then the detailed framework.

It has to be accepted that individual lecturers had little obvious incentive to seek contractual change. The *Silver Book* formally set the teaching year at 38 weeks, and required neither attendance nor accountability beyond that period. It limited the working week to 30 hours, and set norms for the proportion of working time which could be contact time. Seen from outside the sector, the terms of trade looked attractive indeed.

In reality, they were probably rarely observed in the majority of institutions. On the one hand, the level of teaching indicated in the *Silver Book* (16–18 hours for a Senior Lecturer and 13–16 hours for a Principal Lecturer) might be tolerable in further education, but was certainly recognized as unrealistic for higher education. On the other hand, few academic staff could build for themselves the reputation they sought by technically fulfilling their contractual obligations and ignoring research and scholarly activity; they therefore developed research and consultancy activity outside the formal contractual framework. By the time it became necessary to review it for practical reasons, the lecturers' contract was already widely ignored. Yet the mere fact that it existed was at times of difficulty a powerful factor; the rule book had become so far separated from normal working practice that a threat of a 'work to rule' constituted a threat of institutional paralysis. This situation contrasted markedly with the position in the chartered universities, where detailed formal terms and conditions of service for academic staff – expressed in terms of hours or weeks – were rarely considered necessary.

For staff other than lecturers, the position was different. The local government terms and conditions were not in themselves viewed as problematic by either employers or employees. The *Purple Book* provided a detailed national prescription on almost all employment matters. The staff and their union saw this as a protection, and managers used it as an administrative handbook, to be interpreted but not amended. Save for some residual unease on the part of the trades unions about the demise of the national code, and the lack of any formal replacement for it, the debate about terms of trade has bypassed those staff without the label academic.

An initial attempt to introduce contractual changes for academic staff from 1 April 1989 – the day upon which polytechnics and colleges left local authority control – failed. After several months of confrontation, and a period of industrial action by the National Association of Teachers in Further and Higher Education (NATFHE), the first pay settlement in the new sector was eventually agreed in February 1990 with help from the Advisory, Conciliation and Arbitration Service (ACAS). The terms of the settlement included an agreement to establish a working party to discuss lecturers' contracts, with an independent chair appointed by ACAS. This working party was chaired by Ian Smith, Reader in Law at the University of East Anglia, and was to complete its work by 30 June 1990.

The submissions from both the unions and the employers' organization to the working party were published (PCEF July 1990c). The lecturers' side argued for a retention of the upper limit of 30 hours a week to be spent on college duties, and for an explicit limit of 15 hours on 'class contact time', with further limits on the loading of lecturers to be calculated by the number of students and courses for which they were responsible. It sought arrangements negotiated at institutional (not individual) level for remission from these norms, and proposed the retention of the 38 week working year.

This position was sharply dismissed by the employers' side as 'little more than a rehash of the *Silver Book*' (PCEF June 1990a). It responded with a position paper which described the unions' approach to these issues as 'the antithesis of a professional relationship between lecturers and their institutions' (PCEF July 1990c). Its own submission proposed a working year of 45 weeks, within which teaching should not normally exceed 38 weeks, and where research and scholarly activity – though spread throughout the working year – should be particularly concentrated in the seven weeks outside this teaching period. Central to the employers' position was the insistence that each lecturer's workload should be built up on an individual basis, determined by a negotiated balance between the needs of the individual and the needs of the department or institution. This contrasted with the union model (and with previous practice) of all lecturers having a standard teaching workload, with deviations from the norm recognized through remission. The employers sought to have teaching viewed simply as one aspect of the lecturer's role, claiming that to 'give undue attention and quantification to any single aspect of the lecturer's job is incompatible with the concept of the job being professional in nature'.

The two sides could not agree on these issues in the working party (although significant agreement was reached in other issues, including staff development and appraisal). It therefore fell to the Chairman to make recommendations. The Report broadly accepted the employers' definition of 'professional contracts', and agreed that this implied having to move away from 'the old rigid formulaic approach based on defined commitments on hours'. It also supported the employers' view of the working year, judging that the unions' wish to retain the '30 hours per week' rule could not 'survive the new realities'. At the same time, the Report expressed a degree of support for union anxieties about potential overloading, and confirmed that 'professionalism does not just mean the staff doing all that the employers decide to take on' (PCEF 1990c). On that basis, some quantified protections were built into the proposed national contract.

The *Smith Report* (PCEF 1990b) could only be seen as a rejection of the union views. Debate on its implementation quickly turned to one about financial compensation, and was resolved – again largely in the employers' favour – only after a trying three-month long dispute. The changes achieved through this process were fundamental. They reframed the role of the lecturer so that it was not simply defined as formal teaching, with other activities viewed as deductions – or even distractions – from it. They moved away from the assumption that all lecturers had a broadly similar mix of duties dominated by class contact to a position where workloads were negotiated annually on an individual basis. They introduced mandatory formal appraisal schemes, and exclusivity of employment. Most importantly, they shifted the centre of gravity from national to institutional level.

A further version of this process has been running in the further education sector, where the College Employers' Forum (CEF) made its opening move to introduce professional contracts shortly before the colleges assumed independence in April 1993. Resistance has been stronger, both from unions and at college level, partly in response to a somewhat less sensitive version of the contract ('You will be required to work such hours as are reasonably necessary . . . with a minimum of 37 hours per week . . .') and partly a function of the different tradition in further education. The new contract being offered is a more blatant attempt to increase productivity, and contains little protection against overloading, and almost no recognition of the professional autonomy of the teacher (CEF 1993).

In higher education, the imposition of responsibility for deploying staff has posed significant challenges to those now frequently labelled middle managers – heads of department and their equivalents. They are required to conduct appraisals, to allocate duties (not to fix teaching timetables – usually a task delegated to a humbler teacher assisted by a departmental secretary – but to negotiate the balance of individual staff effort between teaching, research and other activities) and to consider individual and group performance. Gray (1989) is unduly kind to the former polytechnics. Describing a typical university department as a group of individuals who 'have the minimum contact with one another consonant with the continued, but little amended, running of undergraduate and postgraduate courses year in and year out and pursue, in the most individualistic of ways, "research"', he judges that 'in the polytechnics, there is generally a greater unity of purpose than in almost any university department.' There are dimensions in which this is certainly the case; two decades of CNAA course development and validation processes have naturally brought some benefits. However, the variety of management practice discovered by Gray in traditional universities – ranging from the most authoritarian and/or unpredictable to the most collegial and/or facilitative – is present in all its glory in the new universities. Institutions seeking to gain the full benefits of the contractual changes have had to invest significantly in the development of their heads of department and will need to continue this investment.

The components of the successful management of this change at local level have been an appeal to reason ('this really isn't much different to how you work now . . .'), reassurance that it is not a licence to increase teaching loads, a modest financial inducement, and the careful preparation of heads of department for a broader role.

Appraisal

The professional contract required participation in a locally developed and approved staff appraisal scheme. Concern to embed appraisal schemes in publicly funded education has been a feature of the thinking of Conservative administrations since at least the early 1980s, when the White Paper *Teaching Quality*, dealing with teaching in schools, called for 'formal assessment of teacher performance' in order that employers could 'manage their teacher force effectively' (DES 1983). Elliot (1988) has chronicled the way in which appraisal schemes in schools, and later in the old university sector, have attempted to resolve the tension between different perspectives on teacher appraisal – the manager's concern with control over the work force and the rights of self-determination which are assumed to be a central feature of the teacher's professional culture. In both the case of school teachers (1983) and the university lecturers (1987), ACAS were called upon to mediate between these perspectives and helped formulate agreements which drifted between compromise and ambiguity.

The model of appraisal propounded in the Smith Report was closely based on that previously adopted by the CVCP/AUT. It stressed the professional development purpose of the exercise, and in a key paragraph on 'Appraisal and Other Institutional Procedures', said:

> The developmental approach to appraisal outlined here can be distinguished from appraisal schemes which have an explicit link with remuneration. The scheme should be differentiated from disciplinary and other procedures for dealing with questions of competence and clearly separate from procedures covering probation or promotion.
>
> (PCEF 1990b: 29)

Described in these terms, appraisal need carry no particular threat to staff. In the traditional universities, its introduction had apparently been accomplished relatively smoothly. Rutherford (1988) discovered strong support at the University of Birmingham for more systematic procedures for the appraisal of individuals, involving an annual interview with the head of department or another senior colleague. Helm (1989) offered an account of a scheme readily accepted by staff at Liverpool. The concerns of staff noted at Liverpool – that records of appraisal should be confidential, and that resources should be made available to support action plans – were doubtless mirrored in many other discussions. The formal introduction of appraisal into the PCFC sector was no more painful.

There is yet little evidence of the impact of the appraisal schemes of the late eighties and early nineties. Rutherford (1992), revisiting the topic at Birmingham, notes a degree of scepticism over the credibility of appraisers, and some suspicion that the scheme is another mechanism to identify dead wood; but these doubts must be set against a significant body of opinion which is enthusiastic about appraisal interviews. At the University of Brighton, they have often been seen by staff as an entitlement, rather than a burden. Is this ready acceptance of schemes indicative of an acceptance of change, or does it suggest that the new appraisal schemes have been integrated into the culture of the professional lecturer without forcing any change at all?

At the individual level, the answers to these questions must be varied. There are clear instances of individuals feeling liberated and motivated by the formal opportunity to review their priorities and goals, and to negotiate time and other support for them; there are also instances of appraisal discussions which fail to uncover serious problems (which may then emerge later in other contexts), or those which promise action – by either party – which is not followed through. Indeed, most large universities could probably find corners in which the appraisal scheme is working fitfully, if at all.

The impact at head of department level can be more readily assessed, and it is a mixed picture. The workload implications are significant, and need to be set alongside other rapidly growing challenges placed upon the head of department's role, including devolved financial management and increasingly stringent health and safety responsibilities. Heads of department originally appointed as academic leaders before 1990 have been increasingly required to adopt the role of manager. This process was well under way in the traditional universities in the 1980s, and was addressed explicitly in the Jarratt Report (1985); but this does not prevent the further shift in balance being resisted and resented on occasions, both by heads and by those whom they lead. Yet the price of this additional strain is worth paying if heads of department – through gaining in a structured way firsthand knowledge of the strengths and potential of their departments – can contribute more fully to the strategic planning of their institutions. What has so far been gained from appraisal systems is a greater sense of the whole – by heads of their departments, by deans of their faculties and by institutional leaders. Gray's earlier and somewhat harsh analysis, in which departments appeared as 'little more than havens of individuality' with little capacity for development into 'cohesive collectivities' (Gray 1989), is beginning to fade. The external pressure for sharp appraisal systems was perhaps based on a wish to maximize the accountability of the individual, but the initial benefits have been collective in nature.

Observation

It was perhaps unfortunate that the introduction of appraisal schemes was required as part of a pay settlement, rather than through a more natural process of recognition that such schemes were a key component of an institution's planning process. In the months following the professional contract settlement, as institutions either modified existing staff appraisal schemes or began afresh, there was an inevitable distaste over the fact that government had required the introduction of appraisal schemes by threatening to withhold grant.

At the next possible opportunity, the Secretary of State again used his holdback powers. Two per cent of each institution's pay bill for academic staff was held back pending confirmation that staff appraisal schemes contained a contractually binding commitment to 'observation and/or other methods of instruction'. At one level, this was an innocuous issue; lecturers in the PCFC sector were perfectly used to being observed – by professional accrediting bodies, by colleagues in team-teaching approaches, and by Her Majesty's Inspectorate (HMI); it was only when government required observation that they became suspicious. At other levels, it was a more difficult issue to manage. The whole thrust of the successful discussions on the professional contract had been to emphasize the full and rounded nature of the lecturer's role, and to cease defining it in terms of full-time teaching with agreed remission; now government was placing teaching (or instruction) firmly back at the centre of the lecturer's role, and making observation of teaching a central part of performance assessment. On 8 November 1991, Kenneth Clarke, then Secretary of State for Education and Science, went as far as saying in a letter to John Stoddart, the Chairman of the Committee of Directors of Polytechnics, 'I do not see how appraisal of lecturers is to be effective unless appraisers have the right to observe teaching.'

The weaknesses of such a narrow view are easily exposed, particularly at a time when even conservative institutions are increasing emphasis on managing the learning process by introducing a variety of forms of student-centred learning. If the key issue is to monitor and improve the quality of the student experience, then observation can play a part, but a relatively small one. Staff were not slow to concede the principle of observation, but to see government pressure for it as a precursor to a requirement for performance-related pay.

Reward systems

That pressure arrived within weeks. The salary settlement incorporating observation, though effective from September 1991, was eventually agreed after a national ballot on 22 January 1992; on 4 March, the Department of Education and Science formally confirmed to the PCEF that the condition for releasing the sum of money held back from the 1992/93 grant would be a

salary settlement which made provision to relate pay more closely to performance, along the lines set out in the government's *Citizens' Charter*. The *Charter*
affirmed that the ways in which people are paid can have a powerful effect
on improving performance. Pay systems in the public sector need to make a
regular and direct link between a person's contribution to the standards of
service provided and his or her reward. This government stance led to a
formal pay offer in the sector of 3.9 per cent, with a further 0.75 per cent to
be distributed selectively.

The negotiations on this package were played out against a background of
unrest across higher education. In the UFC sector government had intervened – constitutionally but without precedent – to veto an agreement between
the AUT and CVCP to increase salaries by 6 per cent across the board, with
a further 1 per cent to be agreed locally and a proposed joint working party
on performance-related pay. The objection to this was that the total package
was too generous, and the performance element too small. (The principle of
discretionary pay had earlier been reluctantly conceded by the AUT, and the
union therefore appeared perfectly happy to sign an agreement structured in
this way, so long as the basic increase was seen to be adequate.)

There was determined resistance to the principle of performance-related
pay from the union side in national negotiations, and the dispute could well
have escalated quite quickly. However, rumours that the November 1992
Budget would contain a draconian public sector pay freeze were sufficiently
strong to usher in a number of fudged agreements in higher education and
elsewhere. The PCFC sector fudge was based on a hurried acceptance at
national level of the 3.9 per cent which was on offer without strings and the
passing of the performance-related pay issue down to institutional level.

In surveying the varied institutional response to this situation, it is clear
that there exists a wide range of attitudes on the part of managers and
governors; some have readily accepted the guidance offered by government,
and moved with enthusiasm into a PRP scheme, while others have expressed
distaste for the principle and have attempted to find minimalist solutions.
Even within an institution like the University of Brighton, where both Board
of Governors and Directorate declared their opposition to PRP, middle management opinion was not always firmly against it. Those seeking to avoid
PRP on a divisive basis sought refuge in special payments for additional
responsibilities, staff development credits and additional promoted posts. Those
wholeheartedly embracing the principles introduced more straightforward
schemes. The University of Central Lancashire, for example, adopted a scheme
categorizing all teaching and managerial staff as having had 'an exceptional
year's performance' (which merited a 7.5 per cent bonus), 'a most satisfactory year's performance' (which merited normal treatment for salary purposes,
but no performance-related bonus), or 'an unsatisfactory year's performance'
(for which an annual increment would be withheld).

The further development of performance-related pay schemes remains on
the government agenda. The School Teachers Review Body struggles with it
each year, but has made little progress towards an acceptable scheme (see

HMSO 1993a); the police service is determinedly fighting off the approach proposed in the Sheehy Report (HMSO 1993b). However, two years (1993/4 and 1994/5) of pay restraint have dented progress somewhat, in that it is difficult to extend the discretionary element of pay when overall increases remain below two per cent.

The satisfactory resolution of this issue does seem to us to be critical to the future of human resource development in education, bearing as it does on the concepts with which we began this chapter – corporate culture and staff morale – and on those aspects of change which we have been intent upon fostering: a stronger sense of shared purpose based upon open communication. It is widely accepted that most academics are principally motivated not by money (unless the sums involved are fearfully large) but by the freedom to engage in research, scholarship and teaching in an appropriate environment. It has not been difficult to reward particular instances of excellence with the existing mechanisms of promotion or accelerated increments; but the implementation of a high profile scheme which brands a small minority of staff 'excellent', a large majority 'satisfactory' and a few stragglers 'unsatisfactory' is likely to undermine both staff morale and relationships between staff and those who manage them. It is also likely to undermine the appraisal system, from which much of the evidence on performance must necessarily be drawn; ironically, the evidence from the appraisal system is not likely to be sufficiently sharp to demonstrate (as legally it must) that differences in pay are based on objective criteria.

The Fender Report (1993) prepared by the CVCP from a traditional university base, but published after the dissolution of the binary line, promotes 'a continuing shift of responsibility for pay and performance to individual institutions and individuals' and accepts the desirability of a link between performance and pay; but it also recognizes that 'the fashion which led to a concentration on individual performance' is being replaced by a growing emphasis on the collaborative performance of teams and the development of individuals within them. It therefore seeks to retain the limited mechanisms previously adopted in the traditional universities to reward exceptional individual performance and to introduce complementary mechanisms for rewarding team performance.

Although the Fender Report does not solve the PRP issue, it does at least move the discussion forward. It recognizes that withholding routine cost of living increases is not a viable way of managing poor performance, it emphasizes the role of the team (unit or department) over that of the individual, and it stresses the need for objectivity and transparency.

Final thoughts

In addition to these areas a number of tough questions remain before the further and higher education sectors. On pay arrangements in higher education, for example, the ending of the binary line has not led to sector-wide unified arrangements. Separate scales, superannuation arrangements, titles and distribution of posts show no immediate prospect of being merged, and this is before such radical ideas as a single spine of pay points to cover all university appointments can be considered.

Such formal problems conceal the demarcation issues facing both sectors. The primary functions of the colleges and universities, of teaching and research, will undoubtedly optimally be met in the future by a more fluid teamwork approach from all staff: teachers, administrators and other, equally professional, support staff. To achieve this, entrenched and defensive attitudes (on all sides) will have to change (see Bocock and Watson 1994).

Further and higher education will also have to deal with one of the other watchwords of the 1990s: *diversity*. Diversity of mission across both sectors can often be appealed to as an alternative to considering desirable but painful rationalization of provision. If, however, it is to result in positive system-wide outcomes, more critical thought needs to be given to management strategies for different types of institution on a collective basis, not least in human resources. The prospect of networking within families of institutions is an attractive one, and could avoid the danger of enervating battles as major problems are fought out, in isolation, at 'plant' level (see Tight 1988).

As will no doubt have been apparent from the beginning of this chapter we, like most other institutional managers, have some fairly rough and ready ideas on what appears to work in the approach to managing change, and what does not. Our primary stress throughout has been on the importance of communication and consultation, recognizing that these are not the same thing. People being managed through periods of significant change, especially when the implications are on the face of things distressing and in that sense at least not chosen, appreciate and are more likely to respond positively to clear information on what is happening and why. They are also more likely to accept changes if they understand them and respect the motives of those driving the changes. Equally, they will have a right to expect consultation, rather than just communication, in areas in which their own experience and expertise can be seen as potentially making a positive difference.

These sound like modest objectives. They are – and a similar level of modesty needs to be reinjected into management discourse. People with not very long personal histories of working in the sector can already count on several fingers the number of new dawns which they have been promised, and the equivalent number of new structures, plans and objectives which they have subsequently found themselves dismantling and replacing for the next policy steer. For managers this means vitally resisting the temptation to oversell the significance and likely impact of change. Managing change successfully, ultimately depends upon understood and shared values and objectives, for the managers and the managed.

3

Developing a Human Resource Strategy

Elizabeth Lanchbery

Editors' introduction

This chapter uses the device of a thinly disguised case study of an HE institution over a three to four year period from early 1988 to illustrate some key
factors for the development of an HR strategy. The institution concerned was
at the cutting edge of the major issues involved, the details of the case study
are very interesting in themselves, and they provide a basis for the author's
strategic recommendations. We feel that it is particularly significant that the
author concludes that the implementation of the HR strategy 'has greatly
facilitated other change processes in the University . . .'

Introduction

A chapter with the title Developing a Human Resource Strategy is the sort
which most people might skip in the hope that it would not really matter, but
this is worth reading because it is more an adventure story than a dry debate.
First, however, it is necessary to define a *strategy*. According to that old standby
The Concise Oxford Dictionary, the meaning is clear. Ignoring the more warlike
inferences, it is an overall plan, the direction of a whole operation, a grand
design. It also has overtones of being advantageous or giving an advantage, and
should not be confused with a stratagem which is a cunning plan or a trick.

It is traditional, given the warlike connotations, for the grand strategy not
to be revealed to the foot soldiers, who are simply told where to go and when.
In organizations such as colleges and universities, which are relatively labour
intensive and rely on a predominantly, well educated, professional workforce,
the obscurity of military grand strategy is hardly appropriate. The sense of
vision for the organization needs to be largely a shared one, although writing
it down is often very difficult without it seeming a collection of trite well-worn
phrases. The overall plan for managing the human element of the organization is critical, therefore, in helping people to share the vision.

The organizational strategy is usually set down in a written plan with specific objectives or goals, some of which will relate to human resources, but the full human resource strategy may not be written down in full or shared fully with the whole community because revealing it may make achieving it much more difficult. The way in which people are managed and dealt with as individuals will, however, signal very clearly the nature of the organization and its strategic vision. Actions do indeed speak louder than words and people will judge the organization by what happens to them rather than by the fine words and corporate 'glossies'!

The case study

The best way to illustrate this is to describe what happened in one institution – a university which started out as a polytechnic – and how by having a sense of strategic direction for the university and for managing the people working in the university, significant change could be brought about without major staff unrest. The story must start somewhere, and the focal point would seem to be 1988, when the board of governors of the polytechnic was planning for independence from the local authority.

There was a personnel department in the polytechnic operating a service entirely under the guidance of the local authority using borough terms and conditions, rules and regulations. All decisions relating to academic staff pay and conditions were taken by borough education staff and, until very recently, all administrative and related APT&C staff gradings had been determined by the Borough Personnel Department. Although the polytechnic had, in theory, been semi-autonomous, the decisions relating to its most valuable resource, its staff, were taken elsewhere. Faced with becoming an independent employer on 1 April 1989, the board of governors decided that, at least in the first years after independence, human resource issues would be critical to the success of the institution and it should employ a senior Human Resource professional at Assistant Director (Vice-Principal) level. This was, in hindsight, a courageous decision. No other institution had this type of post and it was by no means accepted within the polytechnic itself. The notion of recruiting an Assistant Director who was not an academic but was a professional manager and a personnel manager at that, caused some outcry. The fact that the person appointed was a woman and relatively young by senior academic standards did little to help, although that is another story.

What the board of governors, with the Director (now Vice-Chancellor) did, was put HRM centre stage on the senior management team at a time when the organization was about to undergo very fundamental and major changes. The Assistant Director Human Resources (now the Personnel Director) was part of the management team developing strategy in a way that it had never done before. As strategy was articulated, sometimes painfully late at night in hotel conference rooms, human resource thinking was there contributing fully and ensuring that human resource strategy would be pro-active and would act as a major vehicle for bringing about the organizational change required.

The place of the Personnel Director on what was in effect the institution's main board was critical to the development of such a human resource strategy. Without this position in the organization the process would have been much slower and less planned. It was important that the human resource strategy was seen as realistic and lead to realistic achievable plans. There were pressures in the system to maintain the status quo and other pressures to bring about radical change from local authority practice as quickly as possible. The direction for change was part of the overall strategy, but whether and how this could be realistically achieved was a vital part of the human resource contribution.

The sense of vision achieved in those early days still holds although much has happened to the organization. The strategy gave a sense of direction to guide the organization while providing a flexible planning structure to allow it to be opportunistic in responding to the changing environment.

The SWOT (i.e. strengths, weaknesses, opportunities and threats) analysis which led to the overall strategy was very simple and very obvious. There was little disagreement over the general direction, although there was vigorous debate about how to get there. It was recognized that a major strength of the organization was its diversity and, within that, the freedom for members of staff to be entrepreneurial and to pursue new ideas and new developments on their own initiative. Many initiatives were generated at the 'chalk face' and only reached the attention of the top of the organization at a late stage. The great weakness, however, was that there was often no corporate view of an issue and those generating ideas and initiatives were not responsible for resources, often leading to waste of resources and unplanned outcomes. In particular, the unplanned outcomes often resulted in widening the academic/non-academic divide, which was identified as a potentially destructive element in the culture of the institution. The academic view was that support departments existed only to service academics and often did not do it very well. The departments viewed the academics as making entirely unreasonable demands on the system and pressing forward with plans without any regard to resource implications.

It was clear that the next few years would be tough financially and that good financial management would be critical for the survival of the institution. The challenge then was to create an organizational framework which would allow the diversity and personal initiative which were essential to the academic quality and vigour of the institution while ensuring sound financial management.

The institution had been very successful as a polytechnic and there was no perceived need to change the overall character and mission, simply to write it down and make it explicit. The Mission Statement was written down and has stood the test of time. Although some words have been changed, the overall intent remains the same. It is: 'To provide career-related higher education, advanced training and research for the development of individuals and organizations in support of the economy and society'.

Given this statement and the analysis of strengths and weaknesses, two major strategic decisions were taken which needed a major input from human resources. The first and perhaps the most fundamental decision was that the organization must be managed. This may not seem an exactly revolutionary idea, but it was not how many people perceived a higher education institution should be run. The tradition had been that of a collegiate culture, where decisions were taken by committees and groups of peers, and the leaders, heads of school/deans, were *primus inter pares*. This collegiate culture was exemplified in the old universities where deans were often elected for a fixed period and were definitely not considered managers. As part of the new strategy the deans were appointed as managers, given budgetary responsibility and significant delegated authority for staffing issues. The same delegated authority was given to heads of the service and corporate departments. Academic structures remained largely unchanged so as to retain as far as possible the two-way communication and ownership given by these collegiate-type structures. The senior management team of the polytechnic was expanded to include the deans and retitled the Executive so that deans were clearly seen to be part of and party to corporate decision-making.

The second important decision was that the future of the institution would depend on the ability to ensure capital investment and that without investment in the end the organization would die. All educational institutions are labour intensive, typically spending some 65 per cent of revenue on salaries and wages. Assuming that the new funding councils would not have large amounts of capital to give away, the polytechnic needed to free revenue to build up reserves and guarantee future investment. The future, therefore, lay in taking more students, thereby increasing revenue, albeit not proportionally, while keeping the same number of staff, and maintaining staff morale. This increased productivity was essential to a secure future, but it would necessitate significant effort to motivate and reward staff appropriately and to innovate significantly in the delivery of teaching and learning.

Within the corporate plan there were, and remain, two core objectives which relate to HRM:

- Maintaining and developing a flexible, competent and well motivated staff team
- Providing services to support all students and staff.

These strategic decisions had significant implications for both the human resource strategy and for the role and function of the personnel department. The main areas for action identified were:

- To move away from the local authority culture as quickly as practical. (Local authorities have now also moved considerably in HRM.)
- To give local managers as much power as possible within an agreed personnel framework.

- To articulate the role of governors in human resource matters, in particular to ensure that they would not act in the same way as local authority councillors, but would act strategically and allow managers to manage.
- To acknowledge that the trade unions would remain part of the scene, but to stress the importance of the direct relationship between managers and staff and the importance of the individual as well as the collective.
- To gain the ability to change the reward package as appropriate to the needs of the institution.
- To gain the ability to change the organization relatively quickly to be able to respond to the requirements of external influences.

The personnel department

The first priority was to structure the new personnel department so as to meet the needs of the newly incorporated institution. Given the emphasis on delegation of authority to line managers, it was suggested that the recruitment process should be taken over by faculties and departments. The organization was universally critical about the performance of the personnel function, but when managers were offered delegated responsibility they unanimously declined and asked that the personnel department continue to provide a central service. The personnel department, which included payroll, evolved a role with two distinct elements: a service/advisory role and a policing role. This duality of role will be very familiar to most personnel professionals, but the function was a new one within the institution. The personnel department has, over the years since incorporation, gained a high degree of acceptance. It would not have been possible to implement a strategy for HRM without a strong personnel function, not necessarily in numbers, but in expertise and the ability to deliver.

It is, perhaps, worth examining briefly how the personnel function worked to support the strategy. The service role was fairly standard, a complete central recruitment process, from placing the advertisement to issuing the contract and signing on the new member of staff. The selection decision was, however, delegated to the appropriate manager. In faculties, deans were responsible, but in certain cases could delegate the decision. A decision was taken early on that personnel staff could not possibly attend all interviews; it was simply too time consuming. Someone would attend at the request of a manager, but otherwise the personnel department issued detailed guidelines, forms to be completed for equal opportunities and arranged training for managers. The Executive agreed, however, that the Personnel Director should have access to any interview panel on request for quality control purposes and to intervene in the case of any problems. This service function was very important in human resource terms because it ensured the quality of the first contact of a potential employee with the organization.

The personnel department issued all contracts of employment and carried out all the administration relating to pensions and the interface with payroll.

The fact that personnel was seen very much as the guardian of contracts was vital to the subsequent work involved in changing terms and conditions. The payroll function which is normally regarded as simply reactive, managed to set new standards of service and became more user friendly. Managers and staff became used to talking to payroll and using payroll staff as a valuable source of advice. This new approach helped to improve communications generally between the function and the faculties and departments.

The policing role and the advisory role were very much seen together and the acceptance of policing depended critically on the perceived value of advice given. The fact that personnel gave good sensible advice about something seemed to make laying down the law more acceptable. All managers, however much they wanted to do their own thing when it came to employment matters, agreed that, as one employer, the university must have fair systems which were seen to apply to all. The Personnel Director was given responsibility for all issues relating to gradings, structures and the application of the pay system, acting in individual cases on the recommendation of a dean or head of department. Senior managers became accustomed to communicating with personnel, asking for advice and, on occasions, accepting it.

The personnel department was expanded to improve the quality of advice available, and a health and safety office and an occupational health service were established. The ability to deal properly with ill health cases was much appreciated and helped to enhance the credibility of the function. The safety adviser was also welcomed, despite the policing role, because managers realized that safety issues would become increasingly important. In common with other parts of the function, these new specialists experienced the phenomenon known as 'herding cats' or trying to get academics to adhere to procedures. The freedom of expression given to academics was often taken to include the ability to ignore policies and procedures. The policing function could only be undertaken with some element of consent and if the community, managers and staff alike were prepared to acknowledge the need for rules. Personnel had to communicate and explain policies and procedures at every opportunity and many times over. It was not enough to write to deans about something, we had to explain at the Executive, write out, explain again, achieve apparent consensus, and then explain again! The experience of trying to communicate within the culture stood us in very good stead when it came to manage the major changes ahead.

The process of change

The first year of independence was recognized as very important in setting the agenda for change. A plan of activities was drawn up which would signal to staff the way in which the new organization would be run and set the pattern for subsequent changes. There was a need to communicate with all staff informing them of the change of employer and although this could have been treated as a mere formality, it was considered an important first communication. It was also a useful test for the newly designed personnel computer system, and it proved itself capable of generating labels to send letters to staff.

The view taken at the time, on good advice, was that although the individual contracts passed to the new employer unchanged, the collective rights did not. The trade union recognition and all collective agreements not deemed a part of the individual contracts, no longer existed after 1 April 1989. The strategy, devised with the employment committee of governors suggested that the unions should be recognized, but the relationship with the individual staff member should also be recognized and built up over time. A recognition agreement was concluded, in line with the national agreement concluded by the newly formed Employers' Forum, the PCEF.

It is perhaps worth noting that the legal position on contractual transfer has subsequently been clarified and the view expressed in the previous paragraph has been proved wrong. In 1992, NATFHE obtained a High Court declaration on the effects of the EC (now EU) Directive 77/187 (Transfer of Undertakings, Businesses, etc) on the incorporation of FE colleges which took place in April 1993. The terms of the EU Acquired Rights Directive were declared to apply to incorporation, and indeed to any statutory or other contractual employment transfer. This declaration meant all collective agreements, as well as individual terms in the contracts of employment, remained in force after incorporation. Although there was no material retrospective effect on HE, the declaration will affect future transfers and mergers.

In addition to the standard letter, it was considered important to make some changes to terms and conditions of employment and to communicate the change at an early date so as to place change firmly in people's minds. Members of the Executive were offered and accepted new individual contracts, and it was considered appropriate that, as senior management, they should change first. The administrative, APT&C, contract had a number of well recognized problems associated with it. Staff, by custom and practice, took more annual leave than was specified, by notionally working more hours during term time and accruing time off in lieu. The APT&C grading structure had not been revised for many years and there were no proper grading criteria other than using comparators. The first change would therefore be changes to the hours and leave for APT&C staff and a new grading structure.

The process by which the change was made was as important as the change itself. The borough had been highly unionized and had negotiated all changes with the unions. Indeed, the unions felt that they had the right to veto any change or, at very least, to delay change by ensuring protracted negotiations. The new APT&C contract was drafted and discussed with the Executive before being presented to the two unions recognized as representing APT&C staff, NALGO and NUPE. However, the contract was presented only for consultation and not for negotiation. It was decided that it would be sent to staff individually and staff would be asked to sign to accept the new terms and conditions. Those who signed received an additional increment and a slightly higher salary scale to reflect an increased working week of 37 hours instead of 36. The increase in the pay bill was considered acceptable because the polytechnic was experiencing severe recruitment difficulties for APT&C staff and increased pay was considered good for recruitment and retention. It was only realized later that there was a benefit in moving slightly away from the national pay scales, if only to show that the polytechnic was an independent employer.

The contracts were prepared and sent out without union objections and were signed and accepted by all staff except two, one who lost the contract, and one who had a grievance about her conditions. The new contracts were considered an improvement on the old ones and were seen to tidy up a lot of loose ends. The new grading structure was designed to be as simple as possible and to avoid the worst excesses of complex job grading systems such as the system for manual staff inherited from the borough, appeals for which were being heard a year after independence. The new system was fully discussed with the Executive and then once again the unions were consulted. Some changes were made at the unions' request, but the scheme went through very easily and was implemented with no grading appeals. Although the grading scheme was considered as perhaps rather simplistic, it has stood the test of time and is still in use, with minor modifications, in the university today.

As a new employer, it was important to establish the basic policies and procedures and to try and harmonize terms and conditions for all staff where possible. During the first year the following were negotiated with the unions:

- the statement of values as an employer,
- the recognition agreement,
- the mechanism for consultation and negotiation,
- a union facilities agreement,
- the disciplinary procedure,
- the grievance procedure,
- the collective disputes procedure.

These were negotiated and fully agreed with all the unions sitting down together – something of a triumph – as under the borough negotiations for academic and non-academic staff were kept completely separate, and there were problems between the affiliated and non-affiliated unions. It was considered worth negotiating these procedures because they may be the subject of outside scrutiny, for example at an Industrial Tribunal, where agreement with staff representatives is important.

The other important work during the first year was to make a start on changing the academic staff contract. This change was recognized as the single most important change and one that could not be brought about easily. Institutions were advised by PCEF to offer all new academic staff a new style of contract with effect from 1 September 1989. The teaching unions, NATFHE in particular, were implacably opposed to such a contractual change and made it known nationally that industrial action was likely on the issue. The irony was that the academic contract did not represent the actual working practice of most academics and those who worked to its terms were seen as not pulling their weight. The contract was more symbolic than real, symbolizing the academics' freedom of action and ability to manage themselves. Any change was seen as an attack on academic freedom and somehow an acknowledgement that academics were not working hard or doing their jobs properly.

The first step in evolving a new contract was to gather information about what academics were actually doing and what was considered a reasonable pattern of work. The contract was discussed with the executive and governors and the intention made clear: the university would introduce the contract for all new appointments and promotions with effect from 1 September. Some deans were concerned about the prospect of such a change, but with the firm backing of the director the contract was agreed. The unions were then invited to discuss the contract or indeed negotiate the contract if they wished. The response, which was not unexpected, was that they would not now, nor in the future, negotiate locally on changes to the contract. It was made very clear that a new form of contract would be introduced with or without the agreement of the unions, although the offer to negotiate was made in good faith and management wished to agree such a major change if possible.

The Personnel Director personally visited all faculties and addressed large meetings of staff to explain the new contract and why a contract which reflected actual work practice was important. These meetings were somewhat cathartic, but necessary, and although most staff seemed very much against the changes, it was the act of communication that was important, part of the strategy to communicate directly with staff and not always through the unions. The contract was introduced for all new appointments and promotions and NATFHE immediately lodged a collective dispute under the new procedure.

In the meantime some new staff and most promotees were concerned about being offered the contract, particularly as only one other institution had taken PCEF advice, all others were still offering an old style of contract. Some deans were still concerned and did not want to confront staff on this issue, but they all held the management line. The unions took the issue through the disputes procedure which involved many hours of meetings and a final agreement on a form of words. The unions were prepared to accept an undertaking that the intention of the contract was not to destroy academic freedom but to reflect best working practice and that new staff would not be expected to carry a higher workload than other hardworking members of staff.

The personnel department carried a heavy load during this period in every way, seeing individual members of staff, helping managers with individual problems, ensuring that the paper work was in order and communicating with staff directly, often by circulations to all staff by post. The text of these letters was often drafted at least five times because the need to communicate clearly was recognized. As an academic institution the importance of the written word cannot be ignored and, from experience, the message can be ignored if the language is inappropriate – academics will mark your spelling rather than take on board difficult issues!

The polytechnic moved into year two and we were still managing to move down the change agenda. New academics were on new contracts and we had experienced no major industrial unrest. The next step was to change the contract of heads of schools and departments, part of the original plan, but, now demanded by the government which imposed conditions on funding as part of increasing the efficiency of the sector. One of the guiding principles of the HR strategy was to harmonize terms and conditions as far as possible; it seemed appropriate to embark on the harmonization of academic and non-academic heads of department. A new generic title of Senior Staff was proposed and has now become part of university vocabulary. The aim of promoting a managed institution meant that the Senior Staff were and remain a crucial part of the management team and it seemed inappropriate to negotiate with union representatives on behalf of their managers. That year, these staff were excluded from national pay negotiations other than the setting of a minimum rate of pay. It was decided that a representative structure should be established to deal with Senior Staff issues and that trade unions would be excluded from negotiating for this staff group. There was a view that such senior managers should be dealt with as individuals and that there should be no collective bargaining. However, the Senior Staff themselves felt very strongly that they wished to have a representative structure. Despite some reservations, particularly on the part of some governors, it was decided that, to give staff a feeling of ownership of the process and outcome, a consultative committee should be established.

The contract proposed was based on the contract which had been in use for almost a year for new academic staff, modified in line with the APT&C staff contract as some quarter of Senior Staff had previously been on senior APT&C type contracts. The academic heads were initially opposed to the concept of harmonization, arguing that their role was substantially different from that of the non-academic heads. The non-academic heads themselves were neutral about the change and were on the whole prepared to try the new proposals. The Executive staff contracts had been changed from 1 April 1989 and it seemed that the non-academic heads felt closer to the Executive group, whereas the academic heads identified strongly with the academic staff.

The discussions about contracts were linked to that year's pay award and to a major change in grading and pay structure which involved the creation of a pay band without increment points. The contract also assumed the introduction of an appraisal scheme which would be designed with staff involvement and introduced the following year. The discussions were not easy, but were, on the whole, constructive and with the advice of the academic heads of Personnel Management and of Law we arrived at a contract that seemed broadly acceptable. All Senior Staff were asked to vote on the proposals and by a large majority they accepted that all would transfer to the new arrangements. This was very exciting for the personnel staff because it was the first local deal and represented a significant shift in the organization.

After the summer, the national negotiations on changing the academic contract for the whole sector seemed to be heading for industrial action. The new model contract produced for the national negotiating body had been broadly agreed, but issues relating to use of time and academic freedom remained unresolved and no formula could be agreed to pay for the proposed changes. Within the institution, however, some 20 per cent of academic staff were already on the new contract and the process adopted to change the Senior Staff contract had been watched very closely by academic staff and generally considered reasonable. The discussions held with the local union representatives during the collective dispute about the contract had resulted in a constructive relationship, as shown by the relatively rapid negotiation of the range of procedure agreements. The Personnel Director and Vice-Chancellor decided that there was the opportunity to pursue a local deal on the contract and avoid the industrial action which now seemed inevitable. Informal approaches were made to the union representatives with draft proposals for revisions to the new academic contract and a pay deal for all academic staff to move to the contract.

The response, not unexpected, was that there could be no local negotiations, although the proposals had some merits, particularly in the light of the Senior Staff settlement. Informal discussions were, however, possible, so that when there was a national agreement the local interpretation would be ready. The discussions were held very quietly, in the evenings, at weekends, in hotels to avoid creating too much interest or too high an expectation on either side. After six weeks, a proposal was on paper for a contract and a pay deal which the union representatives were prepared to take to their members locally to test opinion. Our negotiations had, naturally, not gone unnoticed on the national management side and we were in receipt of much advice about how much money could be offered for the new contract and in what form. The institution suddenly became the focus for much interest and various visits from national figures. The local union representatives were summoned to head offices and asked to explain what they were doing and came under considerable pressure both locally and nationally to wait for the national negotiations to reach agreement. Both sides had the courage of their convictions and believed that the proposals represented the best deal for the Polytechnic and proceeded to a formal ballot of union members.

The personnel department swung into action and arranged circulation of the full proposal to all staff in advance of the ballot. From that point on, staff were kept fully informed of all developments and letters went out to all staff at least once a week. The final offer was sent to home addresses to ensure that all staff at least opened the envelope. The final outcome was acceptance of the local offer by a comfortable majority, which led to a very rapid settlement of the national dispute along the lines of the local agreement. Despite the consumption of a fair amount of champagne, the agreement was a new beginning rather than the end of the process and it paved the way for local agreements on a whole range of issues, some as part of the national agenda, and others part of the overall HR strategy, for example, freeing up the incremental scales for academic staff and developing new criteria for promotion to Principal Lecturer.

The national agenda running alongside the local priorities gave some problems and distorted timescales, but having a fairly clear sense of local direction allowed overall priorities to be assessed and kept on target. The local agenda is still running and the next major initiative is the harmonization of manual and APT&C staff conditions. The new university is still a part of the national pay arrangements, but it is always prepared to opt out if national negotiations do not deliver suitable arrangements. We are still working on communication and perhaps one day we will feel that we have finally got it right.

Final thoughts

The process of the implementation of the HR strategy has greatly facilitated other change processes in the university, because it engaged everyone, unions, staff and managers in discussion and debate. The strategy has moved on from being centred on industrial relations to other aspects of human resources, for example, appraisal and a current initiative to provide more systematic and where possible, certificated programmes of training and development.

The lessons from this case study are fairly simple and clear and in many ways not revolutionary, but they show that a strategic approach to the management of human resources can work. They are that:

- A human resource strategy only makes sense in the context of an overall organizational strategy.
- The human resource professional needs to operate at top Executive Board level. Without this level of authority, or at least being there when strategy is discussed, any strategy is less likely to work.
- An organization needs a clear sense of vision, one that can be communicated and shared.
- Any strategy is a sense of overall direction and must be flexible enough to bend under outside pressures. There is a sense in which success depends on being opportunistic.
- Managers must be prepared to take risks and be brave and the HR function must be right there with them.
- Communications are vital, if in doubt communicate and communicate again.
- A HR strategy must be continually reviewed and updated.

As we set out to revise the plan for another year, the strategy and the general sense of direction still holds good although the overall goals move ahead of us. As Robert Louis Stevenson wrote in his essay 'El Dorado' (1881) 'To travel hopefully is a better thing than to arrive, and the true success is to labour.'

4

Managing Diversity

Rebecca Nestor

Editors' introduction

Despite the oft-repeated claims that educational institutions are liberal organizations, there is still much to be done in all areas covered by the generic term Equal Opportunities. It is probably the case that schools' and FEs' practice is in advance of that to be found in HE institutions, and, within the latter category, that the new universities are in advance of the old. It is therefore most appropriate that the author of this chapter is employed by one of the oldest of the old universities.

The objective of this chapter is to provide a framework within which to remedy the current situation. It begins by briefly describing the legislative scene and suggesting some reasons for the continued under-representation of women and ethnic minorities at senior levels in education. It examines the progress made at national level in raising the profile of equality issues and sharing good practice and finally sets out an action plan for human resource managers who wish to make a substantial contribution to the management of diversity within their own institution. The author has provided especially valuable guidance in the section on recruitment and selection.

The current situation

Educational institutions have been heavily criticized in recent years for the small numbers of women and ethnic minorities they have appointed at senior levels (see CRE 1990a). Figures for ethnic minority staff are not yet officially collected for HE on a national level although the new Higher Education Statistical Agency plans to collect them from such institutions as are able to provide them from 1994/95 and from all institutions as soon as possible. However, according to the CVCP, in the new universities women make up 46 per cent of lecturers, but only 12 per cent of those on grades above Principal Lecturer. In the old universities, women form 33 per cent of those on the

Lecturer A scale, 19 per cent of those on the Lecturer B scale, 9 per cent of those in readerships and senior lecturerships and only 9 per cent of those in professorships nationally (CVCP 1993 and CVCP 1994c). Among academic-related staff in old universities, women form nearly half of the total numbers in the lower grades; their proportions drop in the higher grades and they form only ten per cent of the professorial-level grade. Among technical staff the patterns are similar, with a sharp drop in the proportions of women at senior technician level; among clerical and library staff, a heavily female-dominated group, women form 86 per cent of those in grade one and 74 per cent of those in the highest grade; and among manual staff, women form 84 per cent of those in grade one, but only 29 per cent of those in grade four (CVCP 1993). It is nearly 20 years since legislation was introduced to address institution-alized discrimination against women and ethnic minorities, yet this pyramid is a familiar and depressing pattern, repeated with variations in the gradient of the slope throughout the rest of the public sector, industry and the professions. It could be argued, however, that educational institutions, by comparison with government departments, local government and some of the big multinationals, have taken fewer and less co-ordinated steps to try and flatten their particular pyramid.

The legal framework

Educational institutions, like other employers, are subject to the Sex Discrimination Acts of 1975 and 1986; to the Race Relations Acts of 1968 and 1976; to the Equal Pay Act of 1970 and the Equal Pay (Amendment) Regulations 1983; and to the Disabled Persons (Employment) Acts of 1944 and 1958. The precise provisions of the law are not dealt with, but this section explains direct and indirect discrimination to set the scene and describes two examples of case law that are particularly relevant to education.

Direct discrimination is defined as 'less favourable treatment on grounds of' sex, marriage, race, nationality, ethnic or national origin. Examples might include action taken on the basis of stereotypes – for example, assuming certain characteristics in people of a particular race; action taken on the basis of acceptability – for example, in the belief that customers would not like a black person on reception; inconsistency – for example, failing to shortlist an Asian candidate because she did not have teaching experience, while shortlisting a white candidate who also lacked that experience. Direct discrimination cannot in law be justifiable.

Indirect discrimination occurs when (i) an employer sets 'a requirement or condition' which individuals have to meet to gain a particular benefit; (ii) that requirement is applied equally to all, but members of one race or sex are less likely to be able to meet the requirement; (iii) there is a detriment to those who cannot meet the requirement; and (iv) the employer cannot justify the requirement without reference to race or sex. An action or policy may be indirectly discriminatory if it meets the first three criteria, but it is only unlawful if it also meets the fourth – that is, if it is not justifiable. An example might be the use of an upper age limit of 30 for research posts: the limit applies to all, but women and ethnic minorities are less likely than white people and/or men to be able to comply with it because a larger proportion of women than men are likely to have spent time in their twenties out of paid employment caring for children, and people from minority ethnic groups may have obtained the appropriate qualifications later in life than white people. There is clearly a detriment to those who cannot meet the criterion, because they are ineligible to apply for the research post or they have to make a special justification for the fact that they are over the age limit. This requirement is therefore indirectly discriminatory and the organisation responsible would need to show that it was nevertheless justifiable.

A key question must therefore be what might constitute a *justifiable criterion*. Since the early 1980s, there have been changes in the courts' interpretation of justifiable in this context. The present position of the courts appears to be as given by the Employment Appeal Tribunal in *Greater Manchester Police Authority* v. *Lea (1990)*:

> It is not enough for it to be shown that a condition was imposed in pursuance of an intrinsically laudable and otherwise reasonable policy if there is no relevant need of the employer in connection with the condition.

Criteria and procedures must be clear, transparent and consistent. The case of *Hay* v. *Lothian Regional Council (1983)* is particularly instructive for the education sector (Scottish Industrial Tribunal, reference SCOIT 913/83). Mrs Hay was a Senior Lecturer A in Business Studies at a college of further education. She applied for the post of Senior Lecturer B, for which the stated selection criteria were a degree and/or professional qualification, preferably a teacher training qualification, and experience in using computers in business teaching. She was not shortlisted. One of the men interviewed, who was later appointed to the post, seemed on the face of it to be less well qualified than Mrs Hay: she had eight years' experience and a Teaching Certificate in Further Education, while he had three years' experience and no such qualification. The employer argued that there was no need to interview Mrs Hay, since she had been at the college for a long time and her experience and work performance were well known. They also said that the deciding factors in appointing the successful candidate were his managerial experience in industry, and the fact that he was seen to have the best 'development potential'. In support of her claim of direct discrimination, Mrs Hay argued that she was better qualified than the successful male candidate and should therefore have been interviewed; she also claimed unlawful indirect discrimination on the grounds that fewer women than men had managerial experience in industry, and that this experience was not necessary for the post.

Mrs Hay was found by the tribunal to have been subject to direct discrimination. The college's selection criteria seemed to shift from those declared in the advertisement to those used as the reason for appointing the successful candidate; the criterion of development potential was particularly vague and susceptible to sex bias; and the statements made by one representative of the college contradicted those made by another. Taking these facts into account, the tribunal confirmed its *prima facie* impression that direct discrimination had taken place. It also accepted that fewer women than men could meet the 'managerial experience in industry' criterion, but disagreed with Mrs Hay that this criterion was unjustifiable.

Leaving aside the question of whether a post-1990 tribunal would have found unlawful indirect discrimination, there are some powerful messages for education here. The strongest is that we have to be much clearer than we have traditionally been about the relative priority to be given in each academic appointment or promotion to teaching on the one hand and other aspects of the post on the other. (For experience in industry, one could substitute research in the higher education context: the principles – and the potential for discrimination – are the same.) Since 1983, some work has been done on defining teaching, research and administration more precisely, and this is useful. But the danger is that HE institutions persist in giving candidates one message – that teaching skills are what is sought – when posts are advertised, and quite another – that teaching plays second fiddle to research productivity or income generation – when it comes to explaining why they were unsuccessful.

According to a survey by A. H. Halsey (1992), women spend a slightly greater proportion of their time than men in teaching undergraduates and correspondingly less of their working time in research activity; men do more supervising of research students than women; and 81 per cent of the university women surveyed (compared with 56 per cent of the men) thought that their teaching commitments left insufficient time for research. When these statistics were adjusted to take into account the fact that women in the survey were on average three years younger than men, they resulted in a similar, though less pronounced pattern. The same survey analysed the effects of sex on the probability of promotion to professor and suggested that the differences between men and women related primarily to doctoral qualifications, research orientation, and research performance (place of graduation was not a significant factor). Men were more likely to hold a doctorate, to be 'research-minded and more productive with consequently better chances of promotion'. If we are to avoid another Hay, we must at least be honest about these priorities; if we are really in the business of managing diversity, we should reconsider them.

In *Enderby* v. *Frenchay Health Authority and Secretary of State for Health* (1993), an equal pay case, the European Court of Justice ruled that it was not sufficient for an employer to show that significant pay differences between female-dominated jobs and male-dominated jobs arose for non-discriminatory reasons. The employer must also show that such pay differences were based on objectively justified factors. In such a case, the fact that a difference in pay between jobs of equal value arose through non-discriminatory collective bargaining was not sufficient objective justification; nor could the fact that market forces played a part in determining the pay differential be a blanket defence.

Dr Enderby, a speech therapist, first claimed that her work was of equal value with principal pharmacists and clinical psychologists in 1986. According to the employers, the difference in pay was due to the separate negotiating structures by which the pay for the relevant professions was determined. The case went from industrial tribunal, to the Employment Appeal Tribunal, to the Court of Appeal, to the European Court. After the European Court's decision in October 1993, it is no longer sufficient for employers to point to separate collective bargaining mechanisms to justify differentials in pay. The education sector, like the NHS and other public sector employers, must now consider whether, for example, the pay, terms and conditions of the female-dominated clerical and library staff group are equal with those of the male-dominated technical staff group; and if they are not, whether there are objective, non-discriminatory reasons why.

The experience of other employers

FHE institutions are not alone in struggling with the difficulties of recognizing, valuing and rewarding diversity. Other employers' experiences have demonstrated the difficulty of achieving outcomes that are entirely defensible either in legal terms or against other forms of challenge. Recent research has suggested that, in organizations studied, women and ethnic minorities have had less chance of achieving promotion than their white and/or male counterparts. An investigation of London Underground Ltd carried out by the Commission for Racial Equality discovered that ethnic minority staff were proportionately less commonly selected for promotion than white staff. The CRE (1991a: 24) suggested that the tests used in the selection process were biased against ethnic minorities. Work undertaken by Hammond and Holton (1991) on behalf of Ashridge Management Group for Opportunity 2000, *A Balanced Workforce?*, cites a survey carried out within the Post Office that showed that despite a well-established equal opportunities policy, some recruiters tended to value 'male characteristics' [*sic*] and, as a result, were not recruiting or promoting women in representative numbers. But it is also true that education can learn from the experiences of other employers. Many government departments include equal opportunities objectives in the performance indicators for their managers. Boots the Chemist has provided equal opportunities awareness training sessions for 40,000 staff. Rank Xerox has run a high-profile positive action advertising campaign to encourage women to join its engineering staff.

The education experience

Within the higher education sector, equal opportunities policy statements are common, but detailed arrangements for implementing them are less so. In 1991, the CVCP carried out a survey of old universities' equal opportunity policies and arrangements. The survey indicated that, while 85 per cent of respondents had an equal opportunities policy statement, only 7 per cent had a designated equal opportunities officer, only 26 per cent had a plan for putting their policies into practice, and only 36 per cent were running any training related to equal opportunities. The subsequent report commented, 'There is a lack of material currently in use in universities and great reliance is being placed on the use of external training consultants and material devised for use elsewhere' (Taylor 1992: 293–4).

Since 1991, institutions have been working to share their experiences and develop good practice. An offspring of the Association of University Administrators, the Higher Education Equal Opportunities Network, which meets twice a year, holds discussions and workshops on such issues as appraisal and equal opportunities, harassment and equal opportunities training; it has a newsletter and has begun its own members' training programme. WHEN, the Women in Higher Education Network, was founded following the report of a ground-breaking research project based in King's College, Cambridge, and written by Andrea Spurling (1990), spent its first three years under the auspices of Nottingham University and is now co-ordinated by the University of Central Lancashire. The Commission on University Career Opportunity, set up by the CVCP in 1993 in emulation of a similar and very successful body in the United States, aims to share good practice between institutions; develop ideas on effective use of the positive action provisions of the Sex Discrimination Act 1975 and the Race Relations Act 1976; and investigate reasons for the glass ceiling that seems to be preventing women and ethnic minorities achieving promotion in substantial numbers. The Commission's 1994 survey found that the proportion of universities with action plans for the implementation of their equal opportunities policies had increased since 1991 from 36 per cent to 37 per cent (CVCP 1994c). The University of Central Lancashire runs a harassment network, which aims to enable other institutions to share their own and Lancashire's experience of dealing with harassment.

The old universities, with their tradition of slow change and, perhaps, a certain complacency, are to some extent being shaken out of their gradualist approach by the shock of the new. Faced with the more radical approach to equal opportunities taken by many former polytechnics and institutes of higher education, and suspecting that the proportions of senior women and ethnic minorities in these institutions might be embarrassingly higher than in their own, some practitioners in the old universities are starting to question the liberal, colour-gender-blind culture within which they have worked until recently. Opportunity 2000, a largely business-led campaign 'to increase the quality and quantity of women's participation in the workforce', now has a significant number of FHE members and a special sub-group looking at equal opportunity issues in higher education. With its focus on leadership from the top towards the aim of fundamentally changing member organizations' culture, Opportunity 2000 represents a challenge that universities are increasingly taking up. The lessons to be learned from successful change management, identified by Ashridge Management College for Opportunity 2000 (Hammond and Holton 1991) are that the impetus must come from the top; that resources – money, time and staff – must be put into the project; that there must be a commitment to changing behaviour; and that there must be involvement of all staff and a general sense of ownership of the project. Some of these principles may be difficult ones for institutions as a whole to act on; but they can and should also apply to individual parts of an institution. Managers intending to promote the recognition and valuing of diversity among their own staff may find the following approach an effective one.

Scope for action

This section sets out the main components of a substantial policy for the management of diversity. The headings used are recruitment and selection; appraisal, staff development and training; dignity at work; support for those with caring responsibilities. This is the area on which most institutions have focused their equal opportunities policies. The basis of a policy should be systematic, fair procedures and selection criteria that do not unfairly exclude categories of applicant. There is also scope for encouragement to under-represented groups.

Recruitment and selection

Starting at the beginning of the selection process, the job in question should be carefully defined. At this stage, it is worth thinking both about the content of the job and how it is presented: neither is unalterable and an imaginative approach here can begin the process of opening up jobs to those who have been excluded in the past. For example, a senior technician's job that is consciously conceived and presented as including a substantial element of working with students, supporting and developing more junior staff and liaising with other departmental managers is likely to be more attractive to women – as well as more accurate – than one that is described purely in terms of the technical tasks involved.

The core of the process – defining selection criteria – follows from describing the job. It is here that the most positive steps can be taken to ensure equality of opportunity. Women often have different career paths from men, returning to education as mature students and beginning to build careers in their forties. Those with disabilities may have been through segregated education and faced low expectations of their abilities; they may also have experienced discrimination in employment (see RADAR 1994). People from minority ethnic groups may have educational qualifications unfamiliar to white selectors or have previously faced discrimination in education or employment. Women are also more likely than men to take a break in their career for childcare, although breaks for the care of elderly parents seem likely to become more common among members of both sexes. For these reasons, selectors should avoid relying on rules of thumb such as years of experience or a standard qualification to assess candidates. Criteria should be as accurate and precise as possible, neither more nor less demanding than the job requires; they should also be flexible, not blindly requiring experience and qualifications but enabling candidates to present themselves with either or both so long as they have the necessary skills. There is a human tendency for selectors to base their criteria on the profile of previous postholders: while this is unavoidable to some extent, it also carries the danger of reproducing the race, sex and age of previous postholders. Characteristics that require a highly subjective judgement on the part of the selector, such as pleasant personality or sense of humour should be rethought. What kind of pleasant personality? What is so awful about the job that a sense of humour is essential? Selectors should be encouraged to think about what the postholder needs to do and work from there.

Job advertisements, of course, should be free from any implication that members of one sex or race are unwelcome. Traditional policies of internal-only advertising will need to be reconsidered if the institution is to avoid reproducing the ethnic and sex balance of its existing workforce. Advertisements should avoid jargon and should be consciously phrased to be clear to those outside the education sector: if they are understood only by the initiated, what chance do we have of a workforce that is representative of society at large? Many institutions use the phrase 'An equal opportunities employer' or something similar; more positively welcoming statements can be included if the job is one in which members of one sex or race are substantially under-represented. For example, an advertisement for Registrar in most institutions could safely say, 'The University of X, as an equal opportunities employer, particularly welcomes applications from women and ethnic minorities, who are under-represented at this senior level. All applications will be treated on merit.' The relevant section of the Sex Discrimination Act and/or the Race Relations Act should be quoted. It is not lawful to guarantee interviews to members of one sex or race. However, people with disabilities who meet the basic selection criteria can be guaranteed an interview and many employers have begun to make statements to this effect in job advertisements. With a little imagination, advertisements can be placed where those who are under-represented will be especially likely to see them, without the need for significant extra expenditure. There are increasing numbers of networks of women in the professional and education sectors and these form excellent media for advertising education posts.

The job details or further particulars provided to candidates are of vital importance, particularly given the high costs of advertising. As much relevant information as possible about the job, the selection criteria and the terms of employment should be given. At this stage the institution is conveying strong messages about its equal opportunities culture and if the information is clear and comprehensive – including details of any equal opportunities initiatives such as enhanced maternity schemes, childcare, extended leave for visits to country of origin or flexible working – those messages stand a better chance of being positive.

A standard application form helps maintain consistency in shortlisting, by ensuring that all candidates present the evidence in similar formats. It can also help by minimizing the amount of unnecessary information (for example, age, sex, nationality, type of school attended, marital status, how many children) candidates provide. It may be necessary to collect some of this information for the successful candidate, but there is no reason why this cannot be done after the appointment has been made. The Commission for Racial Equality recommends that questions on nationality be not asked, and suggests that if employers wish to know whether candidates would require a work permit if appointed, they should phrase the question in these terms. Increasingly, institutions are carrying out equal opportunities monitoring of the selection process, by asking candidates to complete a questionnaire, usually anonymously, giving details of their sex, marital status, race, any disability and sometimes whether they have dependants. Candidates should be reassured that this information will not form part of the selection procedure. (For a useful guide, see CRE 1991b.) If this kind of monitoring is not carried out, large or public sector employers, of whom high standards are expected, are at a substantial disadvantage when defending claims of unlawful discrimination.

Shortlisting and interviewing should be carried out by more than one person to minimize the risk of bias. Some institutions have adopted codes of practice that require selection panels, wherever possible, to contain at least one member of each sex and/or racial minorities. This practice can be very effective, both in public relations terms and as a means of raising awareness internally. It does, however, need to be approached in a positive spirit since otherwise it can degenerate into a meaningless rule under which women and ethnic minorities become token, powerless and resentful observers of a process in which they are not full participants. In departments or institutions with small numbers of women and/or ethnic minorities, it may be useful to look outside to increase the pool of panel members, and reduce the burden on female and ethnic minority members of staff.

The interview itself can act as a powerful channel for communication of the institution's policy on diversity. Good interview practice, in which interviewers know what they are looking for and have the skills to ask the right questions and probe effectively, is vital. The CVCP has recently published a resource manual on equal opportunities in recruitment and selection which covers the whole process but may be particularly helpful in relation to developing good interview practice (CVCP 1994b).

Selectors should keep records of shortlisting and interviewing. This not only provides evidence in the event of a claim of discrimination, it also helps make selection more efficient. A significant factor in making procedures more transparent is the provision of honest and accurate feedback to unsuccessful candidates: full records are essential here if feedback is to be genuinely accurate, and records also help selectors make decisions based on evidence rather than intuition.

Appraisal, staff development and training

Work at the University of Birmingham on equal opportunities and appraisal suggests that women and ethnic minorities may tend to undervalue their achievements and stress weaknesses; and correspondingly that appraisers, who are likely (because they are managers) to be white and male, may accept this assessment at face value (Ryan and Slater 1993). Appraisal systems can usefully have built into them the opportunity for appraisees to change their appraiser; the right to be appraised by someone of the same status; training for appraisers and appraisees in the equal opportunity implications of appraisal; and the right to appeal against an opinion of the appraiser.

A survey by the Equal Opportunities Commission in 1991 found that women were less likely than men to receive work-related training from their employers. Conversely, it is the experience of many staff development sections, in education as elsewhere, that women form the majority of volunteers for the internal courses provided. This is not a paradox. It probably reflects to some extent the distinction between the qualification-led, vocational training surveyed by the EOC and the short courses provided by most in-house training functions, and suggests that while women may be very enthusiastic about, and receptive of training, the longer vocational or professional courses are either not suitable for their needs, or their employers do not consider them worth the considerable investment such courses demand. It is worth carrying out a survey of the training undergone by women, men, ethnic minorities, people with disabilities and older people, to establish whether the EOC's findings are replicated. If they are, a positive policy of encouraging under-represented groups to attend day-release or similar programmes may be very helpful. Educational institutions are well placed to develop their own in-house training programmes, which can therefore be carefully designed to meet the access needs of disabled employees and the childcare or other domestic requirements of parents or those with elderly parents. In addition, some groups may benefit from self-development or career development courses such as the Springboard programme (see Willis and Daisley 1990).

Training more traditionally associated with the management of diversity is generally referred to as equal opportunities awareness training. This provides managers and employees with an understanding of their responsibilities and of the organization's policy, either generally or on a specific topic such as harassment or recruitment and selection. Such training is often best linked to the introduction of a new initiative and can act as a very effective tool for building the support, ownership and commitment of staff. An excellent handbook is available on the design and running of equal opportunities training (see Garrett and Taylor 1993).

Dignity at work

Harassment can be a form of unlawful discrimination. It can also prevent those who are subject to it from doing their jobs well. As such it is the responsibility of the employer to see that all its employees are treated with respect and are able to maintain their personal dignity. In 1991 the European Commission published a Recommendation and Code of Practice, *The Protection of the Dignity of Women and Men at Work* (CEC 1991), which describes the steps employers should take to prevent harassment and deal with it effectively when it does happen. Within the educational sector there is lively debate on this subject, with the King's College, London case of alleged rape in 1993 prompting re-evaluation of institutions' disciplinary procedures as they apply to harassment, and the AUT's attempt to provide a model code of practice on consensual relationships between student and staff (AUT 1993) stimulating wider interest focuses on harassment of students. Insofar as harassment is more likely to take place where there is an inequality of power, this interest in a relatively powerless group is understandable. But in a strongly status-conscious sector like education, harassment of staff by their colleagues and managers must also be an issue.

It is almost impossible to judge the prevalence of sexual harassment. This is partly because what is a joke to one person is harassment to another, and partly because, like rape, it is probably very much under-reported. Several major surveys have been carried out: their conclusions vary, but the most conservative of the confidential surveys suggest that around one in four women has experienced some form of harassment (see Commission of the European Communities (CEC) 1993, for a summary of surveys on sexual harassment). If these surveys give a reasonably accurate picture, under-reporting is a serious problem. The University of Oxford carries out annual surveys among its departmental and college harassment advisers, and the 1993 survey showed 31 cases reported to advisers (University of Oxford *Gazette* 1993) – this in an institution with 6000 staff and 12,000 students, which has set out to try and ensure that people suffering harassment feel able to approach someone about it.

Many institutions have set up some form of adviser network. This may constitute one or two people in each department (usually one male, one female), backed up with a central panel whose members may be approached by those who do not wish their case to be dealt with by someone within the department, or who may become involved if departmental mechanisms have broken down. Alternatively the departmental advisers may be little more than contact people who will more or less automatically refer complainants to members of the central panel, who are expected to be fully trained in counselling and harassment issues. Some institutions have made it a principle of the adviser system that it is wholly separate from the disciplinary system. Others have given investigatory powers to the central panel and in effect set up a separate disciplinary procedure for cases of harassment. All these practices are based upon a recognition that the employer needs to be responsive to complaints of harassment, that the complainant should retain as much control as possible over the process commensurate with the employer's need to take appropriate action, and that the proceedings should be kept confidential as far as possible.

Support for those with caring responsibilities

One university survey of its staff found that a significant number of senior male staff foresaw increased caring responsibilities in the near future in relation to their elderly parents. (A cynic might say that it is only when senior people discover how difficult it is to juggle paid work with work at home that employers start to take the problem seriously.) Universities, with their traditions of long vacations and self-directed work, have nevertheless faced the same problems as other employers in disseminating part-time, flexible working as common practice throughout the workforce. Job share policies, laudable though they are, are meaningless unless they are adopted together with a real change in the culture so that commitment ceases to be equated with long hours and 'part time' no longer means 'low status'.

Using the principles of successful change management, one mechanism for changing this culture might be the adoption and public presentation of a whole package of measures to support those with caring responsibilities (see Working Mothers Association 1993). Because of the relatively slow decision-making processes in education, such measures are often taken on a piecemeal basis and introduced with little or no publicity (it can seem rather pointless to shout it from the rooftops when you manage to agree the provision of an extra two days' leave for caring for sick children). If, however, the institution can co-ordinate its activities so that it opens a nursery or after-school club at the same time as introducing new schemes for enhanced maternity and paternity leave, part-time working, long-service sabbaticals for the care of elderly parents and care leave for sick dependants, presents them as part of a package and trains managers in how to implement the new terms and conditions, it is much more likely to see a result in terms of take-up. Equally, a department or section can take the opportunity to hold discussion sessions on flexible working, review all posts to identify those suitable for job-sharing and publicize its findings, and/or collect information on the need for help with childcare among its staff to feed into the wider institutional discussions.

Conclusion

A diverse workforce will contribute a diverse and valuable range of skills and abilities to an organization, many of which will be lost if homogeneity is the order of the day. Hence the effective management of human resources must encompass the management of diversity. This is inevitable: the question is whether managers try to minimize diversity, hoping that all staff will conform to a single pattern, or whether they welcome it and try to put in place systems for enabling the full participation, contribution and development of all. This chapter has tried to provide a few tools for the latter.

5

The Learning Organization

Jennifer Tann

Editors' introduction

In this chapter the author identifies the key characteristics of a learning organization, but points out that it is a process which can never be completed. However, despite the constraints put in their way, the author detects that further and higher education institutions 'are beginning to develop tentatively as learning organizations'. Amongst the many penetrating insights in the chapter are two which the Editors find particularly apposite: first, that high achievement in formal education is no guarantee of the ability to apply that knowledge and second, that there is a growing recognition in FHEIs of the contribution which staff other than academics can and do make.

Introduction

A participant at a recently held workshop on managing change in the not-for-profit sector, reflected on her day's learning and said that, for her, the major learning point had been that there were some people in her organization, perhaps many, for whom having to hang their coat on a different peg was a major innovation. As a recent CVCP Report written by Fender notes:

> Adverse reaction to change is very common in all organisations. Most people are wary if not hostile. The reasons are well understood. They include a fear of the unknown; a reluctance to change familiar working habits; a general feeling that the change is always for the worse; and a number of specific fears like reduction in career prospects, downgrading of work, loss of status, reduction in responsibility and job interest, and the break up of established working groups and friendships.
>
> (Fender 1993: 34)

Such a statement could have appeared in any part of the public service sector or in manufacturing industry; that it was written in 1993 in a document concerning a strategic framework for the management and development of staff in UK universities may perhaps cause some eyebrows to be raised. Such a statement would have been unthinkable in 1983.

But there is more. The Report cites examples of the ways in which people in universities have been expanding the boundaries of their traditional jobs. Technicians have contributed both to research and teaching. The boundaries between departmental secretaries and graduate administrators have become relatively meaningless at the senior secretary end of the spectrum. These developments are by no means universal and, as the Report suggests, have probably been secured despite rather than because of personnel management structures and processes in universities. Strong forces are exerted towards the maintenance of the status quo and those in more senior positions tend to devalue the contributions of those who are nudging at role boundaries. The contribution made by technicians towards teaching, for instance, may be devalued by academics who claim that technicians do not teach but 'instruct' while graduate administrators seek to maintain the boundary between themselves and senior secretaries. As the Fender Report suggests, 'The suspicion is not that staff have been badly managed but that they have been inappropriately managed' (CVCP 1993: 35).

The current focus in universities old and new on clients and their needs, has led to the emergence of new roles which cut across occupational boundaries, requiring the subcultures of FHE to change. Universities have been changing rapidly since the early 1980s. Some of the major changes such as those resulting from the Jarratt Report (1985) were initiated by the CVCP. Others and sometimes conflicting ones have been required by government. There have been instructions to expand, followed by requirements to maintain a steady state, later enforced by the imposition of penalties for exceeding planned numbers, for instance. The CVCP initiative on academic audit has been, to some extent, replicated by the Quality Assessment Committee, established by the Higher Education Funding Council. These apparent inconsistencies of policy have meant that senior managers in higher education have had greater difficulty securing the commitment of those in the middle who have responsibility for management and oversight of the core activities of an institution namely, teaching, learning and research. Some ten years ago, in the old universities, departmental management was more generally referred to as administration, heads of department were more frequently elected and there was, at least in many institutions, the notion of 'Buggin's turn'. Heads probably spent somewhere between 20 and 30 per cent of their time on administration/management. Nowadays, they spend 50 per cent or more of their time, particularly if they are heads of schools with a fully devolved budget to control, in addition to the overall management of human and other resources (Tann 1994).

The majority of heads of academic departments and academic deans have come to their current positions via achievements in the academic sphere. Many have had little management development unless they have been recruited from or have had prior experience in the public sector or industry. While some institutions have joint consortia for the training of heads of department, many staff development units are directing their attention largely to new academic recruits, providing training in methods of teaching and learning which are more or less mandatory, as well as providing training for support staff at all levels. Few training needs analyses have been carried out into the learning needs of managers at any level in FHE. The Fender Report draws attention to the fact that all managers have a teaching role incorporating a responsibility to stimulate learning by their staff. It goes on to state that 'involvement in their own learning is the most important condition for ensuring staff development' (CVCP 1993: 35). Until educational institutions actively accept that they have a major role in promoting and enabling the learning of their employees, besides the provision of teaching and learning opportunities for others, they will not be identified as institutions concerned with modelling lifelong learning – a core feature of a learning organization.

Individual learning

An essential characteristic of a learning organization is that it facilitates the learning of its individual members and continually transforms itself, yet opportunities to encourage individual learning can be missed. In the process of staff recruitment and selection at all levels in an organization, emphasis is generally placed on education and experience, the emphasis on one or the other being greater in different contexts and cultures. The distinction is pointless since high achievement in formal education is no guarantee of the ability to apply that knowledge, while wide experience is no guarantee of knowledge, understanding or competence. The emphasis on past experience, particularly on output rather than process, leads employers to fail to ask the crucial question for a learning organization during the selection process, 'What did you learn last year?' and 'What are you hoping to learn this year?' They thus lose the opportunity of indicating that the institution not only encourages but demands lifelong learning. FHE has been as remiss in this respect as other employers. Once an individual becomes an employee of an educational institution, bearing in mind the role boundary changes outlined above, there is a need for those in management or supervisory roles to provide coaching and mentoring, for the institution to become a learning organization.

Kolb, whose learning cycle has been of considerable influence amongst educators and trainers, focuses upon problem-oriented learning, starting from the position that what people have learned must be evident from their actions. Problems represent both the motive and the vehicle for learning in Kolb's model. The cycle commences with experience leading on to reflection, conceptualization, deciding and planning and returning to (re)doing (Figure 5.1). Experience is achieved through action, reflection is the meditation on this experience, conceptualizing involves analysis and understanding, while deciding and planning involves choice leading to the cycle being repeated, for learning is never ending. While conscious learning is implicit in Kolb's cycle,

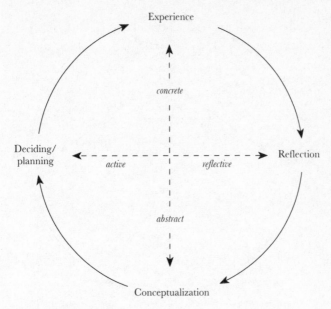

Figure 5.1 Kolb's learning cycle.

it is not explicit. Much learning embodying practical implications is achieved through education rather than experience – issues involving health and safety are an example – and, particularly in a FHE context, the model might, with benefit, be modified to make conscious learning an integrated part of the whole (Figure 5.2).

The introduction of teaching quality assessment has required higher educational institutions to address issues of teaching and learning using language and concepts which are unfamiliar to many academics. The modified learning cycle suggests a way in which academics might become reflective practitioners through the application of reflection in and on, as well as the conceptualization of, experience and learned principles, to the planning of improved educational interventions for students. But this implies a receptivity to individual learning which may not be there in practice, 'but we're professional, we're all good teachers' is too often heard amongst older academic staff, and while the remark suggests arrogance, it is more likely to indicate blindness. The fact that the initial postgraduate education and training of school teachers takes one year does not seem to be relevant to some older members of academic staff, for whom the classroom door remains firmly closed. Change has occurred, however, amongst newer and younger academic staff. Several universities have introduced a qualification in university teaching and a number of staff in those institutions are working towards it.

If there is some resistance to development in what might be considered to be a core area of academic professionalism, how receptive are staff to learning new skills in other areas? The Enterprise in Higher Education initiative has

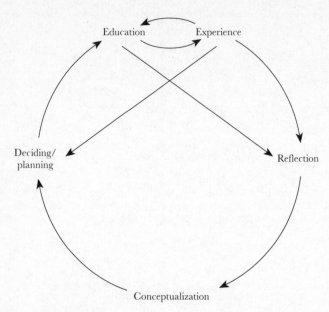

Figure 5.2   Modified learning cycle.

had different emphases in different institutions. In some, the emphasis has been upon the acquisition of IT skills, in others it has been on staff development and in one new university it has been on organizational development. Outcomes have been more or less successful in different institutions, and there have been significant successes in particular departments although learning may not have diffused throughout the institution. However, many staff development managers observe that those who could benefit from training and development do not seek it.

Organizational learning

Organizational learning implies the changing of the behaviour of an organization through a collective learning process. Obviously an organization can only learn through the learning of its individual members, and without individual learning no organization can be a learning organization. On the other hand an organization has not automatically learned when the individuals within it have learned, for while individual learning is necessary, it is not a sufficient condition for organization learning. Organizational learning involves mutual behaviour change, when a change in the behaviour of one individual has an effect on the behaviour of others and there is mutual learning. The key feature of an FHEI, as with any organization, is that effectiveness requires people to co-operate, to think things out together, take decisions and carry out activities. When the behaviour of the FHEI changes in an institutional

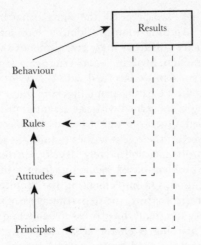

Figure 5.3 Single, double and triple loop learning.
Source: Adapted from Swieringa and Wierdsma 1992.

sense, the organization also changes in an instrumental sense. Swieringa and
Wierdsma (1992) build on Argyris' and Schön's concept of single and double
loop learning (1978), relating it to the three levels of organizational culture
identified by Schein (1993). Single loop learning in an organization can bring
about changes in the existing rules. For example, a department in a HE
institution experiences a steady decline in applications for places on its core
undergraduate course. To remedy the matter the department decides to increase its publicity, to hold open days and produce a new prospectus. Or the
institution may decide to introduce new rules to establish minimum standards to inform undergraduates on their progress each term. Instructions are
sent accordingly through faculties to departments. Changes in behaviour at
the rule level are to do with 'improving on what we already have'. Put
another way, the learning will pose the question 'How?' but less frequently
the question 'Why?' Single loop learning is concerned with improvement
solutions sought and generally found within the existing paradigm.

Double loop learning involves not only changes in rules but also in the
underlying assumptions. In the examples above, the department would begin
to consider its curriculum and whether this meets student needs, as well as
whether the atmosphere in the department, college or university is welcoming. The department required to introduce new rules for informing students
of their progress would address the issue of how this could improve staff–
student relations and contribute to the avoidance of misunderstandings. Thus
double loop learning requires insight and the consequences are more far-
reaching, the number of individuals involved in the change is greater and the
learning process will take longer; 'why?' questions are asked and questions
concern collective knowledge and understanding. Double loop learning may
involve conflict, dispute and contradiction between individuals, departments

and other groups. These are precisely the signals that indicate the need for double loop learning. An indication that double loop learning is required is when enhanced publicity fails to increase recruitment or when colleagues lose a sense of collective mission. Swieringa and Wierdsma (1992: 41) term double loop learning *renewal* since it is concerned with the restoration of insights and assumptions supported by existing principles and values.

Triple loop learning is concerned with the essential principles on which the organization is founded. Questions might be raised concerning the position of the FHEI within its sector, the role it wishes to fulfil, its identity. The department with falling enrolments collectively develops a plan to move from a discipline focus to a problem-based focus and from a didactic to a learner-centred form of education. On implementing the required rules for meeting students to discuss their progress, the department recognizes that this could provide an opportunity to extend the process to academic self and peer review as well. Triple loop learning is characterized by 'Why?' questions as well. FHEIs are experiencing the need for the radical change of triple loop learning when reorganization and structural changes do not solve a problem. But practical solutions are difficult to identify and conflict will often result. In-fighting becomes a displacement activity, while others take avoiding action – the classic fight or flight syndrome. Triple loop learning is concerned with development, the development of new principles by which an organization can achieve more fundamental change.

Evidence of double and triple loop learning is difficult to find in organizations. While the impact of its absence can readily be identified, effective mechanisms which enable it to take place require exploration. FHEIs are by no means alone in largely engaging in single loop learning.

As organizations, FHEIs possess many of the characteristics of a bureaucracy. While their structures are not overly centralist or hierarchical, nor are they strictly functional with line and staff structures, those FHEIs, which have developed a fully devolved system of budget centres, are coming more to resemble multi-divisional organizations. While individuals can learn a great deal within a bureaucracy, although much of it may be one-sided, organizational learning is more difficult. It is in this kind of organization that there is often a considerable discrepancy between what Argyris and Schön characterize as espoused theory and theory in use. Espoused theory concerns the concepts which people say determine their actions, while theory in use concerns the concepts which explain their actions. The emphasis in espoused theory is less on tackling problems collectively and more on talking about them at the level of small groups, departments, faculties and so forth. Academic and administrative colleagues, 'try to convince each other and presumably themselves, via reports and presentations full of rhetoric and rationalizations that they know what has to be done and how they are going to do it' (Argyris and Schön 1978: 57). But more deadly is what Argyris (1990: 12, 14, 24 and 67) terms the 'skilled incompetence' which arises out of theory in use when individuals seek to control but not upset people, when they engage in defensive routines and fancy footwork and manage to prevent effective action.

FHEIs are prescriptive organizations or indeed persuasion organizations in which, particularly when things go wrong, someone else – another department, the faculty head, the centre or even the system – can be blamed. Attempts to achieve single loop and double loop learning are made through committees. But the learning cycle remains uncompleted because although decisions may be made, plans for implementation remain sketchy and feedback loops are not identified frequently enough to ensure that effective implementation results. There is a distinction to be made between what the world ideally should look like, and obtaining consensus about how a particular problem could be solved in FHEIs. Debates about the shape of the teaching year might be prolonged, for instance, and may be so inextricably linked with the concept of modularization that the solving of a standard way of dividing the year by proportion of learner effort is avoided.

A learning organization is one which will consciously permit contradiction and paradox, and a characteristic feature will be variety. FHEIs are uniquely placed to foster variety through people, strategies, structures, cultures and systems. It would be both an irony and a tragedy were the variety which has characterized the sectors in the past to whither and fade as a consequence of FHEIs responses to external pressures. Were this to occur, and there is a danger that it might, FHEIs would be less well placed to learn than they have been in the past while the pressures for change are greater than they have ever been.

The five disciplines

But no institution can seek to enhance its capacity to learn without recognizing that it will never arrive. As Senge (1990: 11) says, 'You can never say, "we are a learning organisation", any more than you can say "I am an enlightened person".' The more people learn, the more acutely aware they become of their ignorance. Thus, an organization cannot be excellent in the sense of having arrived at a permanent excellence; it is always in the state of practising disciplines of learning, of becoming better or worse. It is in this manner that Senge introduces the model of five disciplines that are required to be studied and mastered before organizational learning can be put into practice. To practise a discipline is to become a lifelong learner, and a discipline in Senge's sense is different from emulating a model of best practice which too often leads to piecemeal implementation and failure. Senge's approach has had a considerable impact on organizations in the USA. To what extent is it informative in our FHE sectors?

The five disciplines which, according to Senge, must be developed as an ensemble are:

- personal mastery
- mental models
- shared vision

- group learning
- systems thinking

Personal mastery, a term which carries unfortunate overtones, is the discipline of continually clarifying and deepening the individual's vision, of focusing energy, developing patience and of seeing reality objectively. It is in Senge's words 'the learning organisation's spiritual foundation' (1990: 7). The key issue here is the reciprocal commitment between the individual and the organization, between individual learning and organizational learning. Evidence of personal mastery includes questioning, creative tension and accelerated learning. People with a high level of personal mastery see the current reality as an ally rather than an enemy and have learned how to work with forces of change rather than resist them. In FHE, personal mastery has often been tramlined through the scholarly work of researchers. Excellent scholars may not recognize opportunities for applying their creative skills to wider learning issues within the organization.

Mental models, perhaps more appropriately termed mindsets, are the assumptions, generalizations and images that influence an individual's construct of the world. Too often new insights fail to be implemented because they conflict with existing mental models that limit individuals to familiar ways of thinking and acting. Senge argues that mental models need managing since they not only determine how individuals make sense of the world but how action is taken. This reminds us of Argyris' dictum that 'although people do not behave congruently with their espoused theories, they do behave congruently with their theories in use.' At worst, mental models lead to simplistic stereotyping: 'boys are better at physics than girls.'

Organizational mindsets have determined the espoused theory of what business FHEIs have believed they are in. Many mission statements mention teaching, learning and research. How many mention service? Developing an organization's capacity to work with new mental models involves the learning of new skills and the implementation of institutional innovations that will facilitate the regular use of these skills. One of the ways in which FHEIs could move towards working with new mental models would be to rethink strategy and planning in terms of institutional learning. Scenario planning, successfully employed by Shell in the 1970s, helps to expose corporate assumptions about significant issues and offsets a tendency for individuals to assume, implicitly, a single future. A failure to recognize the creative and liberating aspects of mental models may trap an institution into becoming stuck in a groove shaped by prior assumptions.

Building a shared vision involves a continuous review of the direction in which the organization seeks to go. It provides the focus and energy for learning and involves hearts as well as minds. An organization cannot aspire to learn without a shared vision, be it to achieve a number of 'excellent' ratings in teaching quality assessment, to enhance research selectivity ratings or to forge particular links with the local community. Without a pull towards a goal, inertia may be overwhelming. But do employees in FHEIs share a vision? Or is there the sort of resistance couched in the terms of 'When I joined the sector 15 years ago I did not expect it to be like this?' Anxiety of the future, a revering of the past, and high levels of stress inhibit the translation of visions from individuals to the collectivity. But FHEIs are not unique in this and the majority of people in the majority of organizations are 'in a state of compliance . . . they do what is expected of them . . . but they are not truly enroled or committed' (Senge 1990: 219). In the current environment, a negative shared vision may emerge as institutions begin to pull together when their survival is threatened. But negative vision may be deleterious, for energy that could be harnessed positively is diverted to preventing something from happening. Negative visions carry messages of powerlessness and they are short term. Motivation continues only so long as the external threat exists. Fear can produce extraordinary changes over a short period as the example of how the technological universities moved rapidly to survive the infliction of savage cuts in 1981 demonstrates, but it is aspiration rather than negativism which is a source of continuing growth and learning.

To those familiar with Belbin's work on groups and teams (1981), Senge's rhetoric question, 'How can a team of committed managers with individual IQs above 120 have a collective IQ of 63?' (1990: 9) comes as no surprise. Belbin demonstrates that the blue chip team composed of those with the highest IQs, regularly failed to achieve its objective. Similarly, groups of the most able academics may fail to achieve a target, and FHEIs are now recognizing the important contributions that can be made to problem solving and decision making by staff in other categories who will bring both intelligence and different skills to the group. Shared training in such areas as quality management, customer care and equal opportunities has demonstrated the value of group membership being balanced by different skills and attributes. FHEIs have a steeper learning curve in team learning in some parts of the organization than others. In clinical, science and engineering fields, research teams have been the norm for a number of years, for instance, whereas in the social sciences and humanities they are of more recent introduction and much research is still carried out on an individual basis. Team learning involves dialogue as well as discussion and, as Heisenberg argues, 'Science is rooted in conversations. The co-operation of different people may culminate in scientific results of the utmost importance' (in Senge 1990: 238). A learning team will understand the difference between dialogue and discussion and engineer the movement between the two. Is there a tension between the recruitment and selection policies in FHEIs which have fostered individuality within a culture of collegiality and Senge's concept of team learning? Could some of the most successful scientific research teams be more appropriately described as groups consisting of a loose federation of individuals working on related projects rather than a team in the more generally accepted sense? If this is so, are FHEIs engaging in dysfunctional learning or can dialogue, listening, trust, synergy and a creative rejection of consensus be achieved by a constellation of committed individuals?

Systems thinking, Senge's fifth discipline, is the pivotal one. It is concerned with creative interaction, with feedback loops, with interdependence and with a recognition that individuals, groups and whole organizations are part of the problem which they tend to blame on something or someone else – the HEFCE, the FEFCE, the competition or the economy. Systems thinking shows that the individual and the cause of his or her problem is part of a single system and that the cure lies in the relationship between the two. The essence of this fifth discipline lies in seeing change as a process rather than a series of cross-sectional snap shots and in recognizing circular relationships rather than linear cause and effect.

Finally, Senge's work on the five disciplines makes reference to the distinction between experience and education and between practice and principle. Mastering any of the disciplines requires an understanding of principles and a following of practices. Understanding certain principles is the trap of confusing intellectual understanding with knowing how to do something. Organizational learning involves new understanding and new behaviour underpinned by principles and practices, both of which are vital. And this is where FHEIs have much to learn, for decision making is engaged – in discussion (as distinct from dialogue); rules, codes of practice and principles are devised, but there is a tendency for there to be a shortfall between implementation and action. The Departmental Working Party (a quaint term from the past) may produce an admirable list of recommendations, all or most of which may be accepted by democratic vote. But putting these into practice is quite another matter, requiring different skills and involving different forms of learning.

Final thoughts

For a book subtitled *The Art and Practice of the Learning Organisation* there is an underlying paradox in Senge's bounded and integrated approach since relatively closed systems easily engender the 'not invented here syndrome'. By unpacking the concepts, customized incremental and piecemeal routes towards learning can be identified and implemented by FHEIs. After all, in a period of rapid change, all universities and colleges have adopted quality assurance procedures (see Tann 1993). The majority of universities have staff development units and some have educational development or educational methods units as well. Staff appraisal has been implemented in most universities for more than three years, and personnel departments are striving to achieve a greater adherence to professional selection procedures throughout institutions. Mentoring is becoming an accepted role of senior managers, and both academic and administrative staff can be effective 'boundary workers' scanning the environment for opportunities as well as threats.

Pedler, Burgoyne and Boydell (1991) have identified 11 characteristics of a learning company (Figure 5.4). Six of these characteristics can be identified in parts of a number of FHEIs, namely the learning approach to strategy, participative policy making, formative accounting and control, the existence of boundary workers, a learning climate and self-development for all. But all

	Identified in HE/FE
Learning approach to strategy	√
Participative policy making	√
Informating	×
Formative accounting and control	√
Internal exchange	×
Reward flexibility	×
Enabling structures	×
Boundary workers	√
Inter-company learning	?
Learning climate	√
Self-development opportunities for all	√

Figure 5.4 Characteristics of a Learning Company.
Source: Adapted from Pedlar, Burgoyne and Boydell 1991.

these characteristics imply a more flexible, facilitative and long-term approach than is usually deemed possible in a rapidly changing environment with a downward driving of the unit of resource. In the latter context FHEIs are more likely to become defensive, structured, rule-bound and overly bureaucratic, all of which are, in varying ways, inhibiting to organization learning.

Attitudes to learning in FHEIs range along a dimension from the strategic to the bureaucratic, reactive, apathetic and antagonistic. Initiatives such as Education for Capability, the training of sabbatical officers in students' unions, the empowerment of learners, the encouragement of self-managed learning and, above all, the modelling of lifelong learning by all staff who have a role in managing the human resource in FHEIs, are signs that, despite the difficulties, FHEIs are beginning to develop tentatively as learning organizations. Perhaps in a year or so a typical staff appraisal interview will be conducted along the lines not of 'What courses did you attend last year?' but 'What did you learn last year and what is your learning plan for the present and future?'

6

Effective Communication

Jo Andrews

Editors' introduction

This chapter examines the nature of the various communication channels which are to be found in educational institutions and the influence upon them of the organization's structure. It also explores the barriers to communication and the importance of conducting regular communication audits and attitude surveys. The constraints of space have prevented the consideration of staff newsletters and similar forms of communication, and the interested reader may wish to refer for further information to the educational charity, Heist, which is based in Leeds and concentrates on educational marketing and promotional issues. Heist (1993) has produced an unpublished survey entitled *Staff Newsletters in Higher Education* which is available to enquirers.

The need to communicate

Regardless of their major roles and functions within any organization the most precious skill that all good managers should possess is the ability to communicate. The importance of the need for this skill increases proportionately to the complexity and diversity of the organization. In small compact organizations the communication process – the giving and receiving of information – is likely to operate with greater fluency than in larger organizations with complex hierarchical structures.

As a starting point, however, it is helpful to explore some common misconceptions concerning the communication process. These were postulated by Clampitt (1991) as being alive and well in most organizations. He refers to these misconceptions as myths.

Myth no. 1 – more communication = better communication

This myth addresses the misconception that *everyone wants to know everything about the organization*. However, Clampitt informs us that information is not like money, more is not always better. There is an optimum amount of information that any individual can consume.

Many of us arrive at our pigeonholes after an absence of several days from the institution to be confronted with mountains of paper. There is a magical percentage which, without fail, journeys straight from the pigeonhole to the waste bin simply because it has no relevance or interest for the individual concerned. Everyone does not need to be informed of every decision in an organization – only those decisions to which a useful contribution could be made. It is more effective and efficient to specifically target individuals for communication.

Myth no. 2 – written communication = fulfilled obligation

If the communication is written and sent then the task is complete. This myth assumes that several processes have taken place once a communication has been sent and it assumes that the document has been:

- received;
- read;
- understood;
- agreed with.

It is clearly unwise to consider that a task has been completed simply because a record exists of a document having been sent. Frequently in large organizations written communications go astray or are not read thoroughly. The sender has a very specific comprehension of the message which is being conveyed, but how can the sender be sure that the receiver has understood exactly what it is that is being said?

The whole process of sending written communications without any attempt to encourage feedback carries a risk of antagonizing the receiver for it assumes that the message has been met with agreement. In an educational environment where many employees hold positions of responsibility this particular style can be interpreted as arrogant and can lead to unnecessary hostility.

Myth no. 3 – informing = persuading

It is a fallacy to assume that informing is the same as persuading for *an employee may understand a message given but may not agree with its content.*

Many communications are not complete acts in themselves but require further information and, probably, acts of persuasion in order that recipients respond as the communicator intended.

Myth no. 4 – one channel = efficiency

This myth could well be the case but is not automatically so. There is little point in installing noticeboards on an unused floor of any building. Noticeboards should be installed in places where people congregate. Employee reports merely made available for collection are not generally read while they are read with enthusiasm and interest if sent directly to individual members of staff. The preferred communication channel for the sender may not be the preferred one for the receiver.

If new communication channels are opened then they should be used with the location of the audience in mind.

The organization – communication structure

If we consider the organization as a pyramid, then there are two main types: one *steep* and one *flattened* (Figure 6.1).

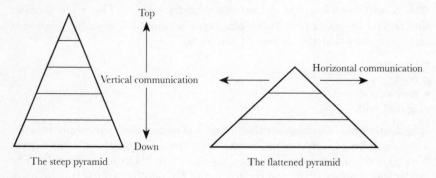

Figure 6.1

The steep pyramid

The steep pyramid is hierarchical in character with numerous managerial/supervisory layers. Roles and responsibilities are clearly defined with highly formalized authority. It is frequently referred to as bureaucratic.

The flattened pyramid

The flattened pyramid has fewer managerial/supervisory layers than the steep pyramid, there being greater flexibility and overlap between the various roles and responsibilities. It is frequently referred to as organic.

Communication flows

Vertical communication is top-down and, ideally, bottom up as well. Horizontal communication is from side-to-side within the layers. These flows of communication are to be found in both pyramid types, but vertical communication predominates in the steep form and horizontal in the flattened form. Top-down communication identifies strategies and objectives, issues instructions and provides performance feedback. Horizontal communication is inter-departmental and concerns the day-to-day or short-term issues arising in a working environment. Unless there is an effective cascade system of briefing within the organizational structure, top-down communication tends to be slower within a bureaucratic organization than horizontal communication in a more organic institution.

In an education environment the horizontal process is likely to be far more active than the vertical one. Hardly a week passes without staff being called to attend one meeting or another at which ideas and news are exchanged with other members of staff across the organization. The nature of the teaching/learning process requires that those teaching in teams regularly meet with other team members to monitor the progress and performance of students. This style of meeting is usually quite formal, but one of the most frequently requested changes to daily operations made by staff in communication surveys is that more information communication channels should exist.

Communication networks: formal and informal

The departmental staff meeting is the most common example of vertical, formal communication. These meetings are frequently chaired by departmental heads who may or may not have issued an agenda well in advance of the meeting. There is rarely an opportunity for all staff to attend these meetings due to timetable clashes, and time usually restricts questions from the floor. The most effective way for these meetings to be conducted is by issuing an agenda at least ten days before the meeting itself and specifically allocating time on the agenda for feedback from the audience.

Vertical informal communication is characterized by an open-door policy which, of course, is down to the particular management style adopted by departmental heads. Other examples of vertical, formal communication are the college newsletter and the employee centred report (discussed later in this chapter).

Horizontal communication in educational organizations also tends to take the form of meetings and memos. Not all educational institutions are able to provide staff with staff-room facilities that are adequate for informal exchanges of news and ideas to take place. Multi-site institutions have particular difficulty in this area.

Where both formal and informal networks do exist they may complement or work quite independently of each other. The most common form of informal networking in any organization is the much maligned grapevine. The grapevine is frequently highlighted as something quite negative in an organization which should be discouraged at all costs. However, a recent study by David Nicoll (1994) identifies the grapevine as an essential component of any organization, not only for the employees, but more interestingly, for management as well.

The role of the grapevine

The grapevine is the prime example of informal communication. In every organization there exists politics and power – politics being concerned with negotiating and power being the authority used to influence or coerce people. Both have positive and negative aspects. If handled correctly individuals may be persuaded to participate in activities from which they benefit, and if mishandled, politics and power are capable of destroying individuals and in some cases whole organizations. In the same way the grapevine (the rumour network) can enhance or ruin informal communication flows.

Where the grapevine is speculative it is likely to arouse apprehension and suspicion, whereas when it is controlled by senior management from the outset, it is a method of distributing new ideas amongst the workforce and measuring the reaction to the proposed changes. 'The grapevine is a good thing for a company and should be utilised to full advantage', claims David Nicoll. 'It's the best way of putting over corporate culture and values – it is ready-made and can never be rooted out.'

It was during a communication research project at the National Employee Communication Centre based at the University of Central England in Birmingham, that Nicoll discovered the extent to which the grapevine was used by senior managers. In the words of one manager, 'You find out what the statistics don't show.' A quarter of departmental heads valued informal feedback as a main source for identifying burning issues for staff. Discipline was a popular reason for using the grapevine with managers sending warning signals through the informal channels in order that individuals might be alerted to the fact that their bad behaviour had not gone unnoticed. This gave employees time to correct their behaviour without any formal record of disciplinary action.

Nicoll describes occupations where the job satisfaction is derived exclusively from personal contact. Many support staff such as porters and security guards are the 'silent but alert guardians when official communications are in full flow'. During the course of my communication survey work, in both the private and public sectors, I have been told time and time again by employees that the one person who really knows what is going on is the Managing Director's secretary.

Nicoll also discovered that, contrary to that which might be expected, the grapevine is remarkably accurate. It does not resemble that game of Chinese Whispers; instead there is '80 to 90 per cent accuracy'. Given that the grapevine is here to stay and that it has advantages for both managers and employees alike, the salient message to be learned from the research is that it is an unwise manager who attempts to interfere with the operations of this informal network. 'There's no need for subterfuge', we are told. The evidence suggests that managers actively participating in the grapevine are not under-mining the value of the more formal communication channels, they might also be utilizing them.

Responsibilities of the sender and the role of the receiver

At the very heart of any organization should be a corporate communication policy. Such a policy keeps all departments functioning throughout the organization and identifies the most qualified source to provide answers to questions. Many organizations simply do not have a communication policy and yet, dissemination of information is a major responsibility of the sender. Indeed, the responsibility for the accurate communication of information lies more with the sender than the listener.

In an educational setting one of the most important areas for communication is across departmental boundaries. Many lecturers find themselves teaming up with colleagues to deliver courses to students in departments other than their own. This creates an environment in which strategic communication issues are top-down while day-to-day information flows are horizontal.

The sender of information must be conscious of the organization's culture – bureaucratic or organic – for information tends to travel more slowly through a bureaucracy. Every sender of any piece of information should be asking him or herself, either on a conscious or sub-conscious level, the following series of questions:

What is my message?

The subject and content of the message should be clear. No communication should contain more than a limited number of messages (three is considered the maximum) and each message should be to the point. The objective of the communication should be clear and should be outlined at the outset – before the message is elaborated upon.

What is my purpose?

There are numerous forms of interpersonal communications – some are to instruct (and do not require or anticipate a reply) others are more persuasive in style. If the message is seeking an answer to a question then all details concerning how the answer can be conveyed should be included. It is vital for senders to be clear in their own minds and to express clearly in the message, what is the purpose and end objective of the communication.

What is the location?

Quite simply the message here is 'consider and target your audience'. There is little point in displaying a newsletter on a single noticeboard which is situated on the wall of a corridor where few people work. One organization where I was involved in a communication audit wrongly considered that they were successfully communicating their Annual Report to their employees by leaving copies at a particular collection point. The communication audit revealed that over 90 per cent of employees at one plant were not receiving these Annual Reports, as the collection point was too far away from their site for them to collect. The collection point was re-located more centrally and thereafter all employees received their own copy of the Report.

Who is my audience?

This question requires a certain sensitivity to the personality type of the receiver. It is quite likely that the tone of a communication to a superior or a subordinate will be different from the tone used to communicate with a colleague. Most organizations (even the more organic ones) have some form of hierarchy and some awareness of status and this affects the way we interact and communicate with each other.

Attention needs to be paid to the receiver's interpretation and understanding of the message, as individuals frequently develop their own particular meaning for, and use of, phrases especially after working for an organization for a period of time. The motive behind the message should also be clear to avoid suspicion.

Perception

This introduces the concept of perception: how we select from information we are given and convert what we have selected into patterns which then trigger our emotions and actions.

Recently after a trip to a secondary school in Northern Ireland I was told this salutary tale by the headteacher there. She had decided that a warm and welcoming gesture to the pupils of the school would be to stand and greet them in the entrance hall as they arrived at the building in the morning. After conducting a staff communication audit, the headteacher found, to her horror, that staff were upset that she had chosen to 'clock them in' in the mornings.

The headteacher had overlooked the fact that both the staff and pupils entered the school through the central foyer and that it could be perceived by staff that she was essentially checking up on them. This story indicates a total mismatch between what one person intended through her actions and what her audience actually perceived as her motives. This lesson encouraged her, as a manager, to detail, in all aspects of the school's communication processes, the intentions behind the actions. With language it is our previous experiences and learning, plus our general attitude, which leads us to codify words into our perceptual set.

It is therefore important that the use of specific terms and jargon are avoided unless it is certain they can be identified with and understood by the recipient of the message. It is the responsibility of the communicator to be concise, to be clear, to identify the objectives of the message and to outline what response, if any, is expected of the listener.

The function of the receiver

Communication is always, without exception, a two-way process. There are good and bad communicators but there are rules which, if followed, can make better *listeners* of us all. They are:

- Concentrate on the message and not the messenger. Your relationship with the communicator is irrelevant. Even if you do not have respect for someone this does not mean that the information given to you should be disregarded – it may be very relevant to you and your work.
- Give the messenger a chance to clarify any areas of confusion or to provide you, the listener, with further information. If the communicator is met with silence then he or she may well assume that you have understood and are happy with the message.
- Ask questions about what is *not* said as well as what is said; the former may be more important than the latter.
- Respond at the time. There is little point in referring back, several weeks or months later to a communication which most probably will have long since ceased to be an important issue to the communicator.

There are various communication techniques which can be adopted by senders and receivers in any organization, but all require total commitment from management to be effective. No communication technique, however technically advanced or sophisticated, improves upon face-to-face communication.

The audit and attitude survey

Whatever method or methods of communication are adopted by an organization, there is an opportunity for senior managers to ask employees which methods they prefer. When a survey is conducted to ask if communication channels are working – then it is merely an audit of communication processes. If, on the other hand, the questionnaire is designed to establish how employees feel about the organization for which they work, that is an attitude survey. Increasingly, educational institutions are using communication audits and attitude surveys to identify the strength and weaknesses of their communication practices.

The communication audit versus attitude survey

The communication audit monitors the effectiveness of the mechanisms of communicating. It focuses upon four main questions:

1. Are the messages actually arriving at their destination?
2. Is there an opportunity (a formal channel perhaps) for people to respond?
3. Is the frequency sufficient, the quality enough?
4. How relevant is the information: how useful, interesting and readable?

Many organizations limit their survey work to the communication audit. This type of audit delves no deeper than to evaluate the *effectiveness of processes* whereas the attitude survey may also assess the effectiveness of *people*.

The attitude survey concentrates to a large extent on what employees think and feel about the organization for which they work. It explores employees' attitudes to their jobs, the people they work with and the roles they have to play in the organization as a whole.

The attitude survey:

- Is more complex.
- Requires more time and attention to the detail of the questions.
- Raises different expectations from employees.

Frequently the communication audit and attitude survey are combined within one questionnaire representing one, comprehensive, communication survey.

The communication survey and its conduct

Communication Audits can:

- *Identify more effective communication methods*
  As outlined earlier in the chapter, if a particular distribution method is being employed for the dissemination of information and it is not reaching the audience, then the communication process has stumbled at the first hurdle. By asking employees if information is actually arriving at its destination, much time and trouble (and occasionally money) can be saved by switching to more efficient distribution methods.

- *Point the way to securing greater employment commitment*
  In every survey I have ever conducted, I insert a question, towards the end of the questionnaire, asking whether employees have welcomed the opportunity to participate in the survey. Without fail, the response to this question has always exceeded 80 per cent, indicating that employees feel fundamentally that they have a contribution to make to organizational policy. If people can see their views influencing and reflected in management practices, then they are far more likely to be co-operative and committed to these practices, for they become participants rather than merely observers.

- *Help organizations develop future priorities in employee relations*
  It is not uncommon in any organization to find that there is a mismatch between what employees see as a priority for them in their work and the priorities that line managers have identified for the same employees. Where two parties are operating to two different sets of priorities a great deal of frustration can be felt by both sides. A communication survey can identify where any mismatch exists and can act as a catalyst for plans to avoid misunderstandings in the future.

- *Illustrate concern and interest on the part of management towards employee relations*
  The very fact that a communication survey is underway is an indication in itself to employees that their views are welcomed.

- *Overcome communication problems between departments*
  In the analysis of organizational structure outlined earlier in this chapter we indicated that the more organic the environment then the more frequently the horizontal communication channels are operating. Not all communication is top-down and in many educational institutions the most common communication processes operate between departments.

  In some instances horizontal communication problems are more difficult to overcome. If we imagine two departmental heads, each responsible as line managers for some 30 people providing some teaching in both departments, it is easy to see how each line manager can assume that certain issues have been dealt with by the other head of department. In this example the problem arises from a situation in which two people have equal status and responsibility in the organization, neither is accountable to the other and both have responsibilities for co-ordination of teaching activities for a large group of people.

- *Pinpoint causes of misunderstandings*
  An earlier point in the chapter considered the problem of people's perceptions of what is happening (or the motives behind what is happening) rather than the reality of actions and intentions. Some people are naturally more suspicious by nature and will probably be quicker to look for hidden agendas than others would in the same circumstances. Many a communication survey I have conducted has highlighted one misunderstanding or another that has arisen largely because the time was not taken to explain the intentions behind a particular action.

Conducting the survey – how is it done?

Before launching into a communication survey certain questions have to be asked and answered:

1. Do we conduct this ourselves, in-house, or employ the services of a consultant?

2. Are we going to survey a sample or everyone?
3. Is this going to be a postal survey or personal, face-to-face, interview technique?
4. We will need a questionnaire – who is going to be responsible for designing it and who will proof-read it?
5. Who is going to process the data, analyse it and prepare the final report?
6. Are we prepared to show a readiness to respond to the results that come through?

Some key *Do's* and *Don'ts* that I have identified after years of conducting these surveys might help to answer these questions.

Do

1. Whenever possible employ an objective external adviser/consultant. Experience tells me that people are very inhibited when the survey is conducted in-house. Quite simply, employees will not be as frank with their answers if they are answering questions asked by another employee of the same organization.
2. Inform people of the purpose of the survey and invite people to participate, rather than force them.
3. Respond quickly in the first instance by reporting back the results – acting upon them can take a little longer.
4. Follow up any areas of interest or concern with further, deeper questions.
5. Act upon the results wherever possible and explain why action cannot be taken if circumstances prevent this.

Don't

1. Expect a good return (more than 25 per cent to a postal survey). People simply are not prepared to give their time to filling in questionnaires, which is why I always recommend random samples for interviewing as well. Some organizations, unable to support the survey with personal interviews, offer a prize to employees as an incentive to boost the percentage returns.
2. Promise a survey then not conduct one.
3. Forget to include all staff. In many educational institutions the academic staff tend to overlook the support staff and their role in the organization. Just as with the example of the Managing Director's secretary and clerical staff who are the most up-to-date with information and therefore have a significant impact on daily activities.
4. Fail to respond to at least some of the suggestions made – your credibility is at stake.

5. Forget to monitor the impact of changes made by repeating the survey, in the same style, at regular intervals, for example every one to two years. Organizations do not remain constant over time – their structures may change and almost certainly some of their staff will move on.

The questionnaire design – some brief guidelines

The design of the questionnaire is perhaps the most crucial point in the whole communication survey. If the questions are badly worded, then they will be misunderstood. If the questionnaire is too long, it will not be read. If the wording leads towards a specific conclusion then the exercise will not be representative of employees' views and feelings. The skill in questionnaire design is getting the balance right.

1. Keep it short and ensure that answers can be given in a yes/no or graded (e.g. 1–5) manner. If there are too many questions invite additional comments.
2. Introduce the questionnaire with a covering letter outlining the purpose of the survey and emphasizing that responses are anonymous and confidential.
3. Allow for an elaboration of answers on a separate sheet which can be detached in order that the questionnaires can be forwarded for data processing while further comments can be categorized.
4. Ask for personal details only if these are really necessary. I have frequently quoted the example of a carpenter I interviewed at an engineering plant some years ago who gave his job title as Carpenter. It was only as I was leaving that he informed me proudly that he was the *only* carpenter working at that particular plant. I pointed out to him that he was therefore highly identifiable and might wish to leave Job Title blank. I have encountered other instances where people have objected to giving this information for they feel that it might disadvantage them in some other way.
5. Remember to proofread and to enlist the help of another proofreader. Frequently the reading of questionnaires is rather hypnotic as there is a rhythm to the questions. It is easy to overlook errors when you are the individual who actually designed the questionnaire.
6. Where personal remarks are made on the questionnaires, aimed at named individuals, these remarks should be shown to the individual concerned and should not appear in the Main Report.

The employee-centred report

All FHE institutions now have to address the legal requirement of publishing their accounts. It is arguable that this is best done within an Annual Report which nevertheless can (and should) present information with the employee in mind.

An employee-centred report satisfies the following functions within the internal communication process:

1. It is one of the few, if not the only documents given to employees which contains the organization's audited accounts.
2. It therefore gives employees a global view of the organization's financial position and frequently categorizes the contributions made to this from the various divisions or faculties.
3. Research surveys have shown repeatedly that an organization's financial position is important to its employees. This may be because of concerns over job security or, in industry, trade unions may require the information for collective bargaining purposes.
4. The most frequently cited reason for interest by employees in finances relates, however, to pride in their organization. A large part of self-esteem stems from valued efforts made at work. The most identifiable contribution of effort to performance is through the annual accounts of any organization.
5. An employee-centred report should also focus upon the employees themselves. In large educational institutions staff frequently complain that there are few opportunities to meet with other staff members during the course of the working week.

   It is not unknown for research areas to overlap or be duplicated by teams working in the same building both unaware of the other work being developed. This once again introduces the problem of the design of many educational buildings. If colleagues' paths do not cross as a result of where their classes are located then there are not always opportunities to exchange thoughts and ideas. Formal meetings have their own agendas so issues of personal interest are not generally aired. The very best employee-centred reports not only cover academic research areas or projects but also focus upon staff achievements in their personal as well as their working lives. It is important for the editor of the employee-centred report to remember that all categories of staff should be included within the report and not just teaching staff.
6. The employee report is a visual statement and images are powerful communication vehicles. All reports should be colourful and contain as many photographs of places and people as space will allow. Although the focus of the report is the previous year's activities there should be a reference to future aspirations reflected in an optimistic and positive literary style.

Concluding thoughts

It is a paradox that those people – lecturers and teachers – whose very jobs depend upon their communication and inter-personal skills when dealing with students, are the very people who are poor communicators when dealing with colleagues.

Regardless of whether the organization is organic or a bureaucracy – and networks formal or informal – the communication survey can identify what channels are working well within an organization and where communication is breaking down. Evidence suggests that employees welcome the opportunity to participate in these surveys and that they also take an interest in the contents of the employee-centred report.

The educational environment does not differ substantially from the commercial and industrial world insofar as a large proportion of its success will depend upon the contributions from a well-motivated workforce. A well-motivated workforce is founded upon commitment and pride in the organization – effective communication provides one of the keys to this success.

7

Managing and Rewarding Performance

David Bright and Bill Williamson

Editors' introduction

There is a great danger that any book on educational management will be written exclusively from a management perspective. This chapter rectifies any potential imbalance by providing a contribution from two authors who see themselves firmly as from the staff side. The authors deal in depth with staff motivation, appraisal and performance related rewards. Their conclusion – that performance management techniques developed for business corporations should not be applied to FHE uncritically and without restraint – will, we believe, prove to be prophetic.

Introduction

British universities operate a variety of different systems for rewarding and recognizing the achievements of academic staff. They attempt to find ways to value people for their teaching, their research and their contribution, through course development or general administration, to the corporate life and well-being of the institution as a whole. The continued commitment of staff to work to the best of their abilities and make this contribution, rests, however, on a precarious balance of negotiated agreements on pay and conditions, promotion opportunities and other conditions, such as opportunities to undertake research or develop teaching. Academic staff are particularly concerned to secure their professional recognition among academic peers. If the systems in place to achieve the balance falter in some way, then staff morale and commitment are threatened.

Indeed, none of these ways which have evolved to acquire the reward and recognition of achievements ever could be entirely satisfactory. All are hindered by the underlying structural weaknesses of the management of higher education in modern societies, and all are in need of reform.

Their central weakness is that they are underfunded and, particularly in the older universities, rather inflexible. The result is that most universities have systems which neither reward achievement well enough nor deal effectively with under-achievement. The consequences for staff morale and work motivation cannot really be estimated precisely. But they are considerable, nonetheless. Academic high fliers are too often tempted abroad for better pay and conditions. Many academics feel trapped in their posts, unable to secure promotion. Some look for rewards elsewhere, in consultancy or career promotion outside their own institutions. Others just coast along, partly satisfied with their work and not being well enough motivated to improve the ways in which they do it.

Most lecturers are, however, conscientious professionals who try to do their jobs well. Throughout the 1980s, they sustained a major expansion in student numbers without a corresponding increase in either the unit of resource or in personal rewards. The institutions within which they work have grown in size and complexity. The management of universities has come to resemble more the styles, structures and attitudes of private companies. The contractual status of university employment has been altered. Tenure is a thing of the past and a growing proportion of staff, particularly in research, are on short-term contracts. Halsey noted pertinently that, despite this, British higher education as a whole 'exhibits high productivity and rising standards of both teaching and research' (Halsey 1992: 137).

Staff are loyal to their subjects, their students and their institutions (Becher and Kogan 1992). But they are, in comparison with their professional reference groups among other highly qualified groups of workers, less well paid and employed under conditions which are not helpful to the maintenance of high levels of professional commitment. Since 1974 their salaries, in real terms, have eroded by as much as one-third in comparison with other top professions (Halsey 1992: 137).

The conditions under which higher education staff work are changing rapidly. Halsey has summed up many of the changes as amounting to a process of proletarianization and has argued that this is, in many ways, inevitable in a modern society (1992). This point need not be debated here. It does have relevance, however, for discussions of systems of reward and recognition. University staff are no different from anyone else; they, too, are motivated by the prospects of promotion, increased earnings and, above all, by professional recognition. The difficulty under the present circumstances of the lowered level of public funding of higher education and the imbalanced age structure of the profession, is that many will be denied such rewards and may, in response to this, perform less well in their roles than they might otherwise have done.

Viable systems of reward and recognition are a key ingredient in the success of any organization. However, there are features of the academic role which are unique and which must be acknowledged, for they bear directly on the motivation of university and college staff and, therefore, on the problem of variation in performance and how it should be dealt with. These features concern the work orientation of subject-based professionals and of the patterns of career differentiation now emerging in further education and the post-binary system of higher education.

Academic staff typically have a strong professional commitment to their subjects and to their students, approaching both with a sense of the open-ended possibilities for further development and change. Because of this, academic staff bring to their work a long time perspective; to research effectively or to teach successfully, requires long-term planning and a high level of dedication to the work involved. Successful career development builds on steady, professional recognition and the performance criteria are not easily measurable, as is the case with industrial or commercial employment, in market terms. The criteria for successful performance are therefore diffuse and qualitative.

Quantitative measures of performance of the sort now being developed and encouraged externally – in the form of research output measures and assessments of teaching quality – are not yet subtle enough to distinguish the qualitatively different levels of performance of different groups of academics. Nor do they separate the steadily successful academic from those Robert Jackson MP, as Higher Education Minister, once called 'tenured mediocrities'. Under present arrangements, there is a real danger that neither the potential high fliers nor the serious underachievers will be adequately managed. Moreover the large group of staff on whom the system depends, who do a good job with little expectation of improving their rewards, are not encouraged to seek to do a better one.

Motivation and performance

Those members of staff who perform well in their jobs – who deliver successful courses, undertake research, contribute to the management of their institutions and meet the range of quality criteria by which they are measured – are not superhuman. They are likely to be professionally committed to teaching and research in their subject, well organized and working in settings where they would like to be well supported to achieve these goals. Even the most competent people will underachieve if they are not properly supported and valued and if the structure of their jobs militates against them realizing their goals.

Those who meet the performance criteria are likely to strike a determined attitude to their own career planning, to be selective in the way they do their jobs and to set high standards for those who work alongside them. Those who are less successful in these terms are not less able people. Failure to match up to changing performance criteria flows from any number of different reasons, including a strong professional sense that the new managerialism is not an appropriate strategy for running institutions of FHE. Others include staff feeling that, since achievement cannot be properly rewarded, it is better not to strive for it. In each case there is a managerial or organizational issue involved and not merely one of individual attitudes, abilities and inclinations.

In what follows we will examine the management and reward of performance in FHE. Performance management has at its heart the belief that organizational effectiveness can be heightened through systems which can identify and measure key performance criteria and reinforce these through the more selective application of rewards. At the same time attention must be given to addressing the issue of under performance through vehicles such as appraisal, staff development and ultimately disciplinary measures.

Staff appraisal

The concept of regular appraisal is disarmingly simple and yet the practice in educational institutions is often not carried out in a satisfactory or beneficial way. Institutions discovered the formal variant of performance appraisal as part of the Jarratt-driven move towards greater managerialism in the late 1980s. Following the publication of the Jarratt Report (1985) and the related legislative changes, many institutions of higher education began the process of introducing systems of appraisal, being heavily influenced by this report. There was an imperative to begin systematic appraisal, as it was resource linked and a governmental requirement (along with the implementation of staff development systems) for the release of an element of the budget to higher education institutions in 1988.

The thinking behind the requirement to introduce formal appraisal systems had three elements to it; the first is that appraisal was a very common management technique in the commercial world of the 1980s and many key players in the determination of education policy at that time were impressed by the techniques of the business community. The second is that appraisal has a natural link to staff development; one could not work without the other. Third, appraisal offered management a way of linking rewards more closely to performance and contribution, a concept strongly supported by Fender (1993), Jarratt (1985), and the Conservative Government.

In essence, appraisal is a method of reviewing and monitoring appraisee performance within a given time period and agreeing courses of action for the future. One key tension inherent in the concept of appraisal, particularly as applied to education, is the degree of linkage to staff development compared with the degree of linkage to managerial control. Randall (1989) notes the different purposes for which an organization might introduce appraisal into its working practices. He cites the following as typical reasons:

- evaluation of staff
- auditing staff potential
- succession planning
- training
- controlling
- development
- motivation
- validation

'Behind these operational purposes' he writes, 'lie more theoretical issues. An examination of an organisation employee appraisal scheme can indicate a great deal about how the organisation "sees" their staff and how they should be managed and developed' (Randall 1989: 157).

The process of appraisal can thus be discerned as one representation of the state of organizational culture. Given that academic freedom has been greatly talked about in recent years by lecturers and their unions, the notion of what type of appraisal system becomes established would appear to be central to the approach of management. A recent study by Buck (1991) suggests that for academic staff, at least, the typical appraisal scheme is likely to veer more towards a development model than the top-down, management model used by many business organizations.

> Although a small number of respondents, particularly academics, referred to apprehension and resistance to the introduction of appraisal, the great majority of those interviewed felt that there had been few problems in negotiating and introducing a system. In part, this seems to have been because university managements appear to have accepted the contention of the AUT, with whom each negotiated at local level, that the appraisal schemes should be concerned only with development and not with managing an individual's performance.
>
> (Buck 1991: 95)

The scheme adopted by Durham University, for example, strives to encompass both strands in its objectives, which are:

* To help individual members of staff to develop their career within the university.
* To improve staff performance.
* To identify changes in the organization or operation of the University which will enable individuals to improve their performance.
* To identify and develop potential for promotion.
* To improve the efficiency with which the University is managed.

(Durham University 1990: 1)

To work effectively, a formal appraisal scheme has to possess a number of characteristics. It should be owned and understood by those expected to work with it. It should have a number of senior managers as champions. It should be linked to a regular process of informal appraisal sessions. It should have a degree of flexibility built into it. It should be fair and address areas of potential discrimination. It should be linked to some aspect of reward allocation (not necessarily pay). It should be clearly seen to fit into other key elements of the organization's approach to the management of people.

While ownership is critical for the effective operation of any scheme of formal appraisal, it is arguable that the context within which the FHE sectors found themselves in recent years did not augur well for successful implementation. For the old universities the linking of appraisal to release of funding created a climate of scepticism, if not opposition, within the ranks of the staff, which culminated in the AUT's boycotting of appraisal as part of its campaign of industrial action over pay in 1989. Thus, formal appraisal was seen by many to have been forced on them by their employers at the behest of their paymasters. Against such a backcloth it is evident that ownership and commitment are not easy to achieve.

For the new universities, the establishment of new corporate identities and the pressure to adopt performance-related pay led to similar difficulties, albeit a few years later, though here again, the emphasis on development rather than on managerial control has given a degree of comfort, as NATFHE has noted;

> schemes of individual staff appraisal and development have been introduced in all institutions over the last twelve months. These have been subject to both national and local negotiation with NATFHE and have been designed to function on the basis of a shared evaluation of strengths and weaknesses and a shared assessment of the development needs and individual and organisational changes needed in order to meet both individual aspirations and institutional objectives.
>
> What these schemes are not designed to do is to link performance with pay.
>
> NATFHE (1992: 5)

Some institutions have attempted to increase the degree of ownership by involving groups of staff in discussions and workshops over the structure, purpose and administrative arrangements for the appraisal system prior to introduction, with amendments being made where perceived improvements were noted. While this is undoubtedly a sensible approach to negotiating change, overcoming the limitations to ownership of appraisal systems created in part by the overriding climate, it remains a significant task for managers.

To overcome these difficulties, senior managers need to work consistently and visibly as supporting champions of appraisal and, indeed, staff development. Put simply, such issues will not be accepted if they are deemed to be mainly the property of the Personnel Department. Another caveat for FHE institutions relates to flexibility. There are a number of different types of staff in post and it is arguable that any appraisal schemes which relate to their terms of employment should have a degree of bespoke tailoring to reflect these differences. Fletcher comments forcefully that overly rigid and inflexible schemes are doomed to failure.

> Doubtless the idea of a universally applied personnel-driven standard procedure that stays rigidly in place (perhaps kept there by the weight of its own paperwork) within the organisation for years on end will lumber on in some quarters for a while yet, but its days are numbered. In its place are evolving a number of separate but linked processes, applied in different ways according to the needs of local circumstances and staff levels.
>
> (Fletcher 1993: 37)

If appraisal is to be valued by academic and non-academic staff, then it has to be more than a vehicle for encouraging self-examination and identifying the supporting role of others. There have to be realistic substantive outcomes. In our experience, a number of appraisal schemes have two inherent weaknesses in this respect: often the appraiser does not have the authority to commit resources to pursue a particular agreed path, and the appraisal process is not itself sufficiently linked to resource allocation.

Peer appraisal is quite common for academic staff in FHE. There are, of course, a number of reasons why such models have value and are preferred by many staff and their unions, associated, as it is, with the staff development mode of appraisal. The limitation with this approach, however, is that as the appraiser is often not the Budget Officer, any ostensible commitment between appraiser and appraisee over funding for staff development, changes in work patterns and other possible outcomes, require further discussion with department heads and probably other departments within the institution.

Additionally, it is a practice in a number of establishments, not to link the appraisal process directly to the allocation of resources but to see it as a feeder channel into institution-wide programmes of staff development. It is difficult to convince a member of staff that appraisal will benefit his or her career if there is no system of committing supporting resources to a planned and agreed course of action. Some institutions have attempted to address this limitation by devolving an element of the overall staff development budget to departmental allocation. Such a practice allows the department to meet at least some of the outcomes from its own funds.

While institutions have made significant efforts to introduce formal systems of appraisal, none of these schemes will achieve a degree of success if the formal structure and administrative arrangements are not supported by a process wherein informal appraisals take place on a regular and varied basis. Put simply, the big 'A' of the formal scheme needs to be underpinned by a series of little 'a' meetings to monitor progress over time and to discuss unplanned interventions. This takes considerable time to carry out properly and institutions need to find ways of supporting both appraisers and appraisees in finding adequate time for these critical activities.

While performance assessment is an important part of any system of appraisal, care should be taken not to use an appraisal system as a disciplinary process. The utilization of disciplinary measures in situations of underperformance should come about by separate procedures. Any attempt to use appraisal in this way would destroy its credibility and would risk creating other, difficult employment relations issues.

Rewards and performance management

For any type of reward system to be relevant to performance management, the following characteristics are needed. It should:

- Support the organization's corporate objectives.
- Be transparent and easily understood.
- Reward contribution and development, measured both in qualitative as well as quantitative ways.
- Possess a degree of flexibility.
- Interact effectively with other elements of the organization's approach to the management of its human resources.

Different types of performance-related pay are now well established in wide sectors of the United Kingdom economy. Surveys in the 1980s by ACAS and by the research organization Incomes Data Services, revealed a trend for organizations which had hitherto restricted such types of reward practice to cadres of senior management, to extend the practice to many other grades and levels of employees. Such a trend has now encompassed the National Health Service, areas of the Civil Service and FHE.

Certainly, the overall trend has been encouraged by a number of human resource management-related factors, some of the most significant of which are:

- The desire to support corporate objectives through the management of performance.
- The need of senior management to utilize the amount of money spent on payroll in the most cost-effective way.
- The need to address recruitment and retention problems of certain groups of staff by establishing a more flexible reward structure.
- The desire of management to adopt flatter systems of grading and responsibility.

In a detailed study of remuneration and benefits, Knell defined performance-related pay in three ways:

(a) where total pay varies depending on personal performance against agreed targets, e.g. piece work or commission earning, payment by results,
(b) where part of total remuneration depends on personal performance, e.g. achievement of agreed targets,
(c) where part of total remuneration depends on company or group performance or profit.

(Knell 1993: 5/1)

Interest in most educational institutions has focused on the second of these, linking some aspect of reward to individual performance, though it should be noted that many businesses are now showing an increased interest in the development of team or corporate-related pay. Such a development could prove difficult in educational settings where corporate objectives are difficult to measure and where achievements cannot easily be related to the actions of particular groups of staff. Such measures run against the grain of the professional orientation of academic staff and their representatives.

A number of individual-based performance pay schemes have been established across the higher education sector in the last few years. These include: a provision in the contracts of senior managers for linking an element of pay to the achievement of key objectives; allowing members of staff to submit applications for additional increments on the grounds of significant contribution; withholding incremental increases where contribution has been deemed to have been not satisfactory, and more generally, moving to individualized salaries for senior academic and administrative personnel.

It must be remembered, however, that incremental pay scales remain the most significant aspect of reward determination for the vast majority of staff in education. NATFHE believes that these scales need attention rather than supplementing with performance additions: 'HE staff are some of the most productive in the country. They should be rewarded with adequate professional salary scales, not bought off with titbits for the few' NATFHE (1992: 7).

Views about the merit of rewarding through performance have been divided since the Secretary of State adopted the concept in 1987. Buck's survey of the old universities captures this division:

> Those academics and outsiders associated with the AUT were generally against this idea of pay flexibility, regarding it as divisive, leading to 'low morale' and the potential exercise of patronage. Some academics were more pragmatic, however, with one noting that 'flexibility had upset a lot of people who got nothing' and seeing a gap between theory and practice in people's response to it.
>
> (Buck 1991: 97)

Any system of performance-related pay needs to be adequately resourced and measured if it is to possess any validity. Some of the typical failings of schemes in practice are first, an insufficient funding level. If employees are to be persuaded that performance-related pay has value, enough funding must be reserved for it to allow those covered by it to benefit and to feel that they have benefited from it. In FHE this should not be too difficult a task in the case of rewarding senior managers. It is more problematic when the institution attempts to apply performance-related methodology to larger and wider groups of staff.

In the latter case there is very real danger that all good and effective staff cannot be rewarded adequately (not possibly motivated) as there are insufficient funds to do so, or a danger that in order to distribute the performance pot to all deserving cases, the proportion going to each individual becomes infinitesimally small and is viewed at best as an irrelevance and at worse an insult. It is very difficult to defend an assertion that institutions have been able to avoid these pitfalls with regard to applications to middle managers and lecturing staff.

Second, there is the issue of ineffective measurement. To link individual pay to performance, it is customary to measure actual performance to predetermined objectives. This requires that the objectives are both realistic and capable of being measured. Some of the early systems in the business world suffered from defects in both of these areas. The objectives should:

• Be agreed between the parties and understood.
• Relate to the employee's role.
• Be precise.
• Be capable of revision.
• Not conflict with other objectives.
• Have an element of 'stretching'.

As a general principle, the more senior the member of staff the less prescriptive and detailed the objectives should be. Thus, the rewarding manager should be able to consider staff performance against objectives which possess all of the above features. If this is not the case, then the system is failing because of inadequate objective setting and lack of skill on the part of the manager. This, in turn, calls into question the usefulness of the pay system.

Third, there is the issue of the equity of the scheme. This potential weakness relates to the two earlier ones. If a performance-related pay system is not deemed to be fairly constructed and operated, then *it cannot work*. As well as the need for adequate resourcing, those administering the scheme need to be fully versed in the skills of setting objectives and assessing staff. They need to be aware of legal parameters, particularly in the area of equal opportunities, and take pains to avoid mismanagement through either giving everyone the same increase or a perceived favouritism, where certain staff members appear to others to have been rewarded for reasons apart from simple performance.

Over the last decade universities, new and old, have been strongly and regularly encouraged to adopt performance-related elements of pay. While such schemes may have motivated senior management, it is doubtful whether such schemes have had any radical positive effect on the performance of the ordinary lecturer or administrative worker. Many business organizations have now turned away from individual related schemes to schemes built around team performance or the annual performance of the organization as a whole. It may well be sensible for the education sector to examine the potential of such practices to help meet its own needs.

Fowler's words of caution regarding performance-related pay are worth considering at this juncture:

> Organisations will need to consider very carefully the operation of any scheme which does not enable the majority of employees to benefit from it; those organisations which have introduced performance pay mainly to improve salary levels will have great difficulty in applying real performance principles; as happened with MBO (Management by Objectives) some schemes are becoming so structured that their operation runs the risk of becoming an end in itself – sophisticated performance-related pay schemes can too easily become the property of personnel managers.
>
> (Fowler 1991: 48)

Fourth, there is the issue of acknowledging and recognizing staff contributions. In addition to changes in payment systems, FHEI's need to give careful consideration to wider aspects of recognition if they are to develop and reward performance sensibly. We would argue that recognition has three sub-variants, these being: financial rewards, other substantive forms of recognition, such as cars and healthcare insurance, and a wider variant, which embraces responsibility, promotion, professional recognition and development and some notion of empowerment, through which members of staff are enabled to set their own agendas. This is particularly crucial in the case of academic staff who have a distinctive, often highly specialized expertise and unique research agendas.

The issue of providing enhancements in addition to salaries is a difficult one for institutions. Apart from the issue of whether the institutions can adequately fund such benefits, it is arguable whether visible benefits for members of staff would help the organization to function more effectively. Universities, new and old, have been managed traditionally through a combination of bureaucracy and professionalism. While salaries and titles reflect differences in position, academic employees have seen little other evidence of status differences, apart from the quality of some office accommodation and the perennial taxing issue of car parking spaces. Thus, when compared to business organizations, higher education institutions have traditionally had fewer, status-dominated structures and have been more harmonized.

It is exactly this type of flatter, more harmonized employment structure that many commercial organizations have been attempting to develop in recent years. It would appear sensible, therefore, for educational institutions to avoid going very far down the road of using non-pay benefits discriminately in an attempt to reward performance. The few examples of institutions embracing this mode of reward suggests that it has not become a widespread practice.

The other branch of reward, related to empowerment and development, is of greater importance to education establishments. Ridley, citing Vroom, puts this into conceptual terms: 'Vroom, for example, puts forward the idea that an individual will be motivated to perform a task if the reward for so doing is valued by that individual, and he or she believes that the effort expended will result in the reward being obtained' (Ridley 1992: 9).

For academic members of staff, a traditional significant freedom and motivating factor has been the right, within course boundaries, to develop and deliver lectures, conduct research programmes and to engage in scholarly work with other members of the academic community through seminars and conferences. A survey conducted by the AUT in 1990 of almost 3000 staff in universities endorsed this argument:

Job satisfaction was viewed by respondents in all categories being the major motivator. This feature is generally accepted as encompassing a number of aspects, including the work itself, colleagues and the work environment. Several other intrinsic features of working in a university such as 'having independence and freedom', 'doing challenging work' and 'using your initiative' were also seen as very important.

(AUT 1990: 27)

These features of the job are also the ones which sustain the creative commitment of academic staff. They are a fundamental requirement of the sustained development of academic institutions, their scholarship and research. Without them, intellectual life can be stifled. The AUT argue, however, that increasing pressures on university staff have led to a reduction in the quality of their working conditions and they see this as an issue which must be addressed urgently in addition to significant salary improvements. The AUT report puts it this way: 'Over three quarters of the sample (77 per cent) revealed that their job had become more stressful in recent years, whereas 3.7 per cent reported that their jobs had become less stressful' (AUT 1990: 21).

The increased stress has come about through a combination of inadequate funding of FHE, a requirement to teach an ever-increasing number of students, a need to continually raise more income externally, a pressure to produce research output, a heavy reliance on short-term contract staff, and a welter of quality related initiatives which require considerable effort in the form of audit procedure. There is no doubt that all of these pressures exist and there is also no doubt that institutions have only limited freedom of action. We believe, however, that in the area of recognition, establishments have some scope for creative action.

Examples of practices which can be of benefit in rewarding performance include: internal funding of research projects conducted by high performing staff, allocating an element of development funding to budget centres to allow heads to reward staff through conference expenses and research visits, rewarding high performing teams through extra library allocation for their subject area and on a wider frame, inviting members of staff to represent the department and the institution at prestigious academic or vocational events. None of these are palliatives for the deep issues referred to earlier, but they can help to demonstrate that the institution values the contribution made by an individual and would very much like to encourage future high levels of contribution and achievement.

Of the issues discussed so far, none are as significant as promotion. It is difficult to disguise the fact that promotion systems in most higher education institutions are less than ideal. They do not fit well the logic and patterns of academic careers and the value staff place on professional recognition as a way of developing their own work, research contacts and commitment to their subjects and their students. These commitments, essential to the vocation of teaching and research, are built on timescales which are far longer than those of the managers of institutions who, understandably, must balance their books, attract students, maintain quality and deal with the myriads of immediate problems to keep their institutions afloat.

Promotion is a legitimate and valued hope for academic staff, but it is increasingly difficult to achieve. There are a number of reasons why this is the case, leaving aside the fact that two different structures remain to inhibit the linking together of the old and new universities. Higher education grew at a rapid pace from the mid-1960s and for much of the 1970s. This growth attracted thousands of young lecturers, a great many of whom are now positioned at the top of their relevant grade and who have been hoping for many years to be promoted. While the issue of blockage applies to both new and old universities, it appears to us that it is greater in the old universities.

The former polytechnics appear to have had a degree of greater flexibility in their systems of promotion:

> In the new universities lecturers can be appointed to lecturer, senior lecturer or principal lecturer as the institution decides. They may also be appointed to any incremental point . . .
>
> In the traditional universities a lecturer may be appointed to the bottom of either the A or the B scale and normally progresses through the scale on the basis of annual increments, although there is potential to advance by more than one increment. Once appointed to scale A a lecturer may be promoted at any time to scale B on the basis of their academic attainments, their abilities and their standard of work . . .
>
> Senior lecturers may be appointed or promoted to any salary point.
>
> (IRRR 1993: 9/10)

While the above extract is generally correct, two amplifications are required. First, in the light of age, experience and qualifications appointments in old universities would often be made at a point up the relevant scale rather than at the bottom, but resourcing limitations often pressurize appointing panels to restrict their consideration to the lower end of the scale. Second, because of the tension between the high number of candidates for senior posts and resourcing pressures, the number of staff in the old universities who are promoted in any one year is very low indeed. This leads to a feeling of disappointment bordering on cynicism for many staff who are regularly told informally and formally that their work is of the highest quality, but as only a few new positions can be funded, other candidates were deemed to be even better. A further belief held by many academic staff which does not help to offset the negative evaluation of their promotion prospects is that while it ostensibly can be achieved through high performance in research, teaching, administration and academic development, it is only the first of these factors that counts with most promotion committees.

In the former polytechnics, staff can progress along a unified scale to become senior lecturers in due course and can also be promoted further for a variety of reasons including academic attainment, responsibility for particular courses or areas of work and managing particular initiatives. This is not to say that all deserving cases are promoted in the sector, as resource implications can play a serious role in determining the shape of the establishment. In the new universities there exists a tradition of wider access to promotion through greater flexibility.

If the institutions are to truly address this part of reward and recognition, considerable thought and action needs to be given over to the establishment of a more flexible system across the sector, which rewards contributions made in a number of ways and which can be perceived as having greater equity by members of staff.

The under-performer

In the world of performance management, it is important to distinguish between the unsatisfactory performer, the person operating at the minimum acceptable level, and the person performing adequately but at a lower level than they are capable of.

With an unsatisfactory performer, the member of staff is functioning at a level which is deemed unacceptable under their contract of employment. If the person is a new member of staff or one who has recently taken up a particular post or function, then staff development, informal appraisal and possibly mentoring have a role to play. If however, the under-performance persists then it may be that the institution has no alternative but to utilize its disciplinary procedure. Such procedures cover both performance and behavioural standards, though some organizations separate these out into different procedures.

For heads initiating disciplinary measures, there are a large number of do's and don'ts. Some of the most critical are:

- Know your institution's procedure and follow it to the letter.
- Take advice from the personnel department where necessary.
- Remember that industrial tribunals can find dismissals to be unfair because of inadequacies earlier in the procedure.

Perhaps the most important fact to realize for any head involved in a disciplinary issue is that the procedure is to be used as an aid to achieving improvement, not to punish transgressors or under performers. Warner and Crosthwaite suggest that:

> Discipline and grievance are more prominent issues in polytechnics than universities, but this disparity may alter because of possible changes which we discuss later. The changes referred to are related to a prediction that as the universities have become one sector the approach to employee relations which will become dominant is that carried out in the former polytechnics.
>
> Some form of employer's forum will replace the more arcane and 'gentlemanly style' of the Committee of Vice-Chancellors and Principals, which currently represents the universities as employers.
>
> (Warner and Crosthwaite 1993a: 26–27)

With a minimal performer, the member of staff is contributing sufficiently to avoid disciplinary action but is not really making a fully effective contribution. This is a difficult but not uncommon problem for heads. It is unlikely that simple financial inducements can effectively address the issue, particularly where under-performance can be caused by a number of factors, including lack of motivation, inability or willingness to address the changing requirements of the role or a mismatch between the competencies of the individual and the needs of external clients. Heads will need to attempt to rectify this issue through a combination of informal and formal appraisal, teamworking and staff development. One of the more successful modes of intervention is encouraging the individual staff member to become more involved in certain departmental activities and, through this, inculcating a more positive general commitment.

In the case of a member of staff who is performing adequately but is capable of doing even more, financial inducements of some kind may be of relevance, as long as the quality of such inducements is at a reasonable level. Institutions should be careful, however, of simply offering sums of cash to members of staff. More creative use of funding and/or time for research, secondments and special projects may well prove to be more effective and fit in more sensibly to the culture of an educational institution.

Final thoughts

This chapter has been concerned with managing performance in institutions of FHE. Consideration has been given to both the 'carrot' and 'stick' types of intervention. Bevan and Thompson (1991) set down the typical textbook features of an organization which has adopted performance management systems. Such organizations:

- Have a shared vision or mission statement.
- Set individual targets which relate to the local unit and the organization as a whole.
- Review processes to identify training, development and reward outcomes.
- Monitor the process and amend where necessary.

There is no doubt that while the policymakers of FHE might not have articulated the above elements to that degree, much of the thinking that lay behind the Jarratt Report and others, reflected the desire to kindle such business-related practices in their sector.

Since the 1980s, further developments have occurred, notably the achievement of corporate independence of the former polytechnics, which have encouraged further development of the performance model. Most institutions of FHE possess the factors set out by Bevan and Thompson. Corporate objectives and mission statements abound; appraisal schemes have been developed, elements of pay for some staff groups are directly related to performance, and formal staff development and training programmes are commonplace.

In this chapter we have attempted to describe some of the developments in the above areas, together with some limitations to their usage and some caveats about their operation. Out view is that, while a degree of performance management has been achieved, and while it is likely that this will continue to grow, the institutions of FHE, given their cultural traditions, structure and financing arrangements, can only utilize and would probably only want to utilize, performance management to a given degree. To that end, the changes that we have seen described in this chapter, while important in themselves and indicative of some profound cultural and political changes in the climate within which academic staff work, do not demonstrate that education organizations will eventually emulate business corporations. It is important to realize that performance management represents a toolbox for the organization rather than a panacea solution to its problems. Thus, FHE establishments should seek to utilize only those aspects of performance management that appear relevant to their needs and not strive to become a caricature of the firm.

In recent years, institutions have adopted some business practices with differing measures of success. Further change is inevitable but should be handled with caution. We agree with Buck's conclusion: 'On balance . . . universities have become more managerial but they have not become managerial *per se*' (1991: 124). They should seek to remain so in acknowledgement of the fact that major changes have been effected in FHE by members of staff who have demonstrated high levels of professional achievement in uncertain circumstances. This is not an argument to maintain the status quo. Present systems of performance management in FHE, as we have made clear, are no longer satisfactory to maintain the achievements of the recent past or to enable the majority of staff to improve their performance in a planned and steady way.

It is not proven that the methods of management of British industry are a solution to the needs of institutions whose performance – in teaching, scholarship, research and retraining – are fundamental to the social, economic and cultural regeneration of the country. It is for this reason that performance management systems in post-secondary education depend for their success, ultimately, on the kind of vision and the support which the state gives to it, which society has for its educational institutions and the values which should govern them.

Market values, as Halsey has shown, have dominated education policy during much of the 1980s (1992). Intellectual labour has been, as he puts it, 'proletarianized'. Many teachers and academics feel, as Halsey's survey results indicate, bitter and bewildered. They remain, nonetheless – this is where the hope for improvement must lie – 'patiently dogged by re-formation of faith in the academic calling' (Halsey 1992: 270).

8

Executive Recruitment

Diana Ellis

Editors' introduction

According to the Editors' own research (see Chapter 1) the recruitment and selection of staff is the most important task for personnel units in educational institutions. However, avid readers of the educational press cannot have failed to notice that, over the last few years, the recruitment of a significant proportion of senior postholders has involved external agencies. This external involvement has not been limited to just heads of institution appointments, but also to other senior managerial positions, especially in the functional areas of human resources, finance, computer services and estates. Will the use of external agencies increase? If so, what impact, if any, will this have on internal personnel units? The author of this chapter puts forward a strong case for a positive answer to the first question but nevertheless, quite rightly, argues that the external agency does not replace the internal role, but supplements it. The acid test will come when external agencies are used on a regular basis to recruit for educational posts which are entirely academic, as opposed to managerial.

Introduction

To educate is to lead, instruct, develop; yet the academic world and the medical world, far from being in the lead, have been slow to take advantage of modern selection techniques in making appointments. No organization which is seeking the best people to fill senior or junior posts can afford to isolate itself from the wealth of expertise and experience which is now available.

People are the life blood of any organization, the very oxygen which quickens it and gives it vitality. Nothing is of more importance to any organization than the people of which it is composed. Their skill and ability will enrich it, their failings and weaknesses will deplete it. This is true wherever management is involved, in business, industry, commerce or in educational institutions.

Good recruitment is not just finding a square peg for a square hole, but the rigorous and energetic seeking of that one particular square peg which, above all others, will fill that one special situation. This will take time and imagination and will require a thoroughly professional approach. However, it will be worth it because organizations with high quality people are successful organizations.

The questions facing academic institutions when they consider employing executive recruiters are: what advantages can a third party bring, which method of recruitment is most appropriate to the post to be filled and what standards of service should be expected from the company chosen? Most clients are unaware of the differences between advertising agencies, selection firms and search firms. They may be aware of additional selection techniques such as psychometric testing and graphology, but be uncertain about their appropriateness and effectiveness.

In the following pages I aim to present some of the advantages of employing executive recruiters in the recruitment and selection of senior staff and also to clarify the different types of recruitment services and their applications. Many of the advantages will become self-evident as we consider the different methods of recruitment, but one factor which should be borne in mind from the outset is the ability of an independent third party to take a critical overview of a situation, to stand aloof from the tensions which build up in any group of people who meet on a regular basis, and to offer impartial advice uninfluenced by personalities or prejudices.

Most Boards of Governors and educational establishments are composed of extremely busy people with many commitments, who work to a very tight schedule and who just do not have the time to conduct in-depth interviews and to research the backgrounds of numerous candidates. The executive recruiter will not only take over these time consuming tasks and ensure that interruptions to the life of the establishment are reduced to a minimum, but will bring a breadth of experience of recruitment and of character assessment which few Board members will ever achieve. Further practical advantages of employing executive recruiters will be considered later, but let us now consider the different recruitment services available.

The recruitment industry consists of three main types of business. The first is search, the second selection (involving advertising) and the third recruitment agencies, and each has a different role.

Search

A *search consultant*, often called a Headhunter, seeks out available candidates through an extensive network of personal contacts. Talent is required to recognize what is being sought, and the best searchers are persistent and determined with the skills to prise loose candidates who have never thought of moving. Search is an art and searchers can be mavericks. Clients are usually best served by high calibre searchers who are working for a top search firm, because the name of a reputable firm will undoubtedly help to open doors. The best search consultants reach and attract outstanding people who could not be recruited any other way. However, searchers can only consider a handful of the available candidates and the search process is not infallible. Sometimes the preferred candidate cannot be tempted to move.

Search consultants work best in small groups and are not the sort of people who like to be constrained by systems and procedures. *Search firms*, or at least firms involved in top level recruitment, will usually be London based, and are not usually industrial or functional specialists as more senior management posts tend to require generalists. A *search practice* is likely to be quite small and composed of talented, flexible and independently motivated individualists. Their work tends to be thought of as appropriate for captains of industry, senior appointments in the City and those holding posts paying over £80,000 per annum.

Selection

The *selection consultant* employs a sophisticated range of techniques to produce a group of applicants from which the best candidate can be selected. Like the searcher, the selection consultant has a database for support with details of candidates who write in seeking help in finding alternative employment. This database also gives breadth of choice. Clients are no longer looking for a gifted maverick as in a search organization, but for competence and experience and a well worked out process. Selection firms work best when they have their own advertising company, the facility to deal with thousands of letters, computer and sorting systems and a name which is recognized for offering a quality service.

Selection firms tend to operate slightly lower down the corporate pyramid with jobs paying in the £30,000–£80,000 salary bracket and consequently in a much bigger market than search consultants. They often offer specialist skills as in education, personnel, finance, information technology, marketing, sales, research and development, etc. Educational institutions and their candidates like assessments to be done by people who understand the academic world.

The larger selection companies are likely to offer a stronger advertising brand, a more extensive database and better quality control system; characteristics which in their turn help them to do their job more efficiently. Selection firms do not have the off-limits problem which restricts the search firms' growth. They can expand and work without client conflict whereas searchers are restricted to companies which are not their clients.

Recruitment agencies

At the other end of the scale, the third category, are the *agencies*. Agencies are like shops which keep databases of job seekers; the client can see what is on offer and only buys if the agency has what is required. The candidates have not been investigated or checked out by the agency.

Advertising agencies

Advertising agencies do not fall under the banner of management selection as they usually provide only the service of art work and the placement of advertisements in the appropriate media.

The difficulties facing educational institutions considering using consultants

The search and selection industry is unregulated and is divided into a myriad of specialist firms who often know nothing about educational issues. There is no common standard or index of quality in the recruitment world and *NB Selection* stands alone in having gained quality assurance with British Standard 5750 and having an Education Practice.

Most companies geared to general recruitment and selection will try to apply to the academic world the rules that work for the commercial world, sometimes with dire consequences. Companies often guarantee to produce a shortlist, within a set period of time, and work rigidly to this timing regardless of academic terms. They will also be unaware that a large number of people are usually involved in a senior academic appointment and will not be sympathetic to the difficulties of arranging meetings of corporations, councils or senates. Generalist recruiters will not be sensitive to the problems that face even the most successful senior business executive appointed to head an educational institution. Lack of academic credibility, or inability to live comfortably with rule by committee, will certainly have disastrous results. Any educational institution seeking assistance with appointments must investigate thoroughly the pedigree of the company they intend using. There have been cases where the consultant, who wins the assignment and meets those who will be making the final decision, is not the person who handles the recruitment process.

How is an educational institution best served?

There may be confusion in the mind of educationalists as to whether they should choose search or selection. The right solution may involve both approaches: a combination of search and selection. The institution should choose a firm that can offer both and advise impartially on what is best. Search and selection are complementary and are simply two of the tools available for the consultant to use to solve the problem. There is no difficulty in the two methods being used in combination, and it is of note that advertising is playing an increasing role, even in very highly paid posts which were formerly considered to be in the area requiring search alone.

Many people question when one approach should be used rather than the other. Some consider that it is dependent on the size of the salary being offered for the job, but this is an over-simplification. Many jobs paying over £100,000 are now advertised, often with no search and support. The key question is not salary but the size of the candidate base. If there are likely to be large numbers of relevant people who might answer an advertisement then there may be no need to search. Search may be appropriate at a low salary level if one is seeking a specialist within a narrow field. It can be appropriate to advertise at very senior levels when the requirement is for someone from a different field, for example, when an educational institution is hoping to attract people from outside the academic world. Selection is in no way inferior to search. It is different.

The executive recruitment service

A good recruitment consultant will spend time at the educational institution wishing to make an appointment. This is vital in order to understand the requirements of the post, the ideas of those who will make the choice and to get a feel for the environment in which the successful candidate will work. The recruitment process for an educational institution normally involves advertising. Consultants should be able to recommend the best media for the specific appointment, to ensure that any advertisement is seen by as many potential candidates as possible.

Traditionally the *Times Education Supplement* and *Times Higher Education Supplement* have been the vehicles for advertising academic posts. The Tuesday *Guardian* runs a close second place but is often read by the same audience. The other daily papers – *The Times, Telegraph* and *Independent* – are best used according to the target market. *The Sunday Times*, used in addition to the *Times Education Supplement* and *Times Higher Education Supplement* is a productive and relevant source for senior academic, management positions. Professional journals are appropriate for specialist posts, for example, *Personnel Management, Law Society Gazette* and *Accountancy Age*.

Consultants will give advice on the placing, timing and wording of the advertisement, which if done well will enhance the image of the institution. The advertisement should contain critical points about the institution, the post and the required qualifications, which will entice candidates to apply for further information. A good advertisement will not only attract the attention of those keen to further their careers, and on the lookout for a move, but also entice those who are busy and happy in their current employment but who identify with the requirements of the post. Many educational institutions wish to cast the net as widely as possible and are often looking for fresh blood. A cleverly worded advertisement will indicate that applicants from less conventional backgrounds are welcome, yet will be specific enough to ensure that the response is appropriate.

Consultants put together information on the institution, the post, the required qualifications and the remuneration. This is available to enquiring candidates together with the institution's prospectus. The strength of the response will vary enormously and the more specialized the post, the narrower the field. The sifting of the response is a delicate matter and those accustomed to handling hundreds of curricula vitae daily will be more adept at identifying potential candidates. A telephone conversation is useful for questioning candidates about certain aspects of their application and assists in narrowing the field. If search is used in addition to selection, the process will have started early and will continue in parallel. Search is a time consuming operation and searchers will often find themselves following false trails. They will need to know where to find sources who can recommend further sources or possible candidates. Few people are averse to a direct approach. Most are flattered that their opinion is being sought or that they have been recommended as potential for advancement.

Consultants must sell the institution and the post to candidates and be sufficiently sensitive to recognize when strong candidates are losing interest or have concerns about any aspect of the appointment.

There is no predetermined number of candidates who should be interviewed for a post by a consultant. If there has been a large response to an advertisement there may be numerous interviews. Consultants have to get to know the candidates in a short space of time, investigate their past careers and assess their relevance for the particular post. They have also to learn something about their personal backgrounds and aspirations. A report is compiled on each of the candidates who is shortlisted and presented to the educational institution. Those candidates who have been found through search will often be concerned about the confidentiality of their interest and for this reason references cannot be sought until a later stage. When possible, a senior referee will be sought for each of the shortlisted candidates found through selection. After the first interview with members of the institution, and when the number of candidates has been reduced to two or three, further references are taken, preferably on the telephone as referees are usually more frank in conversation. In addition, qualifications will be checked as it is surprising how many people fail to be honest about their degrees!

Good consultants will be able to make recommendations on the format of the interviews and tailor the selection process to suit the requirements of the individual institution.

Other methods of assessment

It is at these later stages that other tools and methods can be used to assist the selectors. Psychological testing is one such tool which can be used to assist the selection committee in their understanding of the strengths and weaknesses of each candidate. There has been a clear trend towards using more sophisticated and more scientific methods of selection in senior management appointments. This is because different selection techniques tap different aspects of personality, individual ability and technical expertise. The traditional interview can never be fully replaced by any other method but it can be supplemented by different techniques to enhance prediction of job success. Psychological tests can provide objective information on more complex personality variables such as motivation, extraversion, stress vulnerability, flexibility or cognitive abilities.

The Institute of Personnel Management (IPM) produced the *IPM Code on Psychological Testing* (1993) as a guide to those using tests for selection, development or other purposes. The Code defines psychological tests as any test that can be systematically answered and administered and used to measure individual differences in personality, aptitude or ability in an occupational context. The term psychological testing is often interchanged with the terms psychometric testing or occupational testing.

Tests can be used at various stages of the selection process: (Toplis *et al.* 1991).

- As an aid to shortlisting where it is anticipated there will be an excess of applicants and a test has been shown to be a valid predictor of subsequent job success.
- As a main part of the selection procedure along with a structured interview, or as a component of a more extended procedure, for example, within the context of an assessment centre.
- As part of a detailed check on the most promising candidates only, in view of the in-depth and sometimes expensive nature of assessments.

As a general rule, test results alone should not be used as the sole basis for decision making (IPM 1993: 3), and feedback should be given by people who are not only qualified in the use of tests but are also skilled in feedback processes (IPM 1993: 5). In selection, feedback can be of significant benefit to unsuccessful candidates and leave them with a positive view of a negative outcome.

There are about 5000 tests and a large variety of computer generated interpretations of psychological assessment so it is hard for clients to find their way through the jungle of psychological assessment procedures. Many recruitment companies now have an in-house chartered psychologist to advise on and administer these tests.

Some consultants use graphology, the study of handwriting, to assist in the assessment of a person's character. It certainly provides the stamp of an individual, and is favoured by recruiters in France and Germany where it is used extensively in selection decisions. In the UK, there remains a debate as to whether the results are reliable and sufficiently scientific to add value to the selection process.

Companies who wish to recruit in volume will often turn to response and assessment centres which have the systems to cope with hundreds or maybe thousands of enquiries by offering dedicated telephone lines for each specific client company. A team will handle the enquiries and the curricula vitae, and telephone applications are screened against specific criteria. Application forms are dispatched together with company information. Completed applications are acknowledged or rejected and group interviews and selection centres are organized which provide assessment of the candidates. Companies will often give presentations at these assessment centres and the candidates have individual interviews as well as group tasks and presentations.

Group assessment is rarely appropriate for educational institutions and for specialist or senior level recruitment. Assessment centres within organizations have gradually switched from assessment for selection to assessment for development – the aim being to gain information about the participants' current and potential competencies.

The advantages of using a third party

The advantage of using executive recruiters to assist with academic appointments are numerous. The institution is relieved of an enormous burden and good recruiters can help sell the institution in a way that the institution would not be able to sell itself. A third party has the ability to match carefully the character of the candidates and the character of the institution and can seek out people who would not normally apply to an advertisement placed by the institution.

Search and selection companies will handle all the preliminary screening to prevent the institution's selection committee from wasting valuable time interviewing candidates who could easily be eliminated. Reports and paperwork will ensure that the best possible use is made of the time generally available to the committee.

A top selection company will work rigorously on behalf of its client institution to seek out the best candidates and ensure that the institution's expectations match those of the candidate, and that once an offer is made the candidate accepts. The educational establishment is relieved of the frustrating and time consuming process of making appointments and is left free to do what it does best – to educate.

9

Essential Employment Law

Geoffrey Mead

Editors' introduction

The title of this chapter describes its contents exactly; the author has clearly set out the essential aspects of employment law which affect FHE institutions. However, as the dates of the majority of the key cases indicate, employment law is an ever-changing field of activity and vigilance is required on the part of senior educational managers to keep abreast of changes. Indeed, as this book was in the last stages of production, the government announced on 20 December 1994 that it was to introduce legislation granting to part-time workers the same employment protection rights as full-time employees, regardless of the number of hours per week which they work. We must constantly remind ourselves of the maxim that, 'Ignorance of the law is no excuse.'

Introduction

This chapter seeks to set out the central issues of employment law as they affect managers in institutions of further and higher education. This is an area of vital importance in human resource management, for the consequences of failure to observe legal obligations can be considerable. Legal proceedings brought by an aggrieved employee will cost money to defend, will take up management time and effort, and may eventually result in defeat in a court or tribunal with a requirement to pay compensation. Moreover, litigated cases may attract considerable media attention, normally to the detriment of the employing institution.

Many of these difficulties can be avoided if personnel managers have at least a basic knowledge of the legal obligations of employers. Experience working in the field tells one that employers at the receiving end of court or tribunal proceedings are usually in that position not because they have deliberately flouted a law known to them, but because they acted in a way which they genuinely did not regard as being improper or unlawful. However, such pleas rarely impress the judiciary; the maxim about ignorance of the law being no excuse applies with full rigour in this area.

It is with these thoughts in mind that this chapter attempts to highlight the main areas of law applicable to the employment relationship in FHE. Given the wide variety of types of employment in such institutions, it is of a general nature rather than concentrating on one particular category of employee. Not all issues of employment law are covered; there is no coverage of health and safety, or of discrimination law, these being matters discussed in Chapters 10 and 4 respectively. There is also little coverage of highly complex issues relating to industrial action. Further, issues relating to the specific employment rights of only certain groups of staff, such as academic staff who enjoy tenure, are not considered, although they are, of course, important.

Common law, statute law and European law

Common law and statute law

The rights and duties of employers derive from both the common law and statute law. Common law is that body of law developed by the courts, and as such can be modified by the courts. Statute law is that body of law laid down in Acts of Parliament; it is obviously subject to interpretation and application by the courts, but cannot be modified by the courts.

In the last 30 years, there has been a considerable growth in the amount of statutory regulation of employment, conferring upon employees rights in relation to unfair dismissal, redundancy payments, gender and racial discrimination, equal pay, deductions from wages, and rights as regards trade union membership. Statutory rights are often regarded as building upon common law rights; they are a way of redressing the relatively weak position of the average employee as against his or her employer.

Impact of European law

In recent years there has also been a considerable growth in the extent to which European Community law has impacted upon UK employment law. This has been a source of considerable political controversy, provoking widely different views as to the extent to which the legal systems of 12 very different countries can and should be regulated centrally. The way in which EC law has a practical impact is an extremely complex matter, and what follows is but a brief summary. The sources of EC law are the provisions of the Treaty of Rome (as amended), EC legislation (Directives and Regulations), and decisions of the European Court of Justice.

The passage of a directive requires a member state to introduce laws into the domestic legal system which ensure that domestic law is in line with the requirements of that Directive. In many cases this is successfully achieved, and the applicant simply relies on the provisions of domestic law. However, if the member state fails to do so before the expiry of the time by which they are required to do so, then any individual employed by an organ or emanation of the state is entitled to rely directly upon the provisions of that directive before the national courts; see *Marshall* v. *Southampton and SWHAHA* (1986).

Emanations of the state are bodies or organizations, whatever their legal form, which have been made responsible, pursuant to a measure adopted by the state, for i) providing a public service; ii) being under the control of the state; and iii) having for that purpose special powers beyond those which result from the normal rules applicable in relations between individuals (*Foster* v. *British Gas* plc 1991). Further, in order for there to be reliance on a directive, the provisions of it must be unconditional, clear and precise. There is no reported authority on the question of whether an FHEI is an emanation of the state for these purposes, and the issue must be regarded as being finely balanced. Much will depend on the precise powers and responsibilities of the institution in question, and the funding and expenditure arrangements under which it operates.

Even if the directive cannot be relied upon, because the employer is a private employer, the national court must, so far as possible, construe domestic law as being consistent with EC law (*Marleasing* v. *LCIA SA* 1992). However, if domestic law is incapable of being interpreted consistently with EC law, then domestic courts must not ignore domestic law provisions or distort their meaning; see *Porter* v. *Canon Hygiene Ltd* (1993).

In respect of regulations, these do not need to be implemented by national legislation, and can be directly relied upon. Treaty articles can be relied upon in domestic courts by employees of both public and private employers, so long as those articles impose obligations or create rights which are sufficiently clear, precise and unconditional to be enforced; see *Stevens* v. *Bexley Health Authority* (1989).

Moreover, in *Frankovitch* v. *Italian Republic* (1992), the European Court of Justice held that in cases where an individual employee of a private employer was unable to rely upon the directive (because his employer was private not public), and it had not been properly transposed into domestic law, he could bring proceedings against the government to recover compensation for the loss which he suffered as a consequence of its non-implementation.

Political issues

The field of employment law has been a particularly fertile area of political debate, especially in the last fifteen years. When the government of Margaret Thatcher came to power in 1979, one of its stated aims was to curtail the power of trade unions. They were widely seen as having excessive power, often wielded without concern to the interests of the wider public and frequently unaccountable to members. In a series of Acts of Parliament since 1979, certain consistent trends can be discerned (McCarthy 1992). These are i) a restriction on freedom to organize and engage in industrial action; ii) the repeal or restriction of existing employee rights against employers; iii) the extension of employee rights against employers in some areas, particularly as a result of EC law; iv) the regulation of trade union government and extensions of members' rights against unions; and v) the repeal of aids to union recognition and the extension of collective bargaining.

Courts and tribunals

The great majority of employment law cases are heard by industrial tribunals (ITrs), which are tripartite bodies composed of a legally qualified chairman, and two wing members, one from each side of industry. They were designed to be informal, speedy and inexpensive; this has, in fact, proved not to be true in all cases, which is due in part to the complexity of the body of legislation which they are required to interpret and apply.

Nevertheless, they do have considerable advantages over the courts, particularly in that an individual can be represented by whomsoever he or she wishes, and there is little risk that if defeated, a claimant will be required to pay the legal costs of the other side. Claimants are often represented by trade union officials, or others with an experience in these matters. The great bulk of the decisions of tribunals are unanimous. Appeals on points of law can be made to the Employment Appeal Tribunal, and thence to the Court of Appeal and the House of Lords. For details on tribunal jurisdiction and practice, see Bowers *et al.* (1994).

With this general perspective in mind, it is now possible to examine the main areas of employment law, looking particularly at those issues especially relevant to the FHE context.

Worker status and the contract of employment

Who is an employee?

A person (a *worker*) may carry out work for another person in either of two main capacities; as an employee or as an independent contractor. If the worker is engaged as an employee, the contract is said to be one of employment or of service; if the engagement is as an independent contractor (often known as *self-employment*), it is a contract for services. The distinction between these two capacities is crucial, since many employment protection rights – such as unfair dismissal, redundancy entitlement, equal pay, maternity rights, and health and safety apply only to employees, and not to the self-employed. The tax position of the worker also depends on which capacity she or he works in.

In determining whether a worker is an employee or self-employed, an ITr will take into account a number of factors. For there to be a contract of employment, it is essential that there be an obligation on the employer to provide work, and an obligation on the employee to carry out work when asked; see *Netheremere (St. Neots) Ltd* v. *Gardiner* (1984). If this is satisfied, the tribunal will look to other matters, and is more likely to find the contract was of employment if the worker

- was subject to control as to how and when he or she did the work;
- did not provide his or her own equipment or hire assistants;
- had no responsibility for investment and management decisions;
- was properly integrated into the business;
- was paid during holidays or illness;
- was a member of the company pension scheme; and
- was prohibited from working for other employers; see *Market Investigations Ltd* v. *Minister of Social Security* (1969).

If these matters are finely balanced, the tribunal will ask how the parties themselves described the relationship. No one factor is decisive; an overall view must be taken, and the decision of a tribunal can only be overturned on appeal if it was such that no reasonable tribunal properly directing itself could have reached (*O'Kelly* v. *Trust House Forte* 1983).

Formation of the contract of employment

As with any other contract, a contract of employment can only come into being if there is an offer by one party, an acceptance by the other, an agreement as to the terms which will govern their relationship, and something of value passing from each side to the other (known as *consideration*). This process ranges from the casual – a verbal offer of a month's work on a building site to a person who passes by seeking a job – to the extremely formal – a process involving a written advertisement and application, interviews, selection panels and detailed provisions governing any relationship which may be entered into.

Content of the contract

In all cases some, but probably not all, of the terms governing the relationship are expressly agreed between the parties, although the more formal the process, the greater the number of terms which will be so agreed between them. Although in principle the parties are free to agree to whatever terms they wish, statutes have imposed considerable limitations on this.

A term not expressly made may nevertheless be implied into a contract of employment if it is necessary to give the contract *business efficacy* (*Scally* v. *Southern Health and Social Services Board* 1991), or if such a term is customary in the trade concerned, or for that employer (*Bond* v. *CAV Ltd* 1983).

Implied obligations normally imposed on employers are the duty not to act in such a way as to destroy the relationship of trust and confidence which must exist between an employer and employee (*Lewis* v. *Motorworld Garages Ltd* 1985); a duty to ensure the health and safety of the employee (*Johnstone*

v. *Bloomsbury Health Authority* 1991); and in some cases a duty to alert the employee to contractual rights which might be secured only by specific action from the employee, where the employee cannot reasonably be expected otherwise to know of those rights (*Scally* v. *Southern Health and Social Services Board* 1991).

The duties normally imposed on employees are the duty not to act against the interests of the employer; the duty to obey reasonable instructions; and the duty to adapt to new methods and techniques in performing their tasks, such as using computers rather than other methods of data processing (*Cresswell* v. *Board of Inland Revenue* 1984). Both the employer and employee are under a duty to give reasonable notice of termination of the contract, unless there is an express provision governing this matter.

Written statement of contractual terms

There has since 1963 been a legal obligation on an employer to provide to each employee a written statement of the terms upon which he or she is employed; Contracts of Employment Act 1963, now consolidated in the Employment Protection (Consolidation) Act 1978 (EPCA), as amended. Due to changes introduced by the Trade Union Reform and Employment Rights Act 1993 (TURERA), the obligation is now very detailed and specific. What follows is a summary of the main points.

An employer is obliged to give an employee the written statement of terms and conditions of employment, within two months of the beginning of that employment; s1(1) EPCA 1978. The matters which must be specified in the statement include names of employer and employee; date when employment began; pay rates, method of calculating pay and frequency of payments; hours of work; entitlement to holidays and sick pay and pensions; notice entitlement; job description; place of work; collective agreements directly affecting terms and conditions; and provisions in respect of working abroad (s1(2)–(3)).

There are provisions allowing for matters relating to sick pay and pensions to be contained in a separate document, so long as that is reasonably accessible; s2(2)(a). There is scope for referring an employee to provisions of a collective agreement in relation to certain of the matters referred to above (s2(2)(b), s2(3)); but certain matters must be given in a single document; s2(4).

By virtue of s3, the statement given under s1 must contain certain information relating to disciplinary rules applicable to the employee. If there is any change in the matters specified in the written particulars, the employer shall give, within one month of the change, the relevant particulars; s4(1). Sections 1–4 do not apply in respect of employment which continues for less than one month, or those employed to work less than eight hours/week.

While the statement given under s1 is not necessarily a contract or conclusive evidence of the content of a contract *System Floors (UK)* v. *Daniel* (1982), it is helpful in establishing what the contractual terms were. If an employer fails to provide a written statement or if it is incomplete, an employee can apply to an industrial tribunal (ITr) to determine what particulars ought to have been included; S11. An ITr may only state those terms which have been agreed; they cannot remake a contract and insert terms which should have been agreed.

Equal pay and maternity

Equal pay

The essence of the Equal Pay Act 1970, as amended, is that it confers an entitlement upon an employee to equal pay with a fellow employee of the opposite sex who is doing like work, work rated as equivalent or work of equal value, unless the employer shows that a material difference or a material factor justified the difference in pay; s1(1)–(3). Both men and women can make equal pay claims; in both cases the comparator must be of the opposite sex. Unlike in sex discrimination law, there is not scope for a *hypothetical comparator* (*Collins* v. *Wilkin Chapman* 1994). Pay is not defined in the Equal Pay Act; s1(2) refers to situations where 'any terms of the woman's contract is or becomes less favourable than a term of a similar kind under which the man is employed'.

'Like work' arises where the woman and her comparator are engaged on work of the 'same or a broadly similar nature' and any differences are 'not of practical importance'; see s1(4) and *Capper Pass* v. *Lawton* (1977) and *Thomas* v. *NCB* (1981). 'Work rated as equivalent' refers to a situation in which a job evaluation study (JES) has been carried out in respect of the work of the woman and her comparator, and they have been rated equivalent in respect of heads such as effort, skill and decision; s1(5). The 'work of equal value' head refers to situations where the man and woman are doing work of equal value in respect of effort, skill and decision; no JES needs to have been carried out.

A woman can make a claim under the equal value head even if there is a man engaged on like work; *Pickstone* v. *Freemans* (1988). Further, each aspect of the remuneration package must be equalized (*Hayward* v. *Cammell Laird* 1988). Cross-employer comparisons are not permitted; cross-establishment comparisons are permitted if common terms and conditions exist across the two establishments of the same employer; see s1(6) and *Leverton* v. *Clwyd CC* (1989).

If the claim is under the 'like work' or 'work rated as equivalent' heads, the employer can establish a defence to a claim by showing that the variation was genuinely due to a material difference between his case and hers. If the claim is under the 'work of equal value' head, it is sufficient to establish that there is a genuine material factor justifying the difference. In practice, there is no real difference between these two defences; see *Rainey* v. *Greater Glasgow HB* (1987). The employer must show that the difference was due to objectively justified factors unrelated to discrimination on grounds of sex; see *Bilka Kaufhaus* v. *Weber von Hartz* (1987). The fact that differences arose because of different collective bargaining structures is no defence; see *Enderby* v. *Frenchay Health Authority* (1994).

Pensions (unless paid under a statutory scheme leaving the employer no discretion at all) fall within the definition of pay within Article 119 of the Treaty of Rome, which guarantees equal pay as between men and women; see *Barber* v. *Guardian Royal Exchange* (1990). However, pensions equality must only be conferred in respect of benefits attributable to periods of service after 17 May 1990 (the date of the *Barber* judgment); *Ten Oever* v. *Stichting* (1993). The principles enunciated in *Barber* apply not only to contracted-out schemes, but also to supplementary schemes; see *Moroni* v. *Firma Collo* (1994). It is not unlawful for an employer to pay a lower bridging pension to a woman than a man on the basis that during the age range of 60–65 women, but not men, receive a state pension; see *Birds Eye Walls* v. *Roberts* (1994). In *Neath* v. *Hugh Steeper* (1994), the ECJ held that transfer benefits and lump sum options are not to be regarded as pay, and hence do not fall within Article 119 in any event.

Maternity rights

The statutory provisions relating to maternity rights have been substantially amended by the Trade Union Reform and Employment Rights Act of 1993 (TURERA) which seeks to implement the Pregnant Workers Directive (Directive 92/85 EEC), implemented on 18 October 1994. It appears likely that the relevant provisions of TURERA, which amend/substitute certain sections of the EPCA with new sections, will not be brought into force before that time. This section seeks to outline the new provisions. The law in this area is very complex and this section does no more than highlight the main rights which have existed since October 1994.

An employee absent during her maternity leave period (MLP) is entitled to the benefit of the terms of employment which she would have enjoyed had she not been absent, but there is no entitlement to remuneration; s33. Subject to some exceptions, the MLP begins with the date which she notifies the employer as the date on which she expects her absence to begin (s34); and, also subject to exceptions, lasts for fourteen weeks (s35). Section 36 stipulates the notice that must be given to the employer of the intended absence in order for the right under s33 to be effective. An employee must give notice of her pregnancy and expected date of childbirth at least 21 days prior to the MLP, or else as soon as is practicable (s37).

If her return to work after the MLP is rendered impracticable through redundancy, the employer shall offer suitable alternative employment, on terms which are not substantially less favourable; s38. If an employee has a contractual right to any of the rights in ss33–38, she can choose whether to exercise the statutory or contractual rights, but cannot exercise both; s38A.

By s39, an employee who has the right to maternity leave and has been employed for at least two years by the eleventh week before the expected week of childbirth, is granted the right to return to work within 29 weeks of childbirth, on terms which are no less favourable than those she would have enjoyed had she not been absent. She must inform the employer, in accordance with s40, and by a specified date, of her wish to return to work. If, by reason of redundancy, it is not practicable for the employer to allow her to return, he must offer her any suitable alternative employment; s41. There are detailed provisions regulating the exercise of the right to return to work (s42), and they include the right of the employee to postpone her return to work for medical reasons rendering her incapable of work (s42(3)).

The Act also lays down amended provisions governing suspension from work on maternity grounds, and the right of the suspended employee to remuneration.

The provisions in respect of the right to maternity pay are also extremely complex. In essence, there is an entitlement if the employee has been employed for at least 26 weeks before the fourteenth week before the expected week of confinement, ceased work because of the pregnancy or confinement, and was earning at least the minimum lower limit for payment of national insurance contributions; s164 Social Security Contributions and Benefits Act 1992. The maternity pay period is laid down by s165, and is for a maximum of 18 weeks. The amount of payment is specified by s166, and is 90 per cent of normal weekly pay for eight weeks immediately preceding the fourteenth week before the expected week of confinement; s166(2). She is entitled to a lower rate for the rest of the period, which from 6 April 1993 was £47.95/week.

Common law provisions governing termination

If an employer terminates a contract of employment, the dismissed employee may seek a remedy at common law or under statute, or indeed both. If the termination is in breach of contract, a common law action for wrongful dismissal will be available. Regardless of whether the termination is wrongful in this sense, the employee may claim the dismissal was unfair; the right not to be unfairly (as opposed to wrongfully) dismissed is one contained in a statute. Unfair dismissal is considered below; this section concentrates on the common law rules governing dismissal.

A contract may state that it can be terminated by either side giving a specified period of notice; if such notice is given, the dismissal is not wrongful, no matter that there is no genuine justification for the dismissal. The EPCA 1978 sets down minimum periods of notice, which can be added to but not subtracted from by express contractual provisions. These notice periods depend on length of service; they are one week's notice for someone employed between one month but under two years; one week's notice for each full year of employment for someone employed for two years or more but less than 12 years; and 12 weeks for someone employed for more than 12 years (s49 EPCA 1978).

There are however, circumstances in which dismissal without contractual notice is not wrongful and does not require the employer to make payment in lieu of either the statutory or contractual notice period. This is where the employee is guilty of gross misconduct justifying summary dismissal; this could include theft of the employer's property (*Sinclair* v. *Neighbour* 1967), acts of violence against other employees; disobedience to lawful orders (*Blyth* v. *Scottish Liberal Club* 1983); participating in a strike (*Simmons* v. *Hoover Ltd* 1977) or gross rudeness to the employer. Much depends on the seriousness of the incident, whether that behaviour had occurred before, and whether the employee had been warned that a repetition would result in instant dismissal.

If a summary dismissal is unjustified (that is, wrongful), the principal remedy for the employee is to claim damages for breach of contract. Those damages are that sum representing lost income for the required notice period, subject to a deduction to take account of both the employee's opportunity to find other employment during that period, and the fact of accelerated receipt of the money. As from July 1994, damages can be sought in an industrial tribunal; previously, it was necessary to bring county court proceedings (see Industrial Tribunal's Extension of Jurisdiction (England and Wales) Order 1994).

That situation was criticized as being unnecessarily cumbersome, requiring a dismissed employee who wished to allege both unfair dismissal and wrongful dismissal to pursue remedies in two separate fora, namely the unfair dismissal claim in the ITr, and the wrongful dismissal claim in court. In practice, the majority of employees did not bring county court claims; such actions were normally confined to highly paid employees with long notice periods.

Damages are the primary remedy for wrongful dismissal, and are a sum representing wages during the required notice period. In certain circumstances a court may grant an injunction prohibiting the employer from effecting the dismissal unless and until the employer has followed proper procedural steps; whether this remedy will be granted depends to a large extent on whether trust and confidence still exists between the parties; see *Robb* v. *London Borough of Hammersmith and Fulham* (1991).

If the employer does an act which constitutes a fundamental breach of the contract, that is a very serious breach going to the root of the contract, this does not automatically terminate the contract, but rather puts the employee in a position of being able to choose whether to keep the contract alive or whether to terminate it. Such a breach may occur where the employer unilaterally reduces the pay of an employee, as in *Rigby* v. *Ferodo* (1987); if the employee neither indicates acceptance of the new terms nor resigns in response, but carries on working, the employee is entitled to be paid at the old rate. Hence if the employer wishes to introduce new terms, the consent of employees must be secured, and those who do not consent must be subject to an outright dismissal, for only by such an act can the employer be sure of terminating the contract.

Unfair dismissal

Introduction

The statutory right not to be unfairly dismissed was introduced by the Industrial Relations Act 1971, and is now contained in the EPCA 1978. Although some of the features have changed, especially qualifying periods and the introduction of several automatically unfair grounds for dismissal, the essentials remain the same; the ITr determines as a question of fact the fairness of the dismissal, subject to oversight by the appeal courts, to which appeal lies on points of law. The right not to be unfairly dismissed is now contained in EPCA s54, which provides that 'In every employment to which this section applies every employee shall have the right not to be unfairly dismissed by his employer.' All statutory references are to EPCA unless otherwise stated.

Procedural pre-conditions

By virtue of s67(2) a complaint of unfair dismissal must be presented to an ITr within three months of the effective date of termination (EDT), or within such further period as the tribunal considers reasonable in a case where it is not reasonably practicable to present it within three months.

Some workers are excluded from making a claim for unfair dismissal; the most important such category is for those continuously employed for less than two years; s64(1)(a) EPCA. The qualifying period for those who work between eight to sixteen hours per week used to be five years, but following the decision of the House of Lords in *R. v. Secretary of State for Employment ex. p. Equal Opportunities Commission* (1994), where it was held that this provision was contrary to EC law as being indirectly discriminatory against women, the limit is likely to be amended. An employee who has worked under eight hours per week is not entitled to bring proceedings regardless of length of service, although this exclusion is also of questionable validity following the *EOC* case.

A further exclusion relates to employees engaged on a fixed-term contract of one year or more where the dismissal consists in failure to renew, if, before that term has expired, the employee agrees in writing to exclude any claim in respect of dismissal; s142(1).

Meaning of dismissal

The applicant must show that she or he was dismissed in terms of the definition given in s55(2):

- Where the contract is terminated by the employer with or without notice (*employer termination*).

- Where a fixed term contract expires and is not renewed (*non-renewal*). It is important to note the difference between a contract for a fixed term and a contract for the completion of a task; non-renewal of the latter is not a dismissal.
- Where the employee terminates the contract in circumstances such that he is entitled to terminate it without notice by reason of the employer's conduct (*constructive dismissal*). The employer must have committed a serious breach of contract; it is not enough that the employer acted unreasonably (*Western Excavating* v. *Sharp* 1978). The employee's resignation must have been in reaction to and motivated by the employer's fundamental breach, and thus an acceptance of that repudiation.

The reason for dismissal

The onus lies on the employer to prove the reason or principal reason for the dismissal; some reasons are automatically fair, some are automatically unfair and others are potentially fair. Automatically fair reasons include dismissal in connection with industrial action, where the employee was participating in the action at the time of dismissal, and either i) in the case of official action, all other participants were dismissed and none offered re-engagement within three months or, ii) in the case of unofficial action, it is simply shown that he or she was participating in the action at the time of dismissal; ss237–8 TULRCA 1992.

Automatically unfair reasons include dismissal on grounds of i) pregnancy (s60 EPCA as amended by TURERA 1993); ii) the transfer of an undertaking (Transfer of Undertaking (Protection of Employment) Regulations 1981); iii) trade union membership or activities (s152(1) TULRCA); iv) assertion of a statutory right (s60A EPCA); v) taking steps to ensure health and safety (s57A EPCA).

Potentially fair reasons for dismissal are listed in s57(2) EPCA and are (a) capability of qualifications, (b) conduct, (c) redundancy and (d) illegality of continued employment. The employer can also assert that there was 'some other substantial reason' for dismissal; see s57(1)(b). Once the employer establishes that the dismissal was for a potentially fair reason, the next stage of the inquiry is whether it was fair to dismiss for that reason.

Fairness of the dismissal

By virtue of s57(3) the determination of fairness is made on the basis of whether, in the circumstances, including the size and administrative resources of the business, the employer acted reasonably or unreasonably in treating the reason as sufficient for dismissal, and this shall be determined in accordance with equity and the substantial merits of the case. The burden of proof as regards reasonableness is a neutral one. In practice, a tribunal will request an employer to begin the case in terms of arguing reasonableness.

The general approach of the tribunals is that their function is to determine 'whether the decision to dismiss fell within the band of reasonable responses which a reasonable employer might have adopted. If the dismissal falls within that band the dismissal is fair; if it falls outside that band, it is unfair' (*Iceland Frozen Foods* v. *Jones* 1983). This means that the tribunal will not ask itself whether it thinks the employer did the right thing, but whether dismissal is a response which a reasonable employer would not have adopted.

It is important that an employer does not dismiss the employee until he or she has been consulted about the proposal to dismiss and given an opportunity to put the case as to why he or she ought not be dismissed. A dismissal effected without such warning or consultation will be unfair unless the employer could reasonably have concluded that consultation or warning would have been utterly useless; see *Polkey* v. *A. E. Dayton Services Ltd* (1988) and *Duffy* v. *Yeomans and Partners Ltd* (1993). Most large employers will have a written procedure which is to be followed before a dismissal can be effected; it is important that whatever the reason for dismissal, that such a procedure is followed.

A tribunal will look at the state of the employer's knowledge at the time of the dismissal; the employer cannot justify the dismissal by reference to facts discovered after the dismissal (*W. Devis and Sons Ltd* v. *Atkins* 1977). However, such later discovered facts may be relevant in determining the amount of compensation properly due to the employee for an unfair dismissal.

If an employer wishes to introduce new contracts of employment for a group of employees, the fairness of the dismissal of any of those who refuse to accept those new contracts is determined in the normal way. The fairness will depend on the gravity of the changes introduced, the extent of the employer's need to make those changes, and the proportion of other employees who accept the changes. The higher the proportion who accept, the more likely will it be that the dismissal of those who refuse to accept will be found to be fair; see *St. John of God (Care Services) Ltd* v. *Brooks* (1992).

Remedies

There are essentially three possible remedies; these are reinstatement, re-engagement and compensation. Reinstatement is an order that 'the employer shall treat the complainant in all respects as if he had not been dismissed' (EPCA s69(2)). Re-engagement is an order that 'the complainant be engaged in employment comparable to that from which he was dismissed or other suitable employment' (EPCA s69(4)). By s69(5) and (6) before making an order for reinstatement or re-engagement the tribunal must consider a) the employee's wishes; b) whether such an order is practical, and c) whether it would be just, if the employee contributed to his dismissal. The employer's failure to comply with an order under s69 for reinstatement or re-engagement may result in increased compensation. These remedies are very rarely ordered.

As regards compensation, the award normally comprises a basic award plus a compensatory award. The basic award is calculated by reference to three variables, namely length of service, age and weekly wage. Typically the employee receives one week's wages for each year of service with the employer, although it is one-and-a-half years for all years when the employee was aged over 41. No account is taken of any time beyond twenty years or any weeks' pay over £205; hence the maximum basic award is £6150 (20 years at 1.5 weeks/year, at £205/week). The basic award makes no attempt to connect the measure of compensation to the actual loss suffered.

The compensatory award should succeed in fully compensating the dismissed employee for any type of loss easily reducible to a cash sum. Under s74(1) the amount:

> shall be such a sum as the tribunal considers just and equitable in all the circumstances taking into account the loss sustained by the complainant in consequence of the dismissal.

The main item of recovery is normally loss of wages for the period of unemployment following dismissal, but the employee can also recover for loss of fringe benefits, loss of pension rights, loss of statutory protection, and expenses in looking for work. There will be deducted from the compensatory award any payments in lieu of notice, and an amount representing contributory fault, failure to mitigate loss and the possibility that he or she would have been fairly dismissed anyway (discussed earlier). There is also a maximum level of compensation, currently £11,000. This maximum is imposed after all other appropriate deductions have been made.

Redundancy

Introduction

It was noted above that dismissal on grounds of redundancy is a potentially fair reason for dismissal under s57(2)(c) EPCA 1978. If dismissal on this ground is held to be fair, the employee is nevertheless entitled to a redundancy payment (if such a payment has been claimed); this would be equivalent in amount to the basic award for unfair dismissal, should there be a finding of unfairness.

Statutory definition

The statutory definition of redundancy, now contained in s81(2) EPCA reads.

> An employee who is dismissed shall be taken to be dismissed by reason of redundancy if the dismissal is attributable wholly or mainly to:

(a) the fact that the employer has ceased, or intends to cease, to carry on the business for the purposes of which the employee was employed by him, or to carry on that business in the place where the employee was so employed, or

(b) the fact that the requirements of that business for employees to carry out work of a particular kind, have ceased or diminished, or are expected to cease or diminish.

Judicial interpretation

The first limb gives rise to few problems, since it is normally clear that a business has closed down or is about to close down. The second limb deals with job reduction falling short of a complete closure and often requiring selection if a particular job category is not being wholly eliminated, but merely reduced. A redundancy can occur even if there is no overall reduction in the volume of work to be done; it is sufficient if the work needed to be done is no longer of the same kind as before (*Carry All Motors* v. *Pennington* 1980).

Much therefore depends on how the job or work of a particular kind is defined. In *Murphy* v. *Epsom College* (1984) a plumber was replaced by a heating technician when he indicated that he was unable to maintain the modernized heating system that the college installed. It was held that he was redundant. The work had changed, it was held, from general plumbing to heating maintenance and therefore there had been a reduction in plumbers; hence Murphy was entitled to a redundancy payment.

However, in many cases where there is no reduction in the number of workers, there will be no redundancy. One such case is *Johnson* v. *Notts Combined Police Authority* (1974) where two civilian clerks had their hours changed from normal hours on Monday–Friday to 8am–1pm and 1pm–8pm over a six-day week. They refused, and were dismissed. It was held that they were not redundant as the work remained the same – there was just as much to be done – and the fact that it was at different hours did not change its nature. However, a change from full-time to part-time work probably will constitute work of a different kind, and hence be a redundancy situation (*Lesney Products* v. *Nolan* 1977).

An employee will lose any entitlement to a redundancy payment if an offer of suitable alternative employment is refused; see s82(3) EPCA. A dismissal on grounds of redundancy will be unfair if the employee is selected for an *inadmissible reason* (s59(1)(a)) or in breach of an agreed procedure relating to redundancy (s59(1)(b)).

Collective consultation

Where a trade union is recognized by an employer for the purpose of collective bargaining, that employer is obliged to consult with the union when it is proposed to make redundancies; s188(1) TULRCA. Consultation must begin at the earliest opportunity. Where the employer proposes to dismiss as redundant 100 or more employees within 90 days, consultation shall begin at least 90 days before the first dismissal is to take effect; and where the proposal is to dismiss 10–99 employees within 30 days, then 30 days' notice is required; s188(2).

Consultation must involve disclosing in writing to the union representatives matters such as the reason for the proposals, how many redundancies are contemplated, who it is proposed to dismiss, how the redundancies will be carried out, and how redundancy payments will be calculated; s188(3). The employer is obliged to consider representations made by the union, and although not bound to accept them, is obliged to give reasons for rejecting any which are not accepted. In cases where special circumstances render it not reasonably practicable to comply with all of these obligations, an employer shall do all that is reasonably practicable towards ensuring compliance; s188(7).

If there is a failure to consult, and no *special circumstances defence* the union may bring proceedings seeking a *protective award* for affected employees. Such an award shall be of an amount that the tribunal considers just and equitable; but shall not exceed 90 days' pay in the cases where 90 days' notice is required; 30 days' pay where 30 days' notice was required; or 28 days' pay in any other case.

Business transfers

Introduction

The common law position in relation to business transfers was that if an employer transferred his business to another employer, the transferee owed no duty to take over the contracts of those employees (*Nokes* v. *Doncaster Amalgamated Collieries Ltd* 1940). This position was radically altered by the Transfer of Undertakings (Protection of Employment) Regulations 1981 (SI 1981 No. 1794) (TUPE), which are designed to implement into domestic law the provision of EC Directive 77/187, which is known as the Acquired Rights Directive.

The very general rule with regard to transfers may be stated thus: If an undertaking is transferred from X (transferor) to Y (transferee), the contracts of employment of employees of X are automatically transferred to Y, and employees transferred are entitled to the same rights and privileges as they enjoyed against X.

Defining transfer and undertaking

An *undertaking* includes any trade or business, and need not be a commercial venture (reg. 2(1) TUPE, as amended by TURERA 1993). A transfer may be effected by a series of two or more transactions, and need not involve the transfer of any property (reg. 3(4)); it can be a transfer of only part of an undertaking. In determining whether there is a transfer, the ITr will ask whether the undertaking retains its identify after the event alleged to constitute the transfer. This depends on whether assets (tangible or intangible) are transferred; whether the majority of employees were taken over; whether customers are transferred; whether the activities are similar pre- and post-transfer; whether there is a period of cessation of activities; see *Spijkers* v. *Gebroeders* (1986) 2 CMLR 486; and also *Rask* v. *ISS Kantineservice* (1993) IRLR 133.

Contracting out of service provision

The contracting out of the provision of a service, such as office cleaning, will normally constitute a transfer; see *Kenny* v. *South Manchester College* (1993) and *Dines* v. *Initial Cleaning Services* (1994). This may be particularly relevant to educational institutions which are considering putting certain services out to competitive tender; it will no longer be possible to obtain a lower offer calculated on the basis that the tenderer will be able to offer lower pay to the staff.

Consequence of there being a transfer

Those employees employed by X immediately before the transfer, and whose contracts would otherwise have been terminated, automatically become employed by Y on the same terms and conditions as they enjoyed previously; reg. 5(1)–(3). However, the employee has a right to object to the transfer; if he does, his employment will cease but he will not be regarded as having been dismissed; reg. 5(4A) and (4B).

If an employee is dismissed for a reason connected with the transfer, that dismissal is automatically unfair by virtue of reg. 8(1), and liability for that dismissal will pass to the transferee (reg. 5(2)(b)). Liability will pass even if the dismissal took place before the transfer, if the dismissal was unfair because it was for a reason connected with the transfer; *Litster* v. *Forth Dry Dock Ltd* (1989). Dismissal will not automatically be unfair if it is for an 'economic, technical or organisational reason entailing changes in the workforce' under reg. 8(2). Dismissal because of a refusal to consent to a change of terms will not fall within reg. 8(2); *Berriman* v. *Delabole Slate* (1985).

TUPE also imposes obligations on the transferor employer to inform and consult with the representatives of recognized trade unions about the implications of the transfer (reg. 10). A failure to do so can lead to an award of up to four weeks' pay being made in favour of each affected employee (reg. 11(4) and (11)).

Deductions from pay

The Wages Act

It is provided by s1 Wages Act 1986 that an employer shall not make any deduction from wages of any worker employed by him or her unless (i) the deduction is required or authorized to be made by statute or by a provision of the worker's contract; or (ii) the worker has previously signified in writing his or her agreement or consent to the making of it. Subject to certain exceptions, a deduction which does not fall into one of these categories is a breach of the Act, and an employee can seek redress in an ITr.

By virtue of s1(5), section 1 does not apply to deductions:

   (i) reimbursing the employer for overpayment of wages or expenses;
  (ii) made in consequence of statutory disciplinary proceedings;
 (iii) due to a local authority under a statutory provision;
  (iv) where the employee has consented to money being paid to a third party;
   (v) made on account of the employee's participation in industrial action;
  (vi) made to satisfy a court order that the employee pay money to the employer, where the employee has consented in writing.

Payments in lieu of notice do not amount to a deduction, since wages are payments in respect of the rendering of services; *Delaney* v. *Staples* (1992). The definition of deduction, in s8(3), is a broad one, covering any situation where the wages paid on any occasion are less that the total amount properly payable on that occasion (after deductions), unless the deficiency is due to an error of computation. There may be factual disputes as to what sum was properly due on any occasion, and what deductions were authorized; these must be resolved by the ITr (*Fairfield Ltd* v. *Skinner* 1992).

The only remedy which a worker has in respect of a breach of the provisions in the Act is to make a complaint to an ITr under s5(1). If the ITr finds that an unlawful deduction or payment has been made, it will make a declaration to that effect, and will order the employer to pay or repay the amount of that deduction or excess of what could lawfully have been deducted; s5(5).

Deductions for participation in industrial action

An employee who participates in industrial action may expect the employer to make a deduction from his or her pay. The rules governing such deductions are quite complex, and there follows only a simplified outline. If the employee performs no work at all during a relevant period – that is, participates in an all-out strike – the employer is entitled to make no payment for that period (*Miles* v. *Wakefield Metropolitan District Council* 1987). If the action is partial, involving the refusal to perform certain duties, but a willingness to perform other duties, the employer has an option.

The employer can inform the employee that she or he must carry out all duties, for otherwise there will be no payment at all. If the employee is thus informed, there is no entitlement to pay, even if other duties are carried out, so long as the employer has in no way facilitated or assisted in the execution of such duties (*Wiluszynski* v. *London Borough of Tower Hamlets* 1989). Alternatively, the employer may request that the employee perform all duties that he or she is willing to perform; in which case the employer may deduct from the normal level of wages a sum representing the loss caused by the failure to perform those other duties (*Sim* v. *Rotherham Metropolitan Borough Council* 1986).

In many cases, especially in non-profit-making organizations, it may be difficult to determine just what loss has been caused. There is scant authority on this issue, although it is clear that the onus will lie on an employee to contest the propriety of any deduction, which puts the employer in a powerful position.

Rights of association

Introduction

British law contains extensive provisions which seek to protect the right of individual employees to join or not to join a trade union, or to participate in its activities. These rights can only be effective if an employer is prohibited from discriminating against actual or potential employees on union grounds; this section seeks to summarize the main areas of protection.

Refusal of employment

By virtue of s137(1) TULRCA 1992, it is unlawful to refuse employment on the grounds that employees are or are not trade union members, or that they refuse to accept a requirement to join or leave a union, or make payments in lieu of union membership subscriptions. Employees thus unlawfully refused employment can complain to an industrial tribunal; s137(2). There is a wide definition of *refusal of employment*; s137(5). By virtue of s138 it is unlawful for an employment agency to refuse, on union membership grounds, to provide its services to individuals. It is not unlawful to refuse, on grounds of union activities, to employ them.

Dismissal

By virtue of s152 TULRCA, a dismissal shall be unfair if the reason or principal reason was that the employee was or proposed to become a union member, or had taken part in the activities of a union either outside working hours or within working hours with the employer's consent, or was not a member of a union or a particular union. By virtue of s153, selection for redundancy on these grounds is automatically unfair. An employee dismissed on these grounds is in a superior position, in that a claim for unfair dismissal can be brought even if there was not the two years' continuous employment normally required; and compensation can be much more generous (s156–8 TULRCA). There is scope for joining a union as a respondent to proceedings if the union put pressure on the employer to dismiss the employee (s160 TULRCA).

Action short of dismissal

s146 TULRCA prohibits action against an employee for the purpose of preventing or deterring him or her from membership of or activities in a union, or compelling him or her to join a union. In *Associated Newspapers* v. *Wilson* and *Associated British Ports* v. *Palmer* (1993) it was held that this provision was contravened where an employee was offered additional pay if he agreed no longer to be represented by the union in wage negotiations, although his right to membership remained unaffected.

These decisions were in effect reversed by TURERA 1993; the amended S148(3) TULRCA now provides that where 'there is evidence that the employer's purpose was to further a change in his relationship with all or any class of his employees', but also to prevent or deter membership, the first purpose shall be treated as the employer's purpose, unless the action was something no reasonable employer would take. This opens the way for employers to offer so-called *personal contracts*; these being contracts whose terms are not agreed by collective negotiation, but by individual negotiation between employer and employee.

Industrial conflict

Introduction

In contrast to the law in much of Europe, British law contains no positive right to strike. Such freedom as there is to participate in industrial action derives from statutory immunities to common law liabilities; the courts determine that certain activities will attract liability at common law, and Parliament steps in to restrict those liabilities to an extent that it deems appropriate. Any freedom to strike thus depends on the view of the government of the day as to the proper scope of such action. As was noted above, the general trend in recent years has been towards restricting these immunities.

Common law liabilities

Industrial action may involve the commission of one or more common law wrongs or *torts*; these include inducing breach of contract, procuring breach of contract, interference with contract by unlawful means, conspiracy and intimidation. The most important of these torts for present purposes is that of inducing breach of contract. This will almost always occur during industrial action, in that the union will induce its members to breach their contracts of employment with their employers by refusing to work at all, or refusing to carry out certain of their duties.

If there is prima-facie liability, it is necessary to examine whether the person who would be liable escapes liability by falling within the statutory immunities; the following discussion shall be confined to the tort of inducing breach of contract, although the same principles apply to the other torts.

Statutory immunities

It is provided by s219 TULRCA 1992 that an act done by a person in contemplation or furtherance of a trade dispute shall not be actionable in tort only on the grounds that it induces another person to break a contract of employment. A trade dispute is defined by s244(1) TULRCA as being one between workers and their employer which relates wholly or mainly to issues such as terms of employment, engagement and dismissal of employees, discipline, work allocation, union membership, facilities for union officials, or negotiation and consultation machinery.

If the strike is predominantly about some other matter, it will not be protected; the question of what it is genuinely about is answered in an objective way; *NWL Ltd* v. *Woods* (1979). However, the question of whether the action will further the aims of the union is answered in a subjective way, asking what the tortfeasor actually believed would happen; *Duport Steel* v. *Sirs* (1980).

Strike ballots

In order to obtain immunity, a union inducing breach of contract will have to demonstrate that the action was supported by a valid ballot; s226(1)(a) TULRCA. The balloting provisions are now highly complex, due largely to amendments introduced by TURERA 1993. They may be briefly summarized as follows:

 (i) All of those members who it is reasonable for the union to believe will be called upon in industrial action, and no others, must be balloted; s227(1) TULRCA.

(ii) The ballot must be fully postal, and so far as reasonably practicable, each person entitled to vote shall be sent a voting paper to their home; s239(2) TULRCA.

(iii) The ballot paper must ask certain questions and no others; s229(2) TULRCA.

(iv) The ballot paper must contain a statement that participation in industrial action may involve a breach of contract; s229(4) TULRCA.

(v) The employer must be notified of the intention to hold a ballot, and describe '(so that he [the employer] can readily ascertain them)' which employees it is anticipated will be entitled to vote; s226A TULRCA. The meaning of these words was the subject of *Blackpool and Fylde College* v. *NATFHE* (1994), where it was held that in most cases this will require the union to give names of those who will be voting, for otherwise it would not be possible for the employer readily to ascertain who they are.

(vi) The employer must be notified of the ballot result; s231A TULRCA.

(vii) There must be independent scrutiny of the balloting process; s226 TULRCA.

(viii) The employer must be given at least one week's notice of the action before it commences; s234A TULRCA.

(ix) Majority support of those voting is required; s226(2)(b) TULRCA.

(x) Action which ceases to be authorized may need a new ballot to recommence.

(xi) The action must be called within four weeks of the ballot in order to obtain immunity; s234(1) TULRCA.

Employer's remedies

We have noted above that in respect of individual employees participating in industrial action, an employer can stop or deduct wages, and may dismiss the employee with the possibility of avoiding claims for both wrongful and unfair dismissal. However, an employer will often wish simply to stop the strike going ahead in the first place, and can achieve this by seeking an injunction from the High Court to prevent the action from even beginning.

If the action is not immune from liability (for example, because of a defect in the balloting provision), the call by the union to participate in the action will involve inducing others to commit an unlawful act, which in turn opens up the possibility of obtaining an injunction. In determining whether to grant an injunction the court will have regard to the likelihood that the union will establish that statutory immunity does exist; s221(2) TULRCA, and *NWL Ltd.* v. *Woods* (1979). Injunctions can be and often are granted very rapidly, sometimes only a matters of hours after the employer has learnt of the proposal for action.

If an injunction is either not sought or not obtained, and action takes place which, it is later determined, is outwith the immunities, the union may be liable to pay damages to the employer. However, the union will be liable only if it has authorized or endorsed the action, as defined in s20 TULRCA. If it does not so authorize or endorse it, the action will be unofficial, which in turn leaves those employees who are participating in a more vulnerable position. This is because those dismissed during unofficial action cannot claim unfair dismissal even if they were selected for dismissal amongst those who were participating in the action; s237 TULRCA.

Conclusions

It is clear that no single coherent theme underlies developments in employment law in recent years. While the British government has recently sought to reduce the power of trades unions and limit the legal obligations placed on employers, it has been obliged to implement certain changes due to the requirement of European Community law. This is especially true in the areas of gender equality, and business transfers.

These two main sources of law have ensured not only that there have been a large number of developments of considerable importance, but also that there will be a continuing tension between the aims of the British (Conservative) government and the European Commission. Although the government secured an opt-out of the Social Chapter of the Maastricht Treaty, the influence of European Law on domestic employment law is destined to continue and probably become of ever increasing importance. This raises important constitutional and political issues which will be the source of debate for many years to come.

Table of cases

Associated Newspapers v. *Wilson* and *Associated British Ports* v. *Palmer* [1993] IRLR 336.
Barber v. *Guardian Royal Exchange* [1990] ICR 616.
Berriman v. *Delabole Slate* [1985] ICR 546.
Bilka Kaufhaus v. *Weber von Hartz* [1987] ICR 110.
Birds Eye Walls v. *Roberts* [1994] IRLR 29.
Blackpool and Fylde College v. *NATFHE* [1994] IRLR 227.
Blyth v. *Scottish Liberal Club* [1983] IRLR 245.
Bond v. *CAV Ltd* [1983] IRLR 360.
Capper Pass v. *Lawton* [1977] ICR 83.
Carry All Motors Ltd v. *Pennington* [1980] ICR 806.
Collins v. *Wilkin Chapman* [Employment Appeal Tribunal, March 1994].
Cresswell v. *Board of Inland Revenue* [1984] ICR 508.
Delaney v. *Staples* [1992] ICR 483.
Devis (W) and Sons Ltd v. *Atkins* [1977] ICR 662.
Dines v. *Initial Cleaning Services* [1994] (Court of Appeal, 19 May 1994).
Duffy v. *Yeomans and Partners Ltd* [1993] IRLR 368.

Duport Steel v. *Sirs* [1980] IRLR 116.

Enderby v. *Frenchay Health Authority* [1994] ICR 112.

Fairfield Ltd v. *Skinner* [1992] ICR 836.

Foster v. *British Gas plc* [1991] ICR 463.

Frankovitch v. *Italian Republic* [1992] IRLR 84.

Hayward v. *Cammell Laird* [1988] ICR 464.

Iceland Frozen Foods v. *Jones* [1983] ICR 17.

Johnson v. *Notts Combined Police Authority* [1974] ICR 170.

Johnstone v. *Bloomsbury Health Authority* [1991] ICR 269.

Kenny v. *South Manchester College* [1993] IRLR 265.

Lesney Products v. *Nolan* [1977] ICR 235.

Leverton v. *Clwyd CC* [1989] ICR 33.

Lewis v. *Motorworld Garages Ltd* [1985] IRLR 465.

Litster v. *Forth Dry Dock Ltd* [1989] ICR 341.

Market Investigations Ltd v. *Minister of Social Security* [1969] 2 QB 173.

Marleasing v. *LCIA SA* [1992] 1 CMLR 305.

Marshall v. *Southampton and SWHAHA* [1986] ICR 335.

Miles v. *Wakefield Metropolitan District Council* [1987] ICR 368.

Moroni v. *Firma Collo* [1994] IRLR 130.

Murphy v. *Epsom College* [1984] IRLR 271.

Neath v. *Hugh Steeper* [1994] IRLR 91.

Netheremere (St. Neots) Ltd v. *Gardiner* [1984] ICR 612.

NWL Ltd v. *Woods* [1979] ICR 867.

Nokes v. *Doncaster Amalgamated Collieries Ltd* [1940] AC 1014.

O'Kelly v. *Trust House Forte* [1983] ICR 728.

Pickstone v. *Freemans* [1988] ICR 697.

Polkey v. *A. E. Dayton Services Ltd* [1988] ICR 142.

Porter v. *Canon Hygiene Ltd* [1993] IRLR 329.

R. v. *Secretary of State for Employment ex. p. Equal Opportunities Commission* [1994] 1 AER 910.

Rainey v. *Greater Glasgow HB* [1987] ICR 129.

Rask v. *ISS Kantineservice A/S* [1993] IRLR 133.

Rigby v. *Ferodo* [1987] IRLR 516.

Robb v. *London Borough of Hammersmith and Fulham* [1991] ICR 514.

Scally v. *Southern Health and Social Services Board* [1991] ICR 771.

St. John of God (Care Services) Ltd v. *Brooks* [1992] ICR 715.

Sim v. *Rotherham Metropolitan Borough Council* [1986] ICR 897.

Simmons v. *Hoover Ltd* [1977] ICR 61.

Sinclair v. *Neighbour* [1967] 2 QB 279.

Spijkers v. *Gebroeders* [1986] 2 CMLR 486.

Stevens v. *Bexley Health Authority* [1989] ICR 224.

System Floors (UK) v. *Daniel* [1982] ICR 54.

Ten Oever v. *Stichting* [1993] IRLR 601.

Thomas v. *NCB* [1981] ICR 757.

Western Excavating v. *Sharp* [1978] ICR 221.

Wiluszynski v. *London Borough of Tower Hamlets* [1989] IRLR 259.

10

Making Educational Institutions Safer and Healthier

Patricia Leighton

Editors' introduction

When the former polytechnics and FE colleges gained independence, they also gained a wide range of legal obligations in the health and safety areas. All of these are complex and some of them are quite arcane to the senior educational manager. As a result, health and safety issues may on occasion be treated at arm's length by senior managers – 'Go and speak to the Health and Safety Officer' – and not given their full attention. This chapter provides an invaluable survey of the key legislation and the costs of ignoring it. We should all remember that the author points out 'that the statistics do *not* provide comfort for the idea that (educational) institutions are safe'.

Introduction

Further and higher education institutions are unusual in that most of the time employees are severely outnumbered by non-employees. Students make up the bulk of the non-employees but increasingly institutions invite others to their premises for artistic, sporting and leisure purposes. Many universities, for example, now figure prominently in holiday brochures and those with especially attractive campuses or locations have found such initiatives financially beneficial.

Before exploring the legal and managerial aspects of ensuring safety, health and welfare it is important to address two preliminary questions. First, what are the key features of FHE which have relevance (to include an exploration of recent structural and managerial changes) and second, what, precisely, is covered by the umbrella title 'health and safety at work'? The question of why the topic is now so important for human resource managers in all sectors of employment will also be addressed.

Further and higher education: some key features

The first thing which must be said is that the sector employs over three-quarters of a million people – it is, therefore a significant employer in UK terms. The type of employee varies enormously, from librarian to technician, lecturer to careers adviser. Institutions provide a cross-section of employment which, of course, implies that virtually every legal rule applying to health and safety standards will have relevance.

Institutions are also diverse. Some are very large, and employ several thousand staff, others, such as the relatively few remaining specialist colleges in art, agriculture, teacher education and some rural further education colleges are smaller. Some are a part of large urban communities and are strongly integrated into those communities. Others, particularly universities established in the 1960s are in more rural locations. Some have the majority of students living on campus, others rely on privately rented accommodation or, especially in further education, have a high proportion of students living at home.

In some, the accommodation, both teaching and learning as well as for living, is fairly modern and purpose built. In others, accommodation is cramped, inappropriate or in serious need of repair or upgrading. Some of our more famous institutions have buildings which are old, dark, dingy and cramped. Many institutions have invested strongly of late, but most still have major problems with 'system' buildings of the 1960s and 1970s – as evidenced by legionella scares in some institutions in recent years. All these features have relevance for health and safety law and management, but probably of greater significance has been some of the recent structural changes, not least in industrial relations and human resource management.

FHE has escaped much of the turbulence in other sectors of employment, including the schools sector where employees have from time-to-time engaged in industrial action. However, there are now some signs of mounting pressure and change. It is impossible to provide a full catalogue, but for present purposes the following are of significance:

- All FHE institutions are now autonomous and are the employers of staff. It is the employer who carries the primary health and safety legal duties.
- Although trade union membership is high in comparison with many employment sectors there are planned changes as a consequence of legislation to weaken trade unions by the withdrawal of public funding for training of trade union representatives, including for health and safety training. This will mean that managers will have to plan, organize and monitor health and safety without necessarily assuming that unions will themselves fund training and development.
- There has been a declining role for collective bargaining over pay and a move in some institutions to personal contracts, for generally, senior staff and to local bargaining.

- Many of the developed strategies of human resource management are beginning to have an impact on institutions. There has been a devolution of functions to departmental heads/deans; appraisal is widely used; merit pay is making an impact, especially in senior posts; budgetary accountability is the norm and in a context of concerns about reduced income, there are increasing efforts to improve efficiency and reduce waste.
- One important change for health and safety purposes is a move to outsourcing for staff and increasing use of subcontracting. Typically, institutions employ either one organization to provide a range of services from catering to security (facilities management) or themselves employ individual maintenance, cleaning or other service-based companies. This increases considerably the number of people on institutional premises who are neither employees of the institutions nor students who have a contractual relationship with it. Subcontracting creates additional health and safety problems, which are addressed later.

Further and higher education: the nature of health and safety issues

In January 1993 a headline of the *Times Higher Education Supplement* screamed 'Five student deaths prompt gas safety call'. This had been caused by a series of incidents, some leading to fatalities when student accommodation contained defective gas appliances. Is this a health and safety issue for a university or college? If the accommodation was provided by the university itself, clearly the answer would be 'Yes', and claims could be made if negligence could be shown. If the accommodation was not owned by the university but was on its approved list might there nonetheless be a responsibility? This is a difficult question, but managers in educational institutions should not assume that because the premises or equipment in it is not owned by them that there is no liability. Recommending or approving premises may well have legal implications, and might, if standards are lax, lead to claims.

Beyond these somewhat dramatic incidents it is important to review the scope of the potential health and safety legal agenda. It is also important to have a full awareness of the costs and losses associated with poor health and safety management. The relevance of this in a situation of tight budgets will not be lost.

Educational institutions are not popularly thought to be dangerous places to work. The Annual Reports of the Health and Safety Commission reveal that the serious injury and death rate for employees in service sectors generally is around 50 per 100,000 each year. In railways it is 225, in medical and health care 43, in recreational services 55, but in the whole of the education service it is around 64 (HSC 1993). These figures include only employees, with many of the unrecorded incidents probably involving non-employees such as students and visitors. Data are not disaggregated for further and higher education, so it is difficult to be precise about just how such institutions rate. However, the statistics do *not* provide comfort for the idea that institutions are safe.

The types of accidents and injuries are varied but trips and falls, cuts, scalds and accidents in laboratories have tended to dominate the data. Sports and leisure accidents are also important. Other common types of accidents are collisions between vehicular and pedestrian traffic, injuries through lifting or carrying, or by being struck by a moving or falling object. Less likely to occur are explosions, building collapses and the like, though fire is a mounting hazard.

This is the traditional health and safety agenda. Yet in a context of FHE there are several major issues which face managers beyond that agenda. Included here are:

- Violence and sexual attacks especially against women and ethnic minority students.
- Smoking, and the dangers of passive smoking, drug and alcohol abuse.
- Problems associated with personal and property security.
- Sexual harassment.
- Stress related disorders affecting staff and students.
- Transport accidents, especially between campuses.

There has been considerable media attention on some of the above topics, which are now firmly on the new agenda. Clearly, in strict legal terms, the primary duty of institutions is to its employees. Nonetheless, injuries, incidents and ill-health affecting non-employees can give rise to some legal duties.

The facts and the costs

Responses at institutional level always need clear data. Information can and should be collected at institutional level, but it is also available for both the UK and Europe. The European Foundation for Living and Working Conditions, an EU body with responsibility for researching and policy development in health and safety in its widest sense undertakes large scale and regular surveys of the incidence and distribution of accidents and ill-health (See, for example, European Foundation for Living and Working Conditions 1992.) When information from the Foundation is combined with research data from a number of specialist occupational health institutions across Europe some very clear messages appear.

It is inappropriate to set down the data fully, not least because much of it might not appear directly relevant to educational institutions. The data provides information on the incidence and nature of accidents, the victims and their circumstances and sectors of work. From the data it is possible to identify fairly clearly where accidents are most likely to occur and to whom. For example, accidents are more likely to occur to the young and inexperienced, to those in manual trades and agriculture, to those who work long hours, in repetitive boring tasks, and at night. Part-timers and contract staff are more at risk and where such work is fragmented, poorly managed and under-resourced these factors will increase risks. Information and training has a significant impact on accident rates.

Data on ill-health is equally clear. The UK is considered to have the highest absence rate among employees in Europe – almost 12 per cent per week according to a CBI Survey in 1993 (CBI/Percom 1993) compared to around 3 per cent in Italy and Sweden. This is estimated to cost the UK £13 billion per year or 4 per cent of pay-roll costs. These figures may disguise unauthorized absence (absenteeism) but even so these are worrying figures. The major health problems across the EU, as reported by a representative sample of over 12,000 employees in 1992 were stress (48 per cent), back problems (47 per cent), eye problems (27 per cent) and fatigue (25 per cent) (European Foundation for Living and Working Conditions 1992). It may be tempting to dismiss fatigue as a major problem but it is well established that fatigue is a major contributor to or cause of accidents of all sorts and often leads to stress. It is becoming very clear that long working hours, lack of breaks and constant pressure are possibly the major stress factor and affect women more than men.

The last few years have seen the systematic collection and analysis of the costs of accidents and ill-health. In 1993 the UK Health and Safety Executive produced a report – *The Costs of Accidents at Work* (HSE 1993). Five organizations were surveyed, all appearing to have adequate insurance. Typically, insurance covers loss and damage to property but the major expenses associated with an explosion in a university laboratory or an assault on a student or lecturer are beyond those. Most of the costs of these incidents would be in terms of labour costs, for example, time spent investigating, dealing with the media, counselling staff or students, finding replacement accommodation and hiring extra security staff.

The Health and Safety Executive (HSE) produces useful advice on how individual employers can determine what accidents, incidents and ill-health are costing each year. As an indicator of the financial implications of accidents alone, the HSE study showed that an NHS hospital (the nearest equivalent to an educational institution among the five case studies in the report) was spending 5 per cent of its annual running costs on accidents and their after-math. The economic case for effective well-being, as well as safety policies and management is getting stronger each day.

The causes of accidents and ill-health

Many observers of the health and safety scene have commented on the lack of significant improvement in health and safety standards over the last 20 years despite better building quality, the decline of heavy and dangerous industries, new technology and improved awareness of hazards and risks generally.

This issue is a vital one for effective management because even with huge investment and new equipment, if there is no real understanding of the psychological dimension, significant improvements may not be made. Sir Bob Reid, Chairman of British Rail at a conference organized by the CBI in November 1993 commented, following the enquiry into the Clapham Rail disaster that '. . . all accidents have a human trail'. Accidents do not happen, they are caused. Even in the most sophisticated working environments or with high technology equipment, human error is by far the highest cause or contributor to accidents. Similarly, much ill-health is preventable; it is not inevitable, especially stress. There is little point, many argue, in investing in stress counselling alone; it is preferable to deal with the causes.

There are a number of specific issues which have particular relevance to FHE. One is that health and safety is not always perceived as a major topic of relevance to most academic work; if problems arise they are thought to be capable of resolution by applying common sense. There is, then, a tolerance of a level of accidents or injuries which are thought inevitable or are the expected consequence of a busy environment with lots of young people and perhaps high spirits. Many employers in sectors outside education also draw attention to the difficulty health and safety professionals have in persuading staff to take the topic seriously. It is often seen as routine, mechanistic, boring or marginal. Although there is no specific data from education, it is likely that similar attitudes may well exist. All are agreed that, without the support of senior management, adequate resources and a recognition that health and safety management is the essence of good management generally, improvement will not occur.

The legal framework: an outline

It is important to note and appreciate the basic legal framework applicable to health and safety. It is tempting, in terms of the management tasks facing human resource managers, to concentrate virtually exclusively on the statutory framework, especially the so-called 'Six Pack' of regulations, derived from EU directives, and operative in the UK since January 1993 (The six major sets of regulations, operative from 1 January 1993 cover management, workplaces, work equipment, personal protective equipment, manual handling and the use of display screen equipment. These regulations have received considerable publicity, especially through the Manual Handling, and the Display Screen Equipment Regulations in particular. However, there are other areas of law which deal with health and safety issues which are of equal importance.

An overview of the legal framework is as follows:

(a) The Contract of Employment	(b) Negligence/OLA	(c) Breach of Statutory Duty	(d) The statutory framework, increasingly from the EU
↓	↓	↓	↓
Implied obligations regarding safety through the contract of employment	Remedy where lack of reasonable care has caused an injury	Remedy where breach of safety statute caused injury	Imposition of statutory duties on all at work; prosecutions for breaches

The role of the contract of employment

Contracts of employment of all staff in FHE contain implied obligations as well as express ones, such as terms relating to pay and hours of work. Implied obligations arise as a consequence of case law which has established certain basic obligations on the part of both employer and employee. There are three key areas of relevance to health and safety:

1. The obligation through the contract for the employer to *provide a safe workplace*. The detail of the implied obligation is obtained from safety regulations and any additions due to the nature of the work. Hence, employees have a contractual entitlement to have the statutory provisions delivered through the contract.

2. The obligation of an employer to provide *trust and support*. This is a wide ranging obligation to investigate complaints or anxieties about hazards, to try and find a solution, and to be generally sympathetic to employee concerns, as well as not requiring staff to work excessive hours or in highly stressful environments. In a context where the working hours of academic staff are not usually formally recorded and pressures are growing, this will become an increasingly important issue. It is vital that HR professionals advise line managers of the legal demands in this respect, and the need to be responsive to complaints.

An Illustration: Johnstone v. *Bloomsbury H.A. 1991 2A11 ER.293*
A junior doctor had contracted to work over 70 hours a week but longer if requested, up to 104 per week. He suffered severe stress. His complaints were ignored. It was decided by the Court of Appeal that, despite his contractual agreement, the insistence on long hours, in the light of his health problems was a breach of the implied term of trust and support. The employee has an equivalent obligation to be supportive to the employer. This implies the need to warn of health hazards and to cooperate

with safety procedures and training. This obligation is reinforced by provisions in the *Management of Health and Safety Regulations, 1992*, which requires through Regulation 12 that employees should operate equipment
safely and inform the employer of any health and safety shortfalls (HSE
1992). These are in addition to duties in Section 7, Health and Safety at
Work Act, 1974 requiring care for other people at work and taking care
of their own safety obligations.

3. Employees are required to *obey lawful orders*, but if an order would involve
   health and safety risks if carried out it cannot be lawful. To insist on it
   could amount to constructive dismissal.

This aspect is reinforced by the Trade Union Reform and Employment
Rights Act, 1993, Schedule 5, which implements the EU Framework Directive
on Health and Safety. This protects those who suffer 'detriment' or dismissal
as a consequence of leaving their workplace when faced with 'imminent
danger'.

Schedule 5 of the act sets out that if a safety manager/officer, or member
of a safety committee, or safety representative, or other employee respond to
danger and then suffer a detriment (suspension, reprimand, fine) or are dismissed, the possibility arises of a claim for compensation in an industrial
tribunal, or a claim for unfair dismissal where it is an 'inadmissible reason
for dismissal'.

The only protection for the employer is if the response of the employee was
unreasonable in the light of the information previously supplied to the employee. Given that HR professionals have prime responsibility/overview of
recruitment and training, this is an important issue. Cases will be won by
employers if they have effective management systems and can establish that
the information supplied and reinforced should have enabled the employee to
be safe.

The law of negligence

Legal principles applicable to the work environment have been developed by
judges over many years. They are continually evolving and can respond to
new situations and new hazards. Although the law does not change rapidly
it is nevertheless both active and dynamic. In a given situation, such as an
injury in a gymnasium or in a college laboratory the law's response would be
as follows:

The law of negligence asks two basic questions:

- Was the injured person (student, lecturer, visitor to the college) someone
  the defendant ought to have reasonably foreseen as likely to be injured if
  the activity was not managed carefully?
- Did the defendant reach the standard of care which the reasonably competent person (lecturer, instructor, etc.) would have done in the circumstances?

If the first question is answered 'Yes' and the second 'No', this will, in principle, entitle the victim (plaintiff) to claim that there was a breach of the law of negligence and that compensation (damages) is due. The plaintiff has to prove that the employer failed to take reasonable care, that is, fell below the standard reasonably to be expected. Whether the conduct was reasonable, will probably depend on two issues:

1. Identification of level and nature of risk; for example, the college/university activity, type of students, context, etc.
2. Identification of how the reasonably competent lecturer, college administrator, etc., would have responded to the risk.

Although these rules have obvious application to engineering, in other highly practical and participative subjects the rules can also apply more widely.

A Recent case: smoking – Bland v. Stockport MBC (1992)

This is one of the passive smoking cases where a local government officer alleged that she had suffered severe respiratory problems due to colleagues smoking. She received an out of court settlement as the employer, who was aware of her health problems had failed to take reasonable care for her health.

A Recent case: RSI – McSharry v. BT (1993)

This is another out of court settlement for negligence where employees suffered RSI (repetitive strain injury) after long hours at computers with inadequate office equipment and poor supervision. There are now many successful claims for RSI (more correctly called Work Related Upper Limb Disorder or WRULD). The general view of lawyers is that RSI is a genuine occupational problem and is increasingly leading to successful claims for compensation. Essentially, it is the failure to manage work properly by ensuring breaks, change of activity and a stress-free work environment, rather than the display screen equipment itself which is the evidence of an employers' lack of reasonable care.

Negligence in relation to premises

There are specific legal duties arising from the state of premises where injury is caused to visitors (non-trespassers) through lack of reasonable care in management and maintenance. The law is derived from the Occupiers' Liability Acts (OLA) of 1957 and 1984.

Some key definitions

Occupiers – An organization or people who have a degree of control over premises; control implies the ability to regulate entrance and use of premises; colleges and universities clearly fall into this category. It will include residential, sporting, social facilities as well as leased property on short or long lease.

Visitors – Include everyone lawfully using the premises, teaching and non-teaching staff, students, self-employed people, workers for third parties such as subcontractors, parents and members of the public.

Premises – This includes movable (for example transport and work equipment) and immovable structures. It has special relevance to lifts, stairs, floors, obstructions and adequate lighting, warning of hazards and equipment and procedures for emergencies, such as fire.

Reasonably safe – Taking such precautions by way of maintenance, repair and management as would the reasonably competent occupier in the circumstances.

Some special situations

The law imposes liability on occupiers if an injury is caused to a visitor (this includes students) where the visitor is using premises in an ordinary way. The law requires visitors to take care for themselves, for example, to avoid obvious hazards and to follow instructions. The standard of care owned by occupiers clearly varies according to the risks inherent in premises and the extent and nature of use by visitors.

What if signs are erected warning of hazards? The law says to do that does not, 'without more', exonerate an occupier – *the signs, etc. have to enable visitors to be reasonably safe.* Signs which simply state 'Danger', 'Men Working', 'Take Care', are generally inadequate. They must be specific and offer visitors viable options to avoid injury (S.2(4)(a)).

Impact of subcontractors

The major area for disputes has been where an occupier uses or has used a subcontractor for work of maintenance, construction or repair and an accident occurs which, it is claimed, is directly linked to that fact. The work may have been badly done (roof repairers may have been used but tiles still fell off and injured a student); the work itself creates different hazards (electric cable strewn about corridors cause staff or a student to trip over); or new hazards caused (contractors may interfere with power supplies causing a laboratory technician to be electrocuted).

Clearly, in many of these situations the contractors themselves can be sued for negligence where their carelessness has caused injury. However, occupiers who use such subcontractors may nonetheless be liable also if they have not adequately overseen work and properly managed the premises at the relevant time (S.2(4)(b)). There is much recent case law stressing the on-going responsibility of occupiers.

Using contractors: the new regulations

Regulations 9 and 10 of the *Management of Health and Safety at Work, 1992*, are important. These require that where employers are 'sharing premises, on a temporary or permanent basis, that there should be effective, *co-operation* over the premises' use, and *co-ordination* of activities.' This is especially important when college/university premises are hired out or when management centres are shared with other organizations, or buildings used for teaching are occupied by organizations other than the college or university. Much of this law can be met by providing information, having regular meetings, exchanging work schedules, etc. It is essential that attention is directed to the problem and that there is clear evidence that the use of shared premises has been well planned for and managed.

The Construction (Design and Management Regulations, 1994), intend to further formalize the contractor/client relationship. Construction includes:

- building
- maintenance
- conversion and fitting out
- upkeep
- alterations
- dismantling

There are some derogations, for example, for small contractors (up to five staff and short contracts). The client (college/university, etc.) must appoint a Planning Supervisor who will devise the Safety Plan with the contractor's representative. This reinforces occupiers' liability legislation. The client must also keep a Safety File detailing the materials, substances, etc., used in the work. The contract itself must reflect these new legal obligations to ensure proper attention (and resources) are given to safety.

The statutory framework

Currently, the major statutes affecting educational institutions are:

- The Health and Safety at Work Act, 1974, the 'Six Pack' of new regulations, see p. 123 (establishes the basic legal framework and procedures).
- Regulations on specific topics/hazards – for example, COSHH Regulations 1988; Noise at Work Regulations 1989; Electricity at Work Regulations 1989, Management of Health and Safety at Work Regulations 1992.
- Regulations affecting specific sectors, for example specialist areas of colleges and universities.

The new European approach to health and safety

Due to the impact of the Single European Act and the ability now of health and safety measures to pass through the legislative processes of the EU quickly, progress since 1986 has been rapid. Over 37 measures had been passed by the end of 1993.

It is important to note:

- It is unlikely that any new health and safety law will be introduced other than that required by the EU.
- The priorities of European law are both clear, and are distinctive from traditional UK legislation. Emphasis is placed on:
  (a) Special protections for vulnerable groups, and to curb especially hazardous activities; included in vulnerable groups are people with disabilities, pregnant women, those with existing health problems and young workers.
  (b) Health and safety protections that can promote equal access and equal opportunities at work.
  (c) The responsibility of the organization, especially its senior managers, for health and safety.

Identifying the problem areas

EU law recognizes that some people or in some situations there is an increased risk of injuries or ill-health such as the following:

- Pregnant women
- Young workers
- Work patterns (long hours or being on call, part-time or casual)
- Hazardous occupations/industries or substances
- Asbestos, viruses, bacteria

Many of these target groups or working practices fall directly under the remit of the HR professional.

The EU legislation package

- The Framework Directive (89/391/EEC); now Management of Health and Safety Regulations 1992 (MHSWR) (S.I. 1992 No. 2051)
- Workplace Directive (89/6542/EEC); now Workplace Regulations 1992 (S.I. 1992 No. 3004)
- Provision and Use of Work Equipment Directive (89/655/EEC): now Provision and Use of Work Equipment Regulations 1992 (S.I. 1992 No. 2932)
- Personal Protective Equipment (89/656/EEC); now Personal Protective Equipment Regulations 1992 (S.I. 1992 No. 3139)

- Use of Display Screen (VDU) Equipment (90/270/EEC); now Display Screen Equipment Regulations 1992 (S.I. 1992 No. 2792)
- Manual handling (90/269/EEC); now Manual Handling Regulations 1992 (S.I. 1992 No. 2793)

Additionally, there are proposals or directives on:

- Working Time (to be implemented in the UK by 1997)
- Atypical Work, directive on temporary and agency work passed, now in MHSWR 1992
- Temporary and Mobile Constructive Sites – now in the Construction (Design and Management) Regulations 1994
- Carcinogens – adopted, in amended COSHH Regulations 1988
- Biological Agents
- Pregnant Women, adopted – now in TURERA 1993; health and safety changes operative from October 1994
- Safety Signs, adopted, operative from June 1994
- Physical Agents; this deals with noise, vibration, etc.
- Chemical Agents
- Employment of young workers
- Extractive Industries
- Recommendation of Dignity at Work (1991) – in force

Details of all these are available from the Health and Safety Executive and HMSO/Dillons bookshops. Information on proposals or Consultation Documents is available from the HSE; law from HMSO.

The demands of law on employers

The potential agenda for those in FHE is vast. However, the good news is that the law is coherent and consistent. It requires managers to be proactive, to seek out and identify problems before they surface. For example, it is inadequate to wait for a violent attack on staff working in an isolated environment or when going to their car in an unlit and unguarded car park. The law requires anticipation of likely problems and has adopted a particular strategy to achieve this.

Regardless of topic (noise, hazardous substances, premises, display screen equipment, etc.) the law has the basic demand that employers must demonstrate they have procedures and effective practices for the following:

- Risk assessment, of all potential risks.
- Risk minimization through preventive measures, for example, training, supervision, discipline and safe premises.
- Risk monitoring through auditing, safety committees.
- Consultation, information, for all appropriate people, especially students.

The law applies this approach to health as well as safety issues. It places emphasis on health surveillance, allocating work on the basis of health and safety abilities and the need to re-deploy, provide support, etc., when health

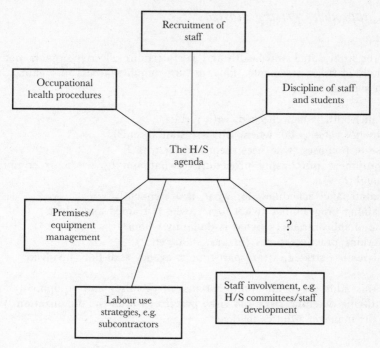

Figure 10.1 The impact of health and safety.

problems surface. These procedures should not be seen as optional extras; they are implicit in the legislation.

The role of the manager in FHE

Health and safety issues will clearly affect all aspects of the organization and virtually all management tasks as Figure 10.1 indicates:

The key tasks

The key tasks for managers in FHE are therefore:

- To be fully aware of the legal rules and their practical impact; to be aware of the psychological factors of health and safety.
- To integrate health and safety guidelines into all aspects of departmental/ faculty decision making.
- To take seriously health and safety standards in induction, training, supervision, staff discipline, career management, appraisal, etc.
- To co-operate with health and safety initiatives, especially by:
  - providing data;
  - participating in risk assessments;
  - participating in committees, discussions.

An approach: getting started

All the legal duties and health and safety require effective organization, especially of risk assessments. This, in turn, requires access to organizational data such as:

- staff health (when checked, with results?)
- absence rates (who, when, why are staff absent?)
- use of premises (who uses them and for what?)
- equipment purchasing procedures (what and by whom is equipment bought?)
- maintenance schedules (for what, how frequently?)
- training programmes (what topics, who is trained and when?)
- use of subcontractors (what is done, by whom?)
- working practices/times (breaks, shifts, etc.?)
- labour use strategies (are part-timers, agency staff fully involved?)

All this adds up to an audit, not just of premises and equipment but of identifying potential risks and risky practices within the organization. What are the manager's duties in this?

Stage 1 – information and risk assessments
The HSE Regulations generally contain useful information on how to carry out risk assessments. Whichever the topic, the key questions are:

What are the risks?
(vibration, excess noise, long hours, violence, etc.

Who is at risk?

How are they at risk?
(deafness, RSI fractures, stress)

How serious is the risk?

---

1. The serious consequence – death, major injury

2. Frequency – eye strain, backache, fatigue, stress, etc.

Stage 2 – responding to risk assessments

Essentially, this stage involves the exploration of options such as:

- change work practices, if necessary;
- improve maintenance of plant, premises and work equipment;
- re-design offices, lecture rooms;
- improve lighting and other security measures;
- provide training for staff and students;
- check contracts of staff and for contractors;
- provide effective supervision of students and effective communication channels.

Final thoughts

Health must be treated similarly to safety. The key likely problem areas include regulating working hours of staff, especially those using display-screen equipment, risks of violence and, perhaps most importantly, stress. Many institutions are moving to Employee Assistance Programmes (EAPs) whereby consultants or in-house specialists are available to provide advice, support and counselling of staff facing stress induced by work, home or a combination of both. Clearly, these are helpful, however, they are no substitution for managers in FHE working towards stress prevention. The causes of stress are increasingly well understood. Many of the causes (long hours, isolation, constant organizational change and boring work) are familiar to those in the education sector.

In all these situations, colleges and universities must be aware of their legal duties, be responsive to anxieties and complaints and have well developed, robust and effective policies. The law is increasingly looking for tangible evidence of policies, for confidence in them and for a full awareness of the potential risks to staff and students. Put succinctly, colleges and universities need to demonstrate that they are on top of this topic.

11

Developing Managers

Elizabeth Walker

Editors' introduction

The Editors consider that one of the most important tasks for senior educational managers is to create a fully-trained management team, especially at middle and first line levels. In addition to the substantial development work required, there is the problem of integrating those managers who have an administrative background and have traditionally been regarded as supporting the academic community with those who hitherto were academics (and in some cases still remain so) and for that reason regarded themselves as the core workers. It is somewhat ironic that the latter group will probably require more management development than the former.

In this chapter the author has explored a strategic approach to management development which nevertheless contains much valuable guidance for immediate implementation.

Introduction

'I have never had any management training.'
'I just picked this job up as I went along.'
'I was thrown in the deep end.'

It is likely that most people reading this chapter will have heard remarks like these, or something very similar. And yet there are thousands of people working more or less effectively at first line, middle management and senior management level throughout FHE who have somehow acquired the skills, knowledge and understanding necessary to carry out those management activities.

Much of the development which has taken place is not recognized as such because it has not been in the context of formal management training programmes. This chapter will provide a brief overview of the formal management development provision, and will then consider mana gement development in its broadest sense. The view will be taken that a strategic approach to management development will be more effective than one-off training programmes for individuals, or isolated pieces of in-house training which do not link back to an ongoing programme of development within the workplace. The place of specific courses and training programmes within a broader development programme will be identified, and the chapter will provide practical advice about where to start with respect to the implementation of a management development programme in a further and higher education institution (FHEI).

Management development provision

The following brief overview outlines the broad categories of management development provision available in the United Kingdom. The nature of management development methods appropriate to address specific development needs will be considered later.

Accredited management development programmes

Traditionally, management development programmes are generally accredited at four levels:

1. Supervisory Level   For those with supervisory responsibilities
2. Certificate Level   For those with first line management responsibilities
3. Diploma Level   For those with middle management responsibilities
4. Masters Level   For those with senior management responsibilities

More recently it has been possible to follow competence based accreditation routes and obtain National Vocational Qualifications in Management at NVQ levels 3, 4 and 5. The issue of accreditation is discussed later in this chapter.

Short courses

Short courses in management are offered by FHE institutions, private management training centres, colleges and individual consultants. There are also some national management development centres for specific occupational areas – for example, the Fire Service College, the Civil Service College, The Staff College (for managers in FHE), and private sector management development centres belonging to large organizations such as Sainsbury's and British Petroleum.

In-house management development programmes

Sometimes these are provided using the expertise from within the organization itself, and sometimes using private training organizations and management consultants or using the services of universities and education management specialists.

The content of management development programmes

Traditional management development programmes have generally covered the following areas:

• Management theory
• Finance, resources and business planning
• Human resource management
• Strategic management
• Management of information
• Estate management
• Project management

These areas of management are common to most occupational sectors, and although clearly some of the content will be different, the basic principles will be the same. Books about management theory and practice generally use examples from a wide range of occupational areas. In addition there will clearly be specialist development needs depending on the specific role and occupational sector within which the manager is working.

Competence based approaches to management development have a more specifically defined content which reflects national standards of management competence developed by the Management Charter Initiative (MCI 1992). The management standards at middle management level are shown in Table 11.1.

A definition of management development

All of the above provision would fall into the category of management development described by Mumford (1980) as formal management development. In order to take a broader perspective and to capture management development in its wider sense it is necessary to adopt a broader approach. Denning *et al.* (1978) describe management development as 'the total process which an organisation adopts in preparing its managers for the growth and change that occur in their working environment'. Jones and Woodcock (1985) describe management development as 'the sum of all the activities available to individuals, to help them to meet their growth needs and keep the organisation viable'. The Management Charter Initiative describes the key purpose of management as 'to contribute to the organisation's effectiveness and continuously enhance its performance'. All of these definitions envisage a very broad

Table 11.1 Management Charter Initiative standards for the middle managers

The key purpose of managers is:

to achieve the organization's objectives and continuously improve its performance.

The following management standards define what a manager should be able to do:

Manage operations
Unit 1   Initiate and implement change and improvement in services, products and systems
Unit 2   Monitor, maintain and improve service and product delivery

Manage finance
Unit 3   Monitor and control the use of resources
Unit 4   Secure effective resource allocation for activities and projects

Manage people
Unit 5   Recruit and select personnel
Unit 6   Develop teams, individuals and self to enhance performance
Unit 7   Plan, allocate and evaluate work carried out by teams, individuals and self
Unit 8   Create, maintain and enhance effective working relationships

Manage information
Unit 9   Seek, evaluate and organize information for action
Unit 10   Exchange information to solve problems and make decisions

Source: Management Charter Initiative 1992.

approach to management development and one which has as its key characteristics the furthering of the performance and objectives of the organization by which the manager is employed.

The changes within higher and further education over the last few years have now produced a situation in which there is a real possibility to develop managers in the context of a clear programme which links with organizational objectives.

The context of management development

The requirements of all FHE institutions to set and work towards strategic objectives, the annual and longer term planning cycles, the introduction of appraisal of individual staff, the inspection guidelines within FHE, and more flexible working patterns, are all factors which form part of the new context. Such factors can contribute to a coherent whole within which the ongoing development of all employees can fit quite naturally without being seen as a separate bolt-on process.

It is possible to address individual management development needs in an *ad hoc* way independently of the strategic thinking, but this is very unlikely to have the general effect of improving management practice across the institution,

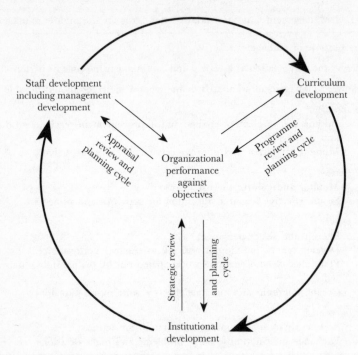

Figure 11.1 The context of management development.

and there will be no framework for linking management development activities which take place away from the workplace with the ongoing work of the manager within their own organization. The starting point needs to be the clear identification of strategic objectives for the institution which arise from the mission statement, or the statement of the fundamental aims of the institution. The strategic objectives inform the annual operating statement of the planned activities and associated development. There follow the phases of implementation, review and planning for the following annual cycle. If we focus specifically on review and development, it is possible to see how management development needs can be identified in the context of organizational objectives, as shown in Figure 11.1. Arising out of those objectives the needs can then be addressed in such a way as to promote the development of individual managers; the development of teams who work with them; the development of groups of managers across the organization; and improved management practice and quality of performance of the organization as a whole. In Figure 11.1 the organizational objectives are central and the ongoing review and development at different levels within the organization feed both into each other and into the meeting of those organizational objectives. Making these links work is crucial in the context of the strategic plan for the organization. *Making the links work* is in fact part of what strategic management is all about. A strategic management approach led by the senior management team throughout the organization because of their guidance would actually make the strategic objectives come alive in the sense that they inform the decision making throughout the organization and provide a constant frame of reference. The strategic objectives inform the strategic planning which in turn informs the curriculum planning, from which follows the planning of staff and other resources, and the delivery of learning opportunities. (Curriculum is here defined in its broadest sense being that experience which runs right through an individual's involvement with a particular institution, from first contact to final departure.)

In an ideal world it would be possible to start with a blank page and plan a management development programme without having to take into account any complicating factors. However, for any FHEI the situation is unlikely to be quite that simple. It is possible, for example, that: appraisal training will have taken place but very little actual appraisal, because of pressures of time; that the responsibility of management development is unclear; that there is a new personnel officer without an academic background working with a staff development officer who has more experience within the institution but who has been given very little time and/or status with which to organize the programmes of staff development; that some academic staff are resistant to the concept of management development and do not wish to see themselves as managers; that far from being a coherent whole different parts of the organization have very different perceptions of its strategic objectives and different systems of reviewing and developing performance with respect to individuals, teams, courses and other programmes; that curriculum development and review and issues of curriculum quality move through a set of procedures which are totally divorced from any mechanism for looking at the implications for the development of individual managers.

It is essential that those responsible for the initiation of management development programmes recognize factors such as these, and are able to take a constructive approach which begins with some strategic thinking about management development rather than with a specific set of management training events. There will need to be consideration of the following issues:

1. What is the purpose of the management development programme? Why does the institution want to develop its managers?
2. How can the development most effectively form part of the ongoing process of organizational development?
3. What is happening already both with respect to any specific development programmes and with respect to any appraisal system?
4. How is it possible to integrate the development with ongoing line management support?
5. How will the development of senior managers, middle managers and first line managers be linked together?
6. How will the resourcing of management development be integrated into the business plans of the organization?
7. What about the issue of accreditation?

The major purpose of management development within a strategic management approach must surely be to develop individuals so as to continuously improve management practice and therefore improve the organization's ability to meet its own objectives. In order to do this there needs to be a mechanism for management development which involves the line managers as key developers of their own staff. This line management support function needs to be recognized and implemented from the top of the organization, so that the chief executive has a clear role in the development of the senior management team. They in turn take responsibility for the development of the middle management staff who report to them, and so the process continues through the organization. Using this model it is possible to use standard personnel procedures (for example, induction, appraisal, line management support) as vehicles for the development of staff, so that development becomes integrated into the ongoing work role. Following this approach let us now consider a possible model.

A model for management development

Let us assume that the organization wishes to adopt a strategic management approach and is competent to do so. This will mean that it is possible to be clear about the responsibilities associated with each of the management levels within the organization. For senior managers most responsibilities will be management responsibilities. This may also be true for middle managers, but will be progressively less so, as they move through the levels of management within the organization. For example, there are many first line managers whose work may consist equally of lecturing and management activities, or for whom management forms a relatively small part of their role. It is the management aspects of the role which are the focus of this chapter.

Clearly it is possible to specify and define management activities throughout the organization quite independently of individual post holders. So the first step (step 1 in Figure 11.2) is to be clear about the management activities which are part of specific posts. The next step (2) is to be able to identify and define the abilities needed in order to carry out those management activities effectively. It would be possible to spend a long time discussing how those abilities should be categorized, but that is not the focus here. Instead I will adopt a pragmatic approach in which the abilities are categorized using the terms *skills*, *knowledge* and *understanding* without being overly concerned about the precise category into which a particular ability falls. Categories are useful to stimulate thinking; however, individuals acquire skills, knowledge and understanding in a variety of ways and not through specifically separate activities, although the focus clearly varies at different times.

In personnel terms, the two steps we have been discussing are the equivalent of the drawing up of job descriptions and specifications. The preparation of these for management posts through the organization is good personnel practice and provides a basis not only for recruitment and selection, but also for

Step 1
Identify management activities for each relevant post.

Step 2
Identify skills, knowledge and understanding needed to carry out ◄──────┐
management activities effectively.

Step 3
Identify development needs.

►*Step 4*
Identify appropriate mechanisms to address development needs.

Step 5
Agree development plan.

Step 6
Implement development plan.

Step 7   additional/new management activities. ──────┘
Review progress and identify◄──── ongoing development needs in the context
                                   of organizational development.

Figure 11.2 A management development model.

the analysis of development needs for ongoing appraisal and for human resource planning in the context of organizational objectives.

Having identified the abilities needed by managers within the organization,
the next step (3) is to identify the extent to which managers already possess
those abilities and the extent to which development is needed. There are
several possible ways of doing this; for example it may be useful to refer to
an external framework such as the MCI national management standards (see
Table 11.1). Whichever method is adopted it is important to have an approach
which is clear, consistent, systematic and sensitive. A strategic management
approach would also require the linking of the development needs analysis
firmly back to the work role and, crucially, to the involvement of the line
manager at some stage in the process.

In addition to the line manager there needs to be a functional specialist
who is taking an organizational perspective. This functional specialist would
have a number of particular responsibilities:

1. To coordinate the process of management development and ensure that it
   happens consistently.
2. To ensure that the line managers have themselves had the development
   which will enable them to develop their staff.
3. To provide a source of ongoing advice, expertise and support for the line
   managers with respect to their management development function.
4. To be one, but only one, of the providers of management development. It

Table 11.2   Some general management development methods

Mentoring
Work-shadowing
Training course
Training package   – software
– paper
Reading
Simulation
Rotating responsibilities
Coaching
Action learning

may clearly be appropriate in some cases for the functional specialist to organize training or a development programme to meet a need which is identified for a number of individual managers. However, line managers need to be aware that many development needs can be met more effectively via other methods. Some methods of management development are listed in Table 11.2.

In the generation of the list of abilities against the job description there will be some generic abilities which occur repeatedly, for example, time management, communication skills, planning skills, prioritizing and delegation. It is therefore sensible to take the list of skills, knowledge and understanding as a whole and identify any gaps with individual managers. The line manager, the individual manager and possibly the functional specialist should also be involved in the next step, step 4, which is to identify appropriate methods for addressing the development needs which have so far been identified. Table 11.2 provides a list of possible management development methods which may be used individually or in various combinations to meet development needs. It is crucial that line managers have the ability to identify appropriate development methods, to ensure that they are implemented, and that the links are made back to the work role. If management development is considered to be entirely the responsibility of a functional specialist and the individual manager who is to be developed, then management development will remain a bolt-on mechanism and not part of a coherent strategic approach to improve management practice throughout the organization. In order to identify appropriate management development methods the line manager needs to be in a position to cost them in order to incorporate development into the business plan for that section of the organization. This in itself will require a considerable amount of time.

Having identified development needs and appropriate development methods, the progress so far needs to be consolidated and formalized as an individual development plan (step 5). The next steps, 6 and 7, are to implement the plan and to review progress at an agreed date. The development plan should therefore be simple, relevant, practical and specific in terms of action, responsibility, cost, timescale, and review. If the planning is overambitious, too vague or too complex, then successful implementation is unlikely. The role of the line manager in ensuring realistic planning, implementation and review is critical.

Having planned the development of an individual manager in the context of that manager's work role and having identified the line management responsibility for ensuring the implementation and reviewing process, the management development should become an ongoing and dynamic process which happens naturally and interacts with the continual development of the curriculum offered by the organization in line with its strategic objectives (see Figure 11.1). Development is identified as a line management responsibility; the development mechanism supports the responsibilities of each post holder.

Therefore, all managers should find themselves supported in the development of their own ability to carry out the development function. The identification of human resource requirements, the processes of drawing up job descriptions and specifications and the analysis of development needs in the context of induction, and then ongoing appraisal, provide mechanisms which are integrated into the functioning of the organization and which ensure that management development needs are addressed. Management development which is always part of the ongoing process of organizational activity is recognized and tied in with strategic objectives so that the organization never needs to launch an isolated management development programme, for example, because of organizational restructuring. Organizational restructuring may require a more intensive period of management development and this will be picked up as the job descriptions and specifications are written for new posts and the processes of development needs analysis previously described are carried out. This approach to management development which focuses on process rather than content is more robust in the face of increasing rates of organizational change, since it does not rely entirely on one functional specialist or one method of management development.

Figure 11.3 shows a possible format for collecting together a complete picture at organizational level of management responsibilities, together with corresponding skills, knowledge and understanding, and appropriate methods for addressing development needs.

Identifying methods of management development

This section of the chapter will consider in more detail the management development possibilities available to those responsible for developing management staff. Table 11.2 shows that there is potentially a wide range of management development methods available. However when development needs are identified, all those involved frequently agree that the most appropriate response to meet the development need is to identify a suitable training course which the individual can attend.

Training courses are popular for the following reasons:

Management level	Responsibilities (taken from job description)	Skills	Knowledge	Understanding/qualities	Appropriate development methods(s) (See Tables 11.2 and 11.3)
Senior					
Middle					
First line					

Figure 11.3 Organizational overview of management responsibilities, abilities needed and appropriate development methods: a possible format.

1. Attending a course is a clear, concrete, visible response which is perceived as taking action to address the development need.
2. The responsibility for meeting the development need is thereby removed from the line manager, the functional specialist and to some extent the individual themselves.
3. The training course therefore becomes a panacea or magic solution which will meet the development need on its own.
4. The training course is seen by the individual as a welcome break from the usual work routine.
5. The functional specialist may have a budget which would enable them to authorize expenditure on the training course more easily than to authorize expenditure on a development need which is addressed within the daily work routine.

While some of the above factors may be reasonable to consider, it would be more useful to take an approach which actually identifies the most appropriate development methods based on rather more logical criteria. These could include the following:

1. Is the development need specific to that individual, or is it a need that other managers within the organization would also benefit from addressing?
2. Is the development need actually located with the individual or is it rather a development need of that person's staff, or of their line manager, or other colleagues with whom they work?
3. Is it a development need at all, or is it a need for more effective administration, more resources, clearer lines of communication, etc.?
4. At what stage is the individual with respect to this particular development need? Could the ability be developed to the level necessary by, for example, development opportunities in the real work situation; or would it be more appropriate for the individual to have an opportunity to attend a training course, so as to develop the ability in a simulated situation first before attempting to put it into practice in the work situation?
5. What is the nature of the development need? Is it, for example, the need for specific technical knowledge which could be read or acquired through a software package? Is it a need for particular skills which have to be demonstrated and practised? Is it a need for professional updating for which attending a seminar may be appropriate?
6. What are the preferred learning styles of the individuals concerned? Do they learn more readily by observation and reflection or by active participation? Is it appropriate to expose the individuals to a range of learning opportunities, or to encourage them to identify for themselves a particular preferred learning style which will suit them in the meeting of this development need?
7. What are the practical and resource implications of the development methods identified? How realistic are the proposals being discussed?

Classifying methods of management development

It may be useful at this stage to consider some theoretical and practical approaches which could provide a framework within which to identify appropriate development methods for meeting the criteria listed above. At a theoretical level, Honey and Mumford (see Honey and Mumford 1986; Honey 1989) have identified preferred adult learning styles and a learning cycle which identifies the stages necessary for effective learning to take place. Their model is described in greater detail in Chapter 5 entitled The Learning Organization. However, it is interesting to note here Mumford's (1989) description of management development processes as *accidental, opportunistic* and *planned. Accidental* or *informal managerial* processes occur within managerial activities which are focusing on the performance of a particular task without having clear development objectives, so the learning is not planned in advance but is owned by managers. Mumford describes the learning in this case as real and direct, but unconscious and insufficient.

Opportunistic or integrated managerial processes are said to occur within managerial activities which have the intention of both task performance and management development so that the development objectives are clear, and the task has been structured with development in mind by both the line manager and the learner. The learning has been planned beforehand and/or reviewed following the learning experience and is again owned by managers. The learning here is said to be real, direct, conscious and more substantial than is the case for accidental processes.

Planned or formal management development processes are described as often taking place away from normal managerial activities, with the explicit intention of development and clear development objectives. The activities are structured for development purposes, not by the line manager or the participant, but by the developers (in the terms of this chapter the *functional specialist*). Such activities are both planned beforehand and reviewed after taking place, with respect to their effect on development. They are described as being owned more by the developers than by the learners (the managers who are participating). The resulting learning is described as being real if it takes place in the course of the job, or detached if it takes place as part of a training course. The learning is more likely to be conscious, but the activity itself is unlikely to take place very often.

Mumford's approach is interesting because it focuses on the unconscious, or unrecognized, learning which was referred to at the beginning of this chapter. Mumford suggests that it is possible to capitalize on the unconscious learning which is occurring naturally as part of everyday experience by making it explicit and so increasing the effectiveness of the learning which takes place. The deliberate use of reflection and conclusion following management activities, so as to improve the planning of subsequent management activities, can make an enormous impact on the standard of management performance. It can also have the advantage of shifting the focus, when difficulties occur at work, away from identifying scapegoats to learning from the experience, so as to improve future performance.

These concepts are explored further in Chapter 5 on the learning organization. However, it is relevant here to consider how the management development processes which Mumford refers to as opportunistic and planned can contribute to the identification of appropriate management development methods. Mumford clearly sees that it is possible to make use of naturally occurring activities and/or to identify specific management development events which take place outside the work role. There is, however, a more structured approach to this whole issue of identifying appropriate management development methods which has been developed by Margaret Levy in her Work-Based Learning Model (Levy *et al.* 1989).

Levy defines work-based learning as 'linking learning to the work role'. She categorizes all planned learning processes in one of three ways:

1. Structured learning opportunities in the workplace – allocated work activities which are productive and at the same time provide an opportunity for learning.
2. Providing appropriate on-job training/learning opportunities – sustained learning/instruction in specific aspects of the job which is carried out in the workplace but does not make a net contribution to productivity.
3. Identifying and providing relevant off-job learning opportunities – opportunities for learning away from where the worker–learner normally works and outside normal productive work activities.

These three categories can be very useful in identifying two significant parameters with respect to development methods. They enable the individual development plan to identify:

1. whether or not the learner will be physically present in the work place during the process of learning, and
2. whether or not the learner will make a net contribution to productivity.

The issue of productivity is often overlooked but is of crucial significance when costing development processes. Clearly if the learner is making a net contribution to productivity while learning, there are benefits to be gained for the organization in terms of cost effective human resource development. If the Work-Based Learning Model is used to identify learning opportunities which occur naturally within the workplace and turn them into more focused and effective learning opportunities by making the development aims and the reviewing mechanisms explicit, then human resource development will be more likely to be affordable and relevant.

Table 11.3 provides examples of development activities which fall into each of the three categories in the Work-Based Learning Model. This should correct any impression which the reader may by now have that there is no place for off-the-job training courses. Thus, a learner may be at the stage at which it is essential for them to receive some off-the-job training before going on to

Table 11.3 Examples of management development activities categorized according to the work-based learning model

---

1. *Structured learning opportunities in the work place*
   Attending a planning meeting on behalf of a senior manager
   Drawing up a departmental budget for the first time
   Taking a turn on an evening cover rota
   Carrying out staff appraisal
   Preparing and presenting a report to the board of governors.

2. *On-job training/learning opportunities*
   Having meetings with the finance officer and the personnel officer as part of
      induction into a new role
   Observing a senior management team meeting
   Shadowing another manager.

3. *Off-job training/learning opportunities*
   Attending a seminar on credit accumulation
   Attending a conference in a specialist subject area
   Attending a skills based management development event
   Spending a day visiting another FHEI
   Going on a study tour.

---

on-the-job training followed by a structured learning activity in which the learner is being productive while continuing to learn. To take a specific example, the ability to participate effectively in recruitment and selection processes often requires the learning to proceed through a series of stages:

- an off-the-job training course which includes skills practice and some input about relevant legislation, followed by
- the opportunity to learn in the work place by observing a recruitment and selection process without participating fully, followed by
- full participation in the recruitment and selection process, with a structured opportunity to reflect on the learning gained from participation.

This process of staged learning would enable the learning acquired in the off-the-job training course to be linked back into the work role in such a way as to establish and maintain the development of the individual learner. The use of complementary mechanisms, such as formal or informal mentoring and line management supervision and support would provide an individual development plan linking into the context of the work role in such a way as to provide robust, relevant and ongoing development.

Costing management development

Management development is seen to be about the long term rather than the short term, and there is an enormous pressure within education to jump reactively to short-term requests for information and visible activity, rather than to think about longer term planning and development. The cost of providing planned management development is, of course, highly visible, whereas the cost of not developing managers is less apparent, particularly in the short term. There has been some interesting work carried out on the development of a cost benefit analysis mechanism, to enable organizations to identify the relative costs of developing staff and compare them with the relative costs of ignoring development needs. This work has been developed by Paul Martinez (1993) using a cost benefit analysis framework. Some preliminary work carried out by further education managers working with this mechanism has suggested that there are many hidden costs associated with lack of staff development and particularly management development. Examples include: the time spent attempting to carry out activities without really knowing how to; ineffective use of meeting time because of lack of chairing skills; considerable time spent in communicating ineffectively with staff; staff and management time wasted in dealing with difficulties caused by poor 'people management' skills; time wasted on inappropriate activities because of the lack of understanding of the management role or management priorities; absence through stress-related illnesses because of poor stress management techniques; very expensive senior management time taken up with industrial tribunals because of lack of understanding of basic employment and discrimination legislation; and resources used inappropriately or expenditure committed without clear knowledge of business planning techniques.

Accreditation of management development

The emphasis in this chapter has been on the process of management development, rather than assessment and accreditation. It is important to be clear about the separation between the development of management ability and its assessment, although some forms of accreditation are set up in such a way that development and assessment are purchased as part of one complete package. This has traditionally been the case with respect to management qualifications such as the Certificate in Management Studies (CMS), the Diploma in Management Studies (DMS) and the Master of Business Administration (MBA). The more recent competence-based approach to development has separated clearly the development route from the assessment route. Specifically in the management field, the Management Charter Initiative has been responsible for developing national standards of management competence for supervisory, first line, middle and senior levels of management. Assessment of competencies with respect to the MCI standards is by way of gathering a portfolio of evidence of competence which is then formally assessed. The development of abilities (so as to be in a position to gather evidence which demonstrates competence) can take place by whichever method seems appropriate; thus the development route is independent of the assessment route.

Table 11.4 A summary of the characteristics of traditional and competence-based management accreditation programmes

Traditional	Competence-based
Focused on input	Focused on outcome
Assessment of assignment, dissertation and exam answers, set for all students	Assessment of portfolio of evidence, specific to individual student
Development route closely linked to assessment route, much of it general to all students	Development independent of assessment route
Development route compulsory	Development route optional
Emphasis on knowledge	Emphasis on skills

The two approaches to management accreditation, traditional and competence based, each have their particular characteristics and their particular advocates (see Talbot 1993). Traditional approaches often define themselves in terms of inputs and are heavily focused on knowledge and understanding. Competence-based approaches define themselves in terms of outcomes and are more heavily focused on skills and abilities. Table 11.4 summarizes some of the characteristics of the two approaches. The traditional qualifications have been offered primarily by Management or Business Schools in higher education institutions and many of the management qualifications are long established. More recently the Association of Business Schools has formed a consortium, the Management Verification Consortium, for the purposes of accrediting competence-based management qualifications. Thirty to 40 business schools offer National Vocational Qualifications (NVQs) in management at supervisory, first line and middle management levels as well as offering the more traditional Certificate Diploma and Masters qualifications in management. Management NVQs are also accredited by a number of national awarding bodies.

A concluding note

The model suggested here has focused on an institutional approach to management development. However, in the absence of a strategic management approach and/or clear organizational objectives the process could be integrated into the functioning of sub-sections of the organization, for example, faculties, schools, departments and other units. The major requirements for the approach to be effective in this more limited context are a clear identification of the objectives of the relevant sub-section of the organization, a clear understanding of the model by the relevant line manager, and the ability and willingness to implement it.

12

Industrial Relations Strategies and Tactics

Roger Ward

Editors' introduction

The author was and, at the time of writing, continues to be one of *the* key actors in industrial relations affairs for the new universities and colleges of FE. He again covers some similar ground to that in Chapters 2 and 3, but from an intimate internal perspective. Above all, the author reveals that, despite the legal autonomy of the independent educational institutions, industrial relations strategy and many tactics are determined by the overall framework set down by the government.

The independence phenomenon

On 1 April 1989 84 institutions of higher education became independent from the supervision of local education authorities in England and Wales. Thus started a process that was to radically transform the human resource management culture, particularly the industrial relations of this new self-managed sector of education. In those few years since independence was gained, the former polytechnics attained the growth targets established for them by their new funding body, the Polytechnics and Colleges Funding Council (PCFC). Indeed, such was their success in the eyes of the Department for Education (DfE) that the demand of polytechnic leaders for full university status became unstoppable. In 1992, as part of the Further and Higher Education Act, the government announced a change in title, and 29 new universities were created. This number has since grown with the upgrading of some of the larger colleges of higher education such as Luton and Derby, with no doubt more to follow.

The language of DfE ministers during the run up to independence contained emotive phraseology. DfE press statements, polytechnic principals and government ministers referred to higher education institutions being *freed* from the *control* of local education authorities. Alternatively, local politicians, particularly in Labour controlled boroughs referred to their colleges being privatized. However, by 1993 the government had become so sure of their success in the former polytechnics and so confident of the ability of such education institutions to run their own affairs, they determined to relieve local authorities in England and Wales of their 460 further education institutions. On 1 April 1993 hundreds of local education authorities were required to hand over control of their general further education, tertiary and sixth-form colleges to a new funding agency, the Further Education Funding Councils for England and Wales (FEFCE and FEFCW). The implications for the further education sector's industrial relations were to be no less significant than in higher education. In both cases the DfE ministers would intervene directly in support of the new employers' ambitions to totally change the contracts of employment of all lecturers and managers. Their intervention was so straightforward and the reactions of the teaching unions so unsuccessful in resisting the new contracts that the DfE is now faced with the choice of extending its new found powers into the schools sector.

For the government, a major plank of their education policy was successfully completed. Higher and further education institutions were seen to have been freed from the yoke of parochial party politics, so often blamed by the government as one of the causes for the United Kingdom's underperformance in higher and further education student participation rates. Justification for the success was there for all to see since participation rates in the former polytechnics expanded beyond the most optimistic forecasts from the DfE. Similar optimism is now expressed over student growth in the newly independent further education colleges. At the end of their first year of independence it would appear that their expected eight per cent growth in student numbers has been exceeded.

The internal policy arguments for a shift away from local control to central government influence had developed during the mid-1980s. The public debate was initiated by ministers in the spring of 1988. Support for the policy of removing polytechnics and higher education colleges from the local authorities became so overwhelming that the educational and policy merits or demerits of the shift largely fell out of the public domain early in 1989. Since then one common thread has permeated coverage in the local and national press and the specialist education magazines. That coverage was not to do with broad educational issues, rather the industrial relations upheavals that followed independence. This was partly because it is generally assumed that the concern voiced in some quarters regarding a possible threat to academic standards had not been realized. Indeed, there seems to be a growing body of opinion to show that standards in many subject areas are improving. Nor was the majority of press comment in the period of incorporation to do with the rights and wrongs of the demise of the role of the local education authority in FHE. Since the ending of the binary line and the granting of university titles to the former polytechnics, a cross-party political policy has emerged that basically supports the removal of all higher education from local education authority influence. More surprisingly is the apparent lack of enthusiasm by the Labour Party to object to the recent independence of further education institutions. At most, any future Labour government seems to have committed itself to a modest increase in the number of college governors to be drawn from local education authority members. The current DfE advice calls for a minimum of one local authority-appointed governor. So, the media debate confined itself largely to one aspect of human resource management, that of the ever-changing industrial relations climate in FHE.

This is surely a surprising outcome and one that few could have anticipated. The UK industrial relations scene in the private and public sectors is widely recognized as a model for the rest of our European Union partners. According to the 1993 EC statistics UK labour costs are amongst the lowest in the world. Nationwide and, indeed, local strikes have become something of an oddity since the late 1980s. Aside from the great set pieces of the miners' clash (1984/5) with Mrs Thatcher and the equally doomed ambulance drivers' strike (1989/90) little occurred to excite industrial relations reporters until the 1994 signal-workers' dispute. Indeed, so sparse had become the industrial relations scene by the late 1980s that most of the media's outlets had even abandoned the title of industrial relations reporters. So swift had been the decline in the traditional industrial trades union membership that where disputes did occur in the 1980s and 1990s, it was more likely to be found in the public rather than the private sector. This is where the impact of polytechnic and the further education institutional independence from local authority political influence led to a fertile ground for trade union activity in the education sector. Just as the trade union reaction to the independence of polytechnics resulted in conflict at local and national bargaining levels, the newly created independent further education institutions also now find themselves in similar circumstances with local and national strikes led by the lecturers' union, NATFHE.

Independence from local authority political and practical management control was proclaimed by the public sector and teaching unions as one of the harsher aspects of Thatcherite policy. In fact, the architect of the legislation and then Secretary of State for Education, Kenneth Baker, did not so much make the polytechnics independent in 1988, rather he transferred the control of funding within the public sector. A new national funding agency was created to take over from the combination of the National Advisory Body for Public Sector Higher Education (NAB) and local education authority direct and indirect political and managerial influence. Formal fiscal and accounting responsibility for the polytechnics and colleges of higher education was ceded to the PCFC on 1 April 1989. This body was soon to establish a funding methodology that required the institutions to compete at their financial margin for students. In the broadest of terms the greater the number of students recruited by an institution resulted in a greater allocation of resources. The reverse was also the case. This tended to drive the former polytechnics and colleges into the market place to sell their services for student growth in competition with one another. This was little more than a natural development from the procedures and structures established through NAB, but with one crucial difference that was to have such an impact on industrial relations. Under the local authority arrangements, institutions had little direct control over pay and conditions of employment for teaching and non-teaching staff. This was dealt with through formal national collective bargaining structures. With independence each institution became an employer in its own right with sole responsibility to determine pay levels and substantive conditions of employment and the independence to set pay and conditions locally as opposed to nationally.

Government involvement

Ultimate control of higher education institution funding derived from the Treasury, through the DfE and thence to the PCFC. The chief executive and accounting officer of each newly independent polytechnic and higher education institution was required, by statute, to report to the PCFC. Through the funding council chief executive the use of public monies was reported to the Public Accounts Committee. This shifting of funding accountability as well as the direct responsibility for monies spent by the new universities and colleges led to the introduction of a new and direct influence on the pay and conditions of all higher education through the Treasury and the DfE.

These two government departments created what became known as the Two Per Cent Holdback mechanism. Originally intended to influence pay developments in the old universities in the UK the advent of the new independent higher education sector gave the Treasury and the DfE an opportunity to substantially extend the scope of the holdback influence. Under powers given to the Secretary of State for Education by the 1988 Education Reform Act the government created a bureaucratic tool that was to become the major problem for NATFHE in its dealing with the employers in FHE. The holdback rule entitles the DfE to withhold up to two per cent of the annual recurrent teachers' pay bill until certain conditions are met by each employer covered by this arrangement. While this approach to pay in the public sector currently remains restricted to the DfE, the principle of directly influencing pay and conditions is not new to governments. In the USA the federal government has been actively withholding funding for state universities since the 1980s in order to enforce social policy such as racial integration and gender balance. In the UK, government involvement in pay and conditions in the public sector is more formal but no less dramatic in impact. Pay Review Boards such as that for teachers retain a theoretical independence from the government but remain influenced by the views of elected government of the day. Ultimately the authority of such Boards and their future lies in the hands of the government that appointed them. Public pay policy is also employed in a more global role where Parliament stipulates public sector pay levels or norms, but in no other arena aside from FHE has the relatively new concept of the two per cent holdback mechanism been implemented.

The advent of the PCEF

The mechanism was used by the DfE to complement the employment policy aspirations of the new employers in the PCFC sector. Just as the funding council had been established in advance of 1 August 1989 so too had the putative employers formed their own representative body. The polytechnics and colleges of higher education each directed well established representative bodies to promote their professional and academic interests. In the case of the polytechnics it was the Committee of Directors of Polytechnics (CDP) and for colleges of higher education the Standing Conference of Principals (SCOP). In the spring of 1988 a joint working party of CDP and SCOP was created to examine the future of industrial relations in the post-independence era. One option was to opt out of the national bargaining framework and deal with all pay and conditions issues at local institution level. This was dismissed as an immediate goal given that a substantial number of the new employers did not have an established human resource department and even fewer employed industrial relations officers with experience of handling multiunion and high density union membership locations. Having reached the conclusion that an element of centralization of pay and conditions was likely to be sustained for some years after independence, CDP and SCOP decided to sponsor an entirely new national body to act as a national adviser on pay and conditions to institutions and to lead on behalf of all the employers. This organization became known as the Polytechnics and Colleges Employers' Forum (PCEF). PCEF was created in the summer of 1988 and by December of that year was listed as an independent employers' association with the Certification Officer of ACAS.

PCEF was established as a company limited by guarantee, and each of the polytechnics and colleges of higher education to become independent was eligible to join as an institution. Voting was by weighted ratios dependent on full-time equivalent student numbers. The elected Board of Management comprised twelve individuals including four places reserved for Chairs of Boards of Governors who, in all cases, were drawn from the private sector.

The election of the first PCEF Board paved the way for a number of disputes between the employers and the unions. During 1989, 1990 and 1991 the philosophy of the PCEF, its strategy and bargaining tactics were perceived, particularly by the unions, as contrary to the inherited local education authority culture of centralized national bargaining on pay and conditions at national level and a collegiate approach at local level. From its inception PCEF stated its desire to retain a national bargaining framework, but one that would allow a much greater local flexibility. A conflict with the unions was inevitable when the largest of the unions in the sector, NATFHE, proclaimed its view that orderly industrial relations could only succeed if they were based on a national framework similar to that enjoyed under local education authority management. This was hardly a novel position reflecting as it did a long cherished belief amongst the mainstream trade unions in the efficacy and equity that stems from national collective bargaining. This was the classical position of practitioners and theoreticians in industrial relations and reflected the dominant culture of the 1960s and 1970s only to decline in the 1980s. The unions that became involved with the PCEF in higher education had developed the terms and conditions of employment inherited by the institutions upon independence through a heavily centralized bargaining machinery. The old unions were not to give up those conditions without a fight.

The potential for dispute between employers and unions became clear to all the employers, DfE and unions concerned at an early stage. The PCEF Board was publicly dedicated to greater local flexibility in the determination of pay and conditions. The unions, on the other hand, had developed their national bargaining experiences through the statutory Burnham Education Committee structure of the 1960s and 1970s. This was replaced by the National Joint Council for Further Education under the auspices of the local authorities employers' body, the Local Government Management Board. It was the NJCs for teaching and non-teaching staffs that negotiated all the conditions of employment and pay levels of staff to be inherited by the newly independent institutions. Under the local authority arrangements NJCs did not include any of the polytechnic or college principals on the management side of the NJC. The management team under the NJC structure was dominated, not by institution leaders responsible for the day-to-day administration and management, but by local authority elected politicians.

The PCEF's approach was to devolve conditions of employment from national to local level within a framework of national guidelines and give greater decision-making powers to the new chief executives and the Boards of Governors. It took the view that the future of pay bargaining may well involve the entire dismantling of inherited national machinery but preferred to await the outcome of devolution of key conditions of employment.

In determining this approach at this inaugural conference in December 1988, PCEF members followed the dominant industrial relations culture of the time. The Thatcher paradigm was at its peak during this period. In this model the notion of nationally negotiated common payscales and conditions is a restrictive practice which distorts the market and forces up unit costs across the sector. The imagery of the time used to convey these so-called distorting effects drew on the housing market and the sharpness of the price gradient between north and south. The creation of the new polytechnic sector aligned with a market rationale for its funding under the PCFC presented a new approach to pay in the education sector. It offered PCEF a unique opportunity to deregulate industrial relations.

In January 1989 the principals of all PCEF member institutions notified their management, teaching and non-teaching staffs of the necessary and limited contractual changes deriving exclusively from incorporation (PCEF 1989a). This included advance notice that the title of employer would change from 1 April and that all disciplinary and grievance procedures would be altered to prevent employees from taking cases for final resolution outside the boundaries of each new institution. In the local authority system grading appeal cases could be determined by a committee system going through the Town Hall to regional and eventually national level decisions. More importantly, managerial and teaching staff in each higher education institution were informed of the employer's intention to introduce significantly different contractual conditions. Specifically, the PCEF recommended that new style contracts would be offered to all teachers appointed or promoted after 1 April 1989. These contracts would be different in design and content from those previously issued through the NJC machinery. The employers took the view that advance notice of substantial variations of contract was prudent in legal and political terms.

The legal principles governing changes in contracts of employment in 1989 were based on the reality that the terms and conditions of an employment contract should not generally be varied without the consent of both parties involved. If the employers had attempted to impose a variant without the employees' consent then they would have been open to the accusation of breach of contract. If any imposed variation had constituted a substantial change in the employees' terms, in other words, a repudiating breach, the employee would have been entitled to resign on the basis of constructive dismissal and then claim for damages. Theoretically the new employers could, if they had so chosen, have terminated the lecturer's contract and offered employees new contracts incorporating amendments desired by the employer. This was dismissed by the PCEF as impractical. Not only would such a move have led to even greater union and staff opposition than was contemplated, but employees with two or more years of continuous service would have been entitled to complain of unfair dismissal to an industrial tribunal. Nonetheless employment legislation at that time provided that an industrial tribunal may find in favour of the employer providing it could be shown that the employer had 'sound business or organizational reasons' for insisting that employees accept new terms and conditions. PCEF adopted a policy in early 1989 that changes in terms and conditions of employment were an unavoidable consequence of incorporation which could be justified as being due to sound business or organizational reasons. This view depended on how the changes were to be introduced. The employers concluded that whatever the outcome of efforts to abandon past local education authority style contracts, it would be essential to consult all staff on an individual basis who may refuse to accept new terms to find out the nature of their objections. In 1989 PCEF attempted to ensure individual employees appreciated the employers' reasons for wishing to introduce contractual change (PCEF 1989e). Such a view of the process of change had not taken into account the fact that NATFHE was developing its own strategies and tactics to derail attempts to replace the old contracts with the PCEF so-called *flexible contracts*.

Prior to incorporation the employers wrote to all employees notifying them of four technical alterations to contracts of employment that arose specifically from independence (PCEF 1989b). The name of each employer altered from the Local Education Authority Board of Governors to the newly named Higher Education Corporation. Where the new polytechnics or colleges were handling their own pay administration systems for the first time this usually involved a change in the date of payment or a move to cashless pay. In such an event consent was to be secured from the employees. Where disciplinary and grievance procedures had traditionally provided stages outside the institution such as the Town Hall or other regional or national local authority appeal structures, these were to be replaced by procedures that ended within the confines of the institution. Finally, employees were advised in March 1989 that the old local authority central bargaining machinery was to be replaced (PCEF 1989c).

The old national arrangements

In the local authorities the Whitley Council and Burnham Committee systems had traditionally determined the pay of all schoolteachers and lecturers in further education colleges, polytechnics and colleges of higher education. This latter group had their own National Joint Council system and during the early 1970s had negotiated a contract of employment for lecturers, senior lecturers, principal lecturers and all managers in further and higher education institutions known colloquially as the *Silver Book* (NJCLA). The nationally negotiated contract of employment for administrative, professional technical and clerical staffs, the APT&C employees, became known as the *Purple Book* (NJCLA). In the summer of 1988 PCEF consulted NATFHE and the non-teaching unions NALGO, GMBATU and the TGWU with a view to introducing a replacement bargaining machinery to the local authority NJCs. The unions, while concerned, expressed a willingness to cooperate. The new employers had long regarded the NJC machinery as unresponsive to the realities of running educational institutions. The NJC machinery was regarded as cumbersome. The lecturers' council consisted of 32 members. Fifteen were appointed not by the college principals but by their political masters in the local authority. The other 17 were appointed by the lecturers' unions led by NATFHE. The employers' representatives were drawn from the Association of County Councils, the Association of Metropolitan Authorities and the Welsh Joint Education Committee. The lecturers' union representatives were appointed from NATFHE, the Association of Principals of Colleges (APC) and the National Society of Education in Art and Design. The APC actually represented the collective interests of the very college principals that were to become the employers of the new independent institutions. These three TUC unions were joined in 1987 by the non-TUC Association of Polytechnic Lecturers by virtue of Section 4 of the Teachers Pay and Conditions Act 1987. The lecturers' NJC specific functions were:

1. Provision for the regular negotiation of pay and other terms and conditions of service.
2. Securing adherence by all LEAs of lecturers and research staff to collective agreements relating to pay and other terms and conditions of service.

3. Clarification and interpretation of such of the Council's agreements as may be required by LEAs and/or their lecturers and/or their research staff.
4. Securing the provision, both locally on all matters affecting relations between LEAs and their lecturers and research staff, and nationally on pay and other terms and conditions of service matters, of appropriate procedures for the resolution of collective differences and disputes.
5. The collection of statistics and information on matters appertaining to the pay and other terms and conditions of service of lecturers and research staff.
6. Cooperation with other joint negotiating committees on matters of common interest.

The NJC was headed by an independent Chair with access to arbitration and a formidable secretarial backup.

The *Silver Book*, as variously updated through mutual agreement between the parties, comprised 93 pages covering the procedures for resolving disputes to specific contractual conditions and national pay scales. Designed at the height of TUC and local authority influence the *Silver Book* and the *Purple Book* represented the apex of public sector national collective bargaining systems. They gave little or no input to local managers in charge of actually managing the education institutions. The NJCs effectively demanded that managers maintained systems rather than innovated. Control and decision making was removed from local management and such limited efforts to introduce flexibility into working practices that were introduced locally usually resulted in procedural wrangling that had a tendency to stifle change. In December 1988 the Board of Management of PCEF was elected on a unanimous vote to abandon the NJC machinery and replace it with a streamlined bargaining structure emphasizing autonomy of decision making at institutional level.

The new national arrangements

The new employers proposed a reduced number of unions and a national bargaining framework to be called the Polytechnics and Colleges National Negotiating Committee (PCNNC). This body was to be charged with the consideration of terms and conditions of all grades of staff to include teaching, APT&C and manual employees. The PCNNC was to make recommendations on behalf of the employers' body and the recognized unions. Crucially these recommendations would not be binding upon the new higher education corporations. These would only have the moral persuasion of a joint recommendation, whenever such a recommendation occurred. The PCEF Board's intent was that the legacy of centrally directed national collective bargaining systems should be deconstructed and ultimately replaced with local autonomy, local determination of salaries and conditions and minimum national coordination. In line with that objective PCEF offered the unions it chose to recognize a national recognition and procedure agreement to last for only 24 months. It was assumed by many that after that period institutions would wish to locally determine pay and conditions of service. In the event, the assumption proved to be only partially realized.

PCEF submitted a draft recognition and procedure agreement to the unions in February 1989 with a stipulation that a new bargaining committee structure must be in place by incorporation the following April. The unions chosen for recognition were APT and NATFHE for the teaching staffs, GMB, NUPE and TGWU for manual staffs and GMB, NALGO and NUPE for APT&C staffs. The new agreement was signed on 17 April with a termination date of 1 March 1991. The unions merely noted the employers' intent to end national bargaining by 1991 and reserved their position.

The new agreement differed in many ways from the Whitley Council-style NJC local authority procedures. The new national bargaining machinery guaranteed the supremacy of the new institutions' Board of Governors. They alone each had responsibility for deciding whether or not to implement any PCNNC recommendations. The agreement brought together teaching and non-teaching staffs into one committee in an early attempt to establish what has since become known as single table bargaining. PCEF also insisted that TUC and non-TUC unions collaborated in negotiations. Previously unions which had been nationally recognized by the NJC were given automatic recognition at local level. This link was broken by PCEF. From that date of incorporation each employer could choose which union, if any, to recognize to suit local circumstances. Compulsory arbitration and the status quo clauses were also abandoned by the employers. So, albeit with some reluctance, all 52,000 employees accepted the first stage of technical changes to their contract subsequent to incorporation and began to readjust to collective bargaining in a more decentralized environment.

The new contracts

Having introduced without conflict the first stage of contractual change PCEF commenced its declared aim of moving to entirely new flexible working conditions for newly appointed teaching staff and promotees. PCEF set a target date of April 1990 for all existing lecturing staff to move from the *Silver Book* to the new PCEF contract. In May 1989 the employers introduced APT and NATFHE to the new contract in an effort to negotiate a joint recommendation under the new PCNNC machinery. The unions replied by submitting a 12.5 per cent pay claim for their 1 April annual pay review and rejecting any alterations negotiated or otherwise to the *Silver Book* in response to PCEF's second stage of contractual change.

The PCEF model contract was intended to be flexible in areas where the inherited contract had created problems for employers. The *Silver Book* restricted the working week to 30 hours maximum and the working year to 38 weeks. Of these only 36 were contracted to teaching, with the remaining period for staff development work. In effect, the contractual year was 190 days' teaching, leaving 14 weeks' holiday. Within the 30 hour week, the *Silver Book* stipulated contact time (i.e. the actual delivery of teaching to students) to a maximum of between 12 to 15 hours per week for higher education principal lecturers and senior lecturers and 21 hours maximum for further education lecturers. Contact time was regarded by PCEF subscribers as particularly unacceptable. This was because nationally negotiated teaching time limits restricted the ability of local management to plan courses timetabled to suit local market needs including the growing demands by students to be taught outside the traditional 9 to 5 working day. Another pressure being faced by the polytechnics was the need to respond to employers who sought higher education training and reskilling provision for their employees during the non-traditional teaching year. With the knowledge that PCFC funding methodology was to be based on demand-led growth and competitive tendering, the higher education institutions embraced the PCEF flexible contract alternative as the most satisfactory option to the *Silver Book*.

The union response was that contractual change was not needed. They claimed the *Silver Book* had operated flexibly enough during the preceding years which had shown a student number growth even before the introduction of PCFC funding methodology. Numerically this was a correct analysis. Full-time student numbers had grown by 47 per cent between 1979 and 1988. The DfE growth projections in student numbers was for a full 90,000 by 1992. Most institutions reported to PCEF in 1989 that lecturing staff did indeed work flexibly. Many staff voluntarily taught more contact hours than that nationally determined by the NJC, and often voluntarily made themselves available for non-teaching duties in excess of their 30 hour contractual week. However, these goodwill efforts depended upon a voluntary approach. This not only cost the employers in terms of overtime payments, but laid itself open to abuse by unions who could take damaging industrial action simply in the form of a work to contract. NATFHE took no time in utilizing this tactic, and in May 1989 commenced to ballot their membership to work to strict *Silver Book* rules in an effort to force PCEF subscribers to withdraw the introduction of the new flexible contract. The intensity of the campaign at local branch level even took the official union structures by surprise. The May 1989 Annual Conference of NATFHE, over the objections of the union leadership, called not only for a work to contract ballot but also a boycott of the student examination process scheduled for June and July.

The rush by the unions to begin industrial action had the effect, not of pressurizing the employers, but of forcing them in adversity to work together to solve a common problem. It was more through NATFHE's initial industrial action ballot than any concept of employer solidarity that forged the PCEF into an identifiable and united organization that retained 100 per cent membership throughout its existence.

PCEF responded to the union action by proposing to them that new style contracts should contain the following terms (PCEF 1989d):

1. Thirty-seven hour working week.
2. Teaching hours of work to be determined at institutional level to suit local needs.
3. All employment to be exclusive with any outside work to be taken only with the express permission of the polytechnic principal.
4. Thirty-day vacation time plus statutory holidays.
5. Abolition of the one-year redundancy notice period.
6. New contracts to be issued to all new starters, promotees, heads of department and other managers by 1 September 1989 and for all other lecturing staff by September 1990.
7. A Joint Contract Working Party to establish the contract details.

The NATFHE work to rule ballot and exam boycott began in late May. This was too late to significantly affect the exam process already under way. In an effort to break the deadlock, the employers proposed a new tactic, and attempted to introduce a new annual pay review date of 1 September instead of 1 April. PCEF offered 5.4 per cent on all basic rates with 2.5 per cent pensionable lump sum to cover the period 1 April to 31 August 1989.

PCEF adopted an early policy of refusing to enter into national union conflict on more than one front at once. The employers settled without dispute the non-teaching unions' July annual review pay claim of 8 per cent, marginally above the Retail Price Index

NATFHE's internal politics reflected the mood of their membership during the early months of independence. Under the new legislation which required regular five-yearly union ballots for the election of General Secretaries, NATFHE became the first union to oust a sitting General Secretary. Geoff Woolf, a full-time lecturer, was elected the new General Secretary to replace the incumbent moderate leader, Peter Dawson.

The new sector entered 1990 with a work to contract and examination boycott still in operation. NATFHE's internal pressures were beginning to tell as they announced a 30 per cent increase in their membership subscription dues. PCEF greeted the new year by advising the teaching unions that in the absence of any national settlement to the 1989/90 pay and conditions negotiations, the employers would serve the nine-months formal notice period to withdraw from the PCNNC machinery, abolish national negotiations and move to local negotiations during 1990. For the remaining nine months of the agreement, PCEF also recommended that the inherited practice of operating the collection of trade union subscriptions on behalf of the teaching unions at no cost would be abandoned. NATFHE entered 1990 in national dispute with the employers, no pay settlement from April 1989 and the withdrawal of a number of trade union facilities previously granted for them at no cost.

The examination boycott, having had little effect in 1989, eventually hit institutions who required lecturers to prepare examination papers in the final term of 1990. The PCEF response was to deduct pay from any lecturer participating in the boycott. Matters came to a head quickly. ACAS intervened and invited both parties for conciliation. The employers were anxious to avoid disruption. The unions were anxious to resolve their outstanding pay claim and a temporary settlement was reached. The unions conceded a delayed annual review date from April to September with compensation to cover the lost months, and the abolition of all national pay and conditions bargaining for managerial staff. The employers accepted that they would participate in a joint ACAS Working Party in an effort to resolve the issue of new flexible contracts to replace the *Silver Book*.

The ACAS Working Party independent Chair, having heard evidence from PCEF and the unions, published his report in August 1990 (PCEF 1990b). Of 13 recommendations two were discomforting to the employers because these indicated the confirmation of national level bargaining by urging consistency of treatment as a desirable goal in regard to the introduction of new contracts of employment. The Chair also urged the creation of a new national joint committee to monitor the introduction of new contracts and provide a national appeals mechanism in the event either side wished to raise a complaint. These two recommendations were reluctantly accepted by the employers along with the other 11 because the total set corresponded to the original PCEF calls for a new contract in line with the two per cent holdback DfE initiative, the significance of which had yet to impact on the sector.

ACAS recommended that a new lecturers' contract to replace the *Silver Book* should contain an exclusivity of employment clause and contractual compliance with employer approved staff appraisal schemes. The PCEF initiatives for appropriate contractual copyright, patent, confidentiality and post-termination restriction clauses were also commended. ACAS recommended local determination of hours of teaching within a band of 14 to 18 per week, 35 days' annual holiday and 'research and scholarly activity' to be undertaken outside a standard 38-week teaching/staff development year. NATFHE's national negotiators rejected the findings, and mounted a well-supported one-day national strike in the polytechnics against new contracts of any sort.

With the ACAS Report largely in the employers' favour, NATFHE and the APCT increased their industrial action programme. However, the next one-day strike called for 6 November was supported by less than one-quarter of the 22,000 teaching staff. This was due largely to the new employers' tactic of deducting pay from all strikers at a rate of 1/190th compared to the traditional local authority pay deduction policy of 1/365th. With support for further action dwindling, the leaders of the APCT and NATFHE finally agreed to recommend a settlement based upon the ACAS recommendations to their members. The eventual agreement reached introduced a replacement contract for the *Silver Book* with an accompanying staff handbook in line with the ACAS recommendations, the abolition of national bargaining for all managerial staff, a pay award in line with inflation and a £500 non-pensionable lump sum plus one additional increment for each individual signing the new contract.

A considerable support system to encourage the employers to introduce contractual change was provided by the Department for Education. They introduced their 2 per cent holdback mechanism to the new sector on 15 November 1989. Secretary of State for Education, John MacGregor, announced that two per cent of the recurrent lecturers' salary bill would be withdrawn from the sector unless 'satisfactory pay settlements' were reached for both the 1989/90 and 1990/91 pay rounds. In addition, the DfE called for 'efficiency' improvements. The Department expanded this policy and advised the PCEF to place all heads of department onto new flexible contracts, subject all employees to staff appraisal and contractual exclusivity of work clauses in line with the ACAS Working Party Report, and finally to appoint all new start staff and promotees onto a new flexible professional contract as commended by the ACAS Working Party with or without the unions' acceptance of the Report. In December 1990 while NATFHE's activists were deliberating their leaders' recommendations to abolish the *Silver Book*, the Department once again intervened. On this occasion in a letter from A. J. Wiggins, Deputy Secretary at the DfE to the PCEF, each employer was advised that in the event of NATFHE rejecting the ACAS proposals and the PCEF's final offer, the Department 'will be ready to advise . . . arrangements which will enable institutions to apply to the (Funding) Council for an appropriate share of the (2 per cent monies) in respect of arrangements made locally'. Equally, the Department advised that in the event of a national settlement on pay and contracts the 2 per cent holdback monies, £12 million would be released to the sector.

This threat to end all national pay bargaining for lecturers halted any resistance by APCT and NATFHE members to the abolition of the *Silver Book* and the introduction of new flexible contracts.

In the eyes of the education press the price of peace was worth it. 'It would be wrong to regard the provisional settlement of the long running and bad tempered dispute about the pay and contracts of polytechnic and college lecturers as a victory for either the employers or the trade unions . . .' ran the editorial of *The Times Higher Education Supplement* for 7 December 1990 '. . . it will be a victory for both sides and consequently the sector.' However, 'the great gain for the employers is that they have at last received the unions' agreement to a proper professional contract designed for actual working conditions . . . which will replace the old *Silver Book* conditions of service written with further education in mind.'

The DfE released further advice to the sector immediately following the unions' formal acceptance of the new flexible contracts for all staff in January 1991. The Department wrote to the PCEF advising that £13 million would be withdrawn from the sector in the following pay round which the Secretary of State concluded 'would be helpful to the employers during the coming negotiations in their endeavour to build upon the progress made in the 1990 settlement.' In September the Secretary of State then advised that the next settlement should introduce performance-related pay and rigorous staff appraisal schemes to be monitored at the point of delivery.

The government's powers

Why did APCT and NATFHE wait for so long to mount a credible defence against the effects of the 2 per cent hold back mechanism apparently weighted against their interests? Curiously the largest of the two teachers' unions accepted the Department's assumed powers with little more than verbal protest. The smaller of the two unions, APCT, decided to challenge the mechanism in court and nearly succeeded. In July 1991 the APCT opposed Department intervention in the collective bargaining process through a Judicial Review of the Secretary of State's powers. The High Court ruled that although the Secretary of State was entitled to continue to withhold funds from institutions until he was satisfied with the outcome of pay negotiations, he had also exceeded his powers. While dismissing the APCT case, the High Court ruled on 31 July that the Department could not withhold monies from an individual institution; only from the sector as a whole. The net effect of this judgment was that the Government amended the legislation to strengthen the Secretary of State's powers by allowing him to deduct 2 per cent of the recurrent salary bill of any individual institution that chose to reject DfE guidance on pay and efficiency.

The basis of the powers of the Secretary of State for Education to intervene in further and higher education pay and conditions negotiations lies in Section 134(6) of the Education Reform Act 1988 to make grants to the funding councils subject to conditions. This does not involve the making of a Statutory Order, the Secretary simply makes his requirements known directly to the funding councils for further and higher education.

In response to the APCT campaign against such intervention the DfE clarified its powers in a letter to the national employers:

> It does not follow ... that the attachment of conditions is a mere bluff. On the contrary, if the Secretary of State attaches a condition to the grant or to part of the grant and that condition is not met, the Secretary of State may withhold the relevant sum from payment.

Because of doubts raised by the APCT Judicial Review results strengthened powers were given to the Secretary of State which were embodied in Section 68 of the Further and Higher Education Act 1992.

Throughout 1992 the APCT alone amongst the teaching unions branded the 2 per cent holdback powers of the Secretary of State as a confidence trick. In a circular dated 25 February 1992 to all PCFC sector Principals and Chairs of Governors the APCT demanded:

> ... we are faced with a confidence trick, a trick which is being perpetuated on lecturers and governing bodies of PCFC institutions by the Government and PCEF/PCFC.

> If the Governors of Polytechnics and Colleges do not stand up for their constitution in this case what could be the next target of the DES? The salaries of Directors? The colour of chalk? The recent history of (DfE)

interference shows they are interested in interfering only as a symptom of addiction to power . . .

The APCT campaign was based on the detailed DfE guidelines circulated to employers by the PCEF in July 1990.
On 18 July, 1990 the DfE wrote to the PCEF advising that:

we think it essential for there to be changes in the contracts of employ-ment of members of the academic staff more generally to promote flexible working practices. These should provide:

(i) arrangements for the working time of staff members which provide the institution's management with the flexibility to make proper use of the institution's resources, human and material, throughout the institution's working week and year in accordance with the institu-tion's needs;

(ii) subject to agreed holiday provision, for staff to be accountable to management for the use of their time during those weeks when they are not required to work at their institutions.

We recognize that these are significant changes: institutions may well wish to proceed with them in different ways, but we should expect arrange-ments leading to changes along these lines to be introduced as part of the 1990 pay settlement at least for new recruits and for staff promoted to higher grades. The effective date should be within the next academic year.

We should expect institutions to introduce no later than next aca-demic year a system of staff appraisal which takes into account national guidelines.

It seems right that full-time staff should not take on outside work without the consent of their employers: but that equally institutions should encourage members of staff to undertake other professional activities where they can do so with benefit for, at least without prejudice to, the work which they do for the institution. We should expect contracts of employment to reflect these principles.

With the powers of the Secretary of State to intervene in free collective bargaining procedures strengthened as a result of the APCT Judicial Review, the DfE continued to press the national employers for yet more flexibility. The process of government guidance for more local pay determination con-tinued unabated. Following the annual Chancellor's Autumn Statement on public expenditure in 1991, the DfE once again wrote to the PCEF on 2 September. The Department emphasized that it expected any settlement 'to build upon earlier progress'. The DfE called for 'further extensions of the scope to settle pay locally.' This time the 2 per cent monies were to be withheld from each institution until it reported to the Funding Council that it had implemented performance-related pay systems for all heads of depart-ment and other senior staff. The DfE also supported the PCEF call for the introduction of staff appraisal. Secretary of State the Rt Hon Kenneth Clarke wrote to the PCEF Chair on 8 November 1991:

> I do not see how the appraisal of lecturers is to be effective unless appraisers have the right to observe teaching. If the present terms [proposed by the PCEF] were watered down I should not release the £13m [2 per cent holdback sum].

DfE powers were not limited to conditions alone. At the same time they successfully called upon the old universities employers' organization to actually reduce their intended pay award to academic staff as it exceeded the rate of inflation. The completion of the Thatcher paradigm in the higher education sector was the call by the DfE for the introduction of performance-related pay for all lecturing staff as a condition on the 1992/93 pay round. Although stoutly resisted by the teaching unions a settlement was finally reached in which the employers implemented an annual PRP pay element of no less than 0.75 per cent on a set criteria exclusively determined by the employer. By 1992 the Secretary of State had extended his 2 per cent holdback powers to the newly independent further education sector in addition to the higher education polytechnics, colleges and universities. In November of that year, following the established pattern of writing to the PCEF immediately following the Chancellor's Autumn Statement, the Rt. Hon John Patten MP, Secretary of State, advised both sectors of his condition that pay settlements must be restricted to between 0 and 1.5 per cent 'in order to keep the growth of paybills as low as possible'. In a break from the traditional policy of concentrating the 2 per cent holdback in the arena of teachers' pay, these restrictions applied to teaching and non-teaching staff.

By this period the objectives set by PCEF to abolish the *Silver Book* restrictive practices had all but been achieved, but despite the success of the employers in devolving all conditions of employment to local level and concentrating principally upon pay negotiations at national level, the fact remained that national pay bargaining systems had survived more or less intact. Despite the radical change in conditions of employment, the abolition of the *Silver Book* in higher education, the devolution of decision making from national to local, and the express use of the 2 per cent holdback mechanism to assist the employers to achieve their bargaining objectives, the teachers' unions APCT and NATFHE had succeeded in retaining the national bargaining framework for annual pay negotiations at least.

It remains to be seen what lessons can be drawn from this particular and peculiar example of government intervention in the pay and conditions bargaining process. By 1993 the PCEF accepted that national pay bargaining, though not conditions of employment negotiations, would remain in force in their sector. With the introduction of the new flexible contracts, staff appraisal at the point of delivery and performance-related pay, the new university Vice-Chancellors concluded that further intervention from the DfE would not produce any greater benefits than those which could be achieved by bilateral talks between the unions and PCEF.

At the request of PCEF and with the support of the CVCP, the old university national representative body, the apparatus for the 2 per cent holdback was withdrawn from the higher education sector. The advent of the 1994/95 pay round marked a return to free collective bargaining without the direct involvement of the DfE holdback.

The advent of the CEF

In the meantime the newly independent further education colleges had formed their own employers' organization, the College Employers' Forum (CEF). Created with the help of the PCEF, the CEF was immediately faced with the 2 per cent mechanism.

On 23 March 1993, Tim Boswell, the Parliamentary Under-Secretary of State for FHE advised the CEF of the Department's intention to withhold funds unless certain conditions set by the Secretary of State were obtained by the employers' body. With the background of success in the higher education sector few were surprised by the contents of Minister of State Tim Boswell's letter to the further education employers in February 1994. 'I am aware of a number of restrictive practices embodied in the *Silver Book*... The model contract which the CEF has drawn up eliminates these restrictive practices.' By this time unions had already embarked on their programme of strike action in one last effort to save the *Silver Book* conditions so clearly identified by the DfE as unacceptable and already abolished in the new universities.

That further education employers now face a period of conflict similar to that endured by the higher education sector cannot be doubted. The DfE have declared their intentions to use the 2 per cent holdback mechanism as before and the further education employers have created their own national employers' organization to push through substantial contractual change for lecturers. The challenge for the unions is to repel the encroachment of the 2 per cent conditions. Having failed to do so in higher education, few will give the unions much chance of success. The challenge for the DfE is to determine exactly how far it should go in the application of the 2 per cent holdback mechanism.

Final thoughts

The use of the holdback mechanism allows the employers to justify their drive to introduce new working practices and contracts of employment while still claiming the existence of free collective bargaining in FHE. The statutory Pay Review Board has replaced national bargaining for schoolteachers, yet no such radical changes in their contracts of employment has been tackled. This, despite the fact that through the Pay Review Board system theoretically there ought to be greater government influence than exists in higher and further education. It is now clear that the combination of free collective bargaining backed up by the influence of the 2 per cent holdback mechanism actually creates a more powerful influence on the teachers' unions, the employers and conditions of service than the more widely publicized statutory Pay Review Board system. It now only remains to be seen how long it will be before the government extends the holdback mechanism to the schools sector.

13

Managing Information

John McManus and Emily Crowley

Editors' introduction

The computerization of human resource information has proceeded apace over the last decade or so, but it is still a topic which causes trepidation in the hearts and minds of some personnel managers. The authors of this chapter have produced a clear and concise, step-by-step analysis of how to select an appropriate information system and implement it. We feel that it will be warmly welcomed.

Human resource information systems

The nature of computer systems used in human resource management has changed radically in the past ten years. The degree of this change is reflected by the way the systems are described, moving away from the concept of a computerized personnel information system (CPIS) to human resource information systems (HRIS). These are likely to encompass payroll, personnel and pensions functions, and have significant interfaces with many other parts of the institution, including finance and staff rostering. This chapter seeks to discuss some of the complex issues which should be considered when selecting an HRIS, both from the business and technical perspective.

The business case

As institutions respond to the competitive pressures of the 1990s, the value of information used to support the HRM function has been recognized. Personnel systems have in the past been given lower priority when corporate information needs were considered, and management typically have focused upon financial systems to provide the information to drive the business.

However, one of the major challenges for organizations today is how to maintain a skilled and flexible workforce which can support the business process in the most effective manner. Employee-related costs may account for up to 75 per cent of the total budget. Without access to an HR system, the ability to extract meaningful information from the different data sources within an institution may be an impossible challenge, particularly as the value of information is increasingly measured against the speed which it may be supplied.

Many human resource professionals, in all sectors, have seen the focus of their role change from the administrative to the strategic. Personnel administration as an overhead has fallen from requiring around 40 per cent of time and resources in the 1970s to under 25 per cent today. In addition to this, industrial relations activity has declined from 15 per cent of time to under 10 per cent today, reflecting the weakening of the collective wage bargaining process since the 1970s. This has helped to change expectations of the type of information needed to support the HR role. Increasingly HR professionals are asked to respond to *ad hoc* enquiries on labour trends and succession planning, to predict future skill shortages or to model the impact of organizational restructuring. Over 20 per cent of the HR department's time may be spent responding to requests from senior management, with a similar proportion responding to line management. This new role of personnel manager as information manager requires the support of advanced HR systems.

Market developments

Although over 75 per cent of large organizations have a computerized HR system, this proportion appears significantly low when contrasted with the universal presence of accounting and payroll systems. In addition, many of these HR systems were introduced in the early 1980s when a typical system configuration was likely to comprise a number of 'dumb' terminals linked to a central mainframe. The software used was often complex, requests for information would be submitted to a central information technology (IT) department for coding as a report. This arrangement did not easily support the concept of users creating their own screen-based enquiries, using a query language.

The rate of development of computer technology has seen a movement away from this central approach to the introduction of personal computers (PC). These have been used initially for word-processing tasks, such as the production of recruitment letters and employment contracts. Often, when needs have changed in such areas as benefit administration, PC-based packages have been introduced to work as stand-alone modules. This solution has been seen as a quick and effective alternative to the cost and effort required to re-develop mainframe systems. The price, however has been the difficulty and complexity incurred in operating, managing and reconciling a set of physically separate but logically related systems.

However, most organizations are now re-assessing the overhead required to manage a disjointed set of systems. The effort of downloading information from mainframe to PC can be significant, particularly if the content of the information is likely to change. The risk of data inconsistency between separate systems is substantial, particularly as organizations are exposed to the present climate of change. Increasingly, the search is for an integrated payroll and personnel system, which runs on PC or Unix-based platforms.

Selecting an HRIS

Fit with business and IT strategy

The integration of business and HR strategy is a fashionable discussion topic within management theory at present, much as the linkage of IT and business strategy was in the 1980s. However, the planning decisions carried out at board level require qualitative information about the entire organization, as well as the ability to assess the rate of change to determine trends. The starting point for selection of an HRIS should be a careful top-down assessment of the information needs dictated by corporate strategy. These may include:

- ability to consolidate data across the institution;
- ability to model different mixes of departmental unit and structure;
- human resource budgeting.

Setting up the project

In many implementations, the personnel director acts as project sponsor, as he or she has the best understanding of the department's information needs. However, he or she may also be expected to work within a fixed set of constraints. In many situations, the personnel manager is given a firm brief by the IT department on the technical options available including:

- hardware platform – mainframe, mini, PC;
- operating system including network configuration;
- database management system;
- compatibility with financial and administration systems.

In addition, the budget set aside for the project is allocated by finance. What may be helpful guidelines from these departments often become overriding constraints, thus the would-be project sponsor often begins the project with an impossible brief.

This situation is often in evidence when reviewing the sales process of software suppliers. Typically, their route to a sale will be through the finance director, rather than the personnel director, who is seen as influential to the sale, but not essential. Without the approval of finance, most suppliers recognize that it would be an unusual organization indeed that would sanction the purchase of business software. Similarly, the IT department is seen as key to the sales process. One major supplier will always attempt to speak to the IT director as early as possible following an enquiry. They have found from experience that much time and effort may be invested in demonstrating the functionality and ease of use of their software to personnel, for the software to be rejected by IT because it would require a database upgrade, or improved terminals. Their comment was that 'personnel have no power to influence the IT department.'

Project structure
It is unlikely that this approach will provide the best solution for the institution and it is not typically in evidence when organizations invest in financial applications, or rostering systems.

By establishing a project team or steering committee which draws its membership from outside personnel, the needs and constraints of different parts of the institution are likely to be represented far more realistically. Team members would include representatives from:

• personnel – typically the project sponsor;
• finance;
• IT – typically supplying the project manager;
• payroll;
• academic departments.

A balance must always be found between a large team, which represents the breadth of the widest range of institutional views and establishing a manageable size. Four to six members has been found to be a practical working number.

Project roles
The role of the project sponsor and project manager should be carefully distinguished. The project sponsor will typically sit at board level in the organization, representing the corporate view and with the ability to sell the benefits of the project. The project manager will have the day-to-day responsibility for control, ensuring that deadlines are met and liaising with team members and suppliers. Ideally she or he should understand and appreciate the HR function and its information needs. It is not unusual for an enthusiastic sponsor to attempt to undertake the role of project manager as well, which is often not realistic given the demands upon the time of senior personnel. The project management role may be given to the last person to undertake a similar exercise in the organization, which is the reason usually given for allocating the task to a member of the IT function. However, the individual may not have an in-depth understanding of the complexities of HR needs. One other concern is that an IT professional may place a higher priority upon the quality of the technical solution than the benefit for the institution.

As the quality of project management is very closely linked to overall project success, many large establishments will invest in the use of an external manager with prior experience of HR system selection. This also may be used to guarantee continuity of resource to the project, where a changing academic and governmental environment may place variable demands upon internal management. The benefits which the establishment should seek to achieve by this may include:

- impartial assessment of business requirements;
- expertise within the HR systems marketplace;
- proven IT project management skills.

Approach and timescales

Depending upon the approach to the project, the business may be able to use a formal methodology for planning and control. Examples of these include public sector project management methodology (PROMPT), and its successor Projects IN Controlled Environments (PRINCE), project management methods used within the public sector. The major consultancy practices will also typically employ a formal methodology, such as that employed within KPMG, known as selection and implementation of information packaged software (SiiPS). The benefit of adopting a formal structure for the project include:

- proven approach;
- set of deliverables at clearly defined project stages;
- clear documentation to form the basis for decisions;
- reflect the specialist needs of package selection projects.

Use of a proven framework typically strengthens the estimating process when considering project duration. At this stage, the project manager will construct a detailed plan for the selection phase of the project, up to contract negotiation. He or she should also create a high-level plan for the implementation phase to provide focus to the selection process, but this will require revisiting when the selection has been made. Timescales will vary considerably depending upon the size and complexity of the institution, together with the resources available to the project. Up to six months' elapsed time would be a realistic minimum from project initiation to selection.

Defining detailed user requirements

This stage is critical to the successful selection of software and its subsequent implementation, although it is often a temptation to short cut this process. A detailed checklist provides a benchmark when comparing the products of different software suppliers, and also provides formal documentation for the reason for selecting particular software. It is of particular importance with human resource information systems (HRIS), where software suppliers will often sell the benefits of their product's flexibility. This may disguise a need for significant development effort on the buyer's part, which is often not clear until after the software has been installed.

Objectives

The starting point should always be the *business objectives* defined by corporate strategy. These should include:

- scope of the new system;
- specific institutional issues;
- identification of key system users.

One essential task should be to define formally, and quantify wherever possible, the anticipated benefits of the new system. These should have been stated as part of the business case for the project, but should be understood and agreed by the system users. These provide a formal measure of the ultimate success of the project, and may be used as part of a final review process.

Identifying the business need

The core requirements are identified from reviewing procedures, inputs and outputs. This should be approached from two perspectives:

- what happens now (current system);
- what we want to happen (required system).

An example of this, important in educational institutions, is the ability for employees to hold multiple posts, and for one post to have multiple sources of finance. It is usually helpful at this stage if at least one member of the project team can broaden the scope of this approach from their knowledge of what is technically possible with state of the art software and currently being done in comparable institutions.

When discussing these areas with users, many will naturally focus on the system they have at present. This is particularly true if users have little experience with other systems or organizations, as it can be difficult to imagine the alternatives. If the users are not challenged, the new systems may simply automate or upgrade present systems, without perceptible benefit. One helpful approach may be to ask users to consider current problems, such as:

- time constraints;
- use of manually compiled reports;
- use of spreadsheets to extract and model data;
- queries they are unable to answer at present.

Care should also be taken to challenge and validate statements relating to the inputs and outputs of the system. Often distribution of reports has been done on an historical basis by a set frequency. This may continue long after the business need for the information has passed away. Again, users may express their needs in terms of a report, when in fact a better solution could be provided by an enquiry screen. At this stage, the emphasis is placed upon *what* is to be delivered, not *how* is to be done.

Existing user access restrictions should also be carefully assessed. Historically, the contents of an HRIS have been considered to be extremely sensitive and information carefully limited to a chosen few. Many major organizations are moving away from this approach. One multi-national has chosen to allow all employees to update their own personal details, such as education and training records. They also permit a browse facility so that managers are encouraged to source their own recruitment requirements for particular roles. This has involved a radical restructure of their information systems, access requirements have changed from a small user group in personnel to potentially hundreds of their academic and administrative staff at many locations around the institution. However, needless to say, security is still carefully maintained around sensitive areas, such as grade, salary and benefits.

Broader views
A very different view of information needs may be obtained from the departments within an organization. Often, requirements are driven from the perspective of the internal personnel function. Academic departments and administration may have very different needs, including scheduling, absence control and monitoring, course costing and task allocation. Again, symptoms of a mismatch between the service currently provided by the present HRIS and department needs may include the use of custom databases or spreadsheets, or even simple stand-alone personnel systems independent of the core system. This has been prevalent in multi-site institutions, where line management have become frustrated with the inability of central systems to meet their individual needs. The time taken to request different report styles or formats from the IT department may seem unacceptable in either time or cost. One particular frustration often seen with older systems is the difficulties of importing information from a spreadsheet or a word-processing system. Equally, response times may seem extremely slow if the central system is physically located in a different building. Security is an issue which requires careful thought, as it is important to assess whether department managers are able to view information for other departments, for example, if they wish to compare their staff utilization against similar departments. This is often not supported under traditional security hierarchies. The existence of such mini-systems may not even be known at the centre, as they will often not rely upon central IT staff for support. This can create serious conflicts when assessing priorities for software selection. It must be recognized, pragmatically, that if departmental needs are not met within the new software, the users are unlikely to surrender their local systems.

Interfaces to other systems

One of the most complex issues at this stage of the project will be to document the interface requirements. These may well include:

- financial system;
- payroll;
- pensions;
- time and attendance;
- timetabling;
- manpower planning.

The relationship with information service providers, such as payroll bureau systems should also be considered at this stage. Where payroll processing is managed by a third party, there may be contractual restrictions on data access which should be fully considered at this stage. Alternatively, if the institution may consider outsourcing payroll in the near future, this option should be built into the business requirements.

The trend in human resource planning is to use an integrated database for personnel, payroll and pensions to reduce the overhead of duplicate data, with the risk of data redundancy and inaccuracy. However, this need not be an automatic constraint. For example, pensions systems may be maintained separately, with a data upload once a month from personnel to pensions, with the pensioner's payroll being processed within the payroll system. The source or ownership of the data should be agreed at this stage, for example:

- Are new starters to the system entered by payroll or personnel?
- Who is responsible for maintaining salary details?
- Who controls the employees' home cost centre?

Documentation

The user requirement statement produced at the end of the process must be a formal, structured document, signed off as accurate by *all* those to be involved as users or operators of the new system. Without this firm, agreed foundation all the following phases are likely to be slower, more expensive and riskier than necessary. It will form the contract between users and project team.

Technical options

It is unlikely that the users will have a free hand when choosing software. Typically, they will have to work within the constraints of an (existing) legacy system in terms of hardware, database and operating software. However, many projects are initiated by changes in the technological platform of the organization, for example, a move away from mainframe systems to Unix-based or client-server platform. In this case, there may be some flexibility, particularly if several systems are to be replaced at one time.

A careful and accurate description of the current technical environment should always be included within information issued to suppliers. As HRIS are redeveloped to exploit new technology, many suppliers may claim total portability of their products, for example, between different database systems or versions of Unix. It is essential to understand whether their existing customers are using an identical environment to your own, or one that is similar, in which case a higher degree of risk can be assumed.

Equally, one initially attractive option is to utilize existing PCs through the use of client-server products which allow a powerful central processor to provide the main power for the system, with less powerful terminals (typically PCs) requesting information from the centre. While HRIS in the 1980s often included a rudimentary wordprocessor or spreadsheet, many users now look for products which support easy 'cut and paste' to the in-house standard software. This is most typically seen within HRIS which conform to Microsoft Windows-based standards, using applications such as Microsoft Word and Excel, or Lotus AmiPro. What users often do not appreciate is that the software suppliers may expect a high specification from each PC, which may involve a substantial upgrade or replacement cost.

The IT department should also advise upon any strategy which may involve future changes to the operating environment, for example, a move to relational database software. This may be less clear cut where new technologies are under consideration. One current example is the use of smart cards within HRIS. Smart cards, which are plastic and typically credit-card sized, incorporate a silicon chip which contains information about the card owner. They have many potential applications, including security systems, identification badges, and employee benefits administration. However, the standards within this marketplace are still being established so the institution may find it difficult to define a precise specification of their needs.

Assessing the software options
When a formal requirements document has been compiled, it should be given a final review to make sure that each statement has a business justification. It is a common failing of selection projects to produce a wish list which would be extremely costly to implement. One successful technique is to assign a priority to each requirement, either essential or desirable, or use a scoring metric to assess the importance to the institution. When this is complete, the document should be signed-off by the users, and issued to a selected long-list of potential suppliers. This will vary according to the technical environment of the institution, by its size. There are more than 100 different suppliers and the market is very competitive. Readers are advised to consult an appropriate directory, contact the IPD or the Association of Personnel Software Suppliers, which is a trade organization. A short pre-qualification exercise will prevent a scattergun approach, as each detailed supplier response will require time to assess and evaluate. A long-list of between four and six would be a typical length.

One of the values of assessing the supplier's response at this stage is that some may be eliminated, from their inability to fit the institution requirements. This should be identified by careful application of a formal assessment method, typically based upon a scoring matrix.

The next stage will be to visit both the suppliers and their users (reference sites), wherever possible drawn from an environment as close to one's own as possible. Discussion with higher education institutions comprising the relevant MAC initiative family may prove helpful in identifying such a reference. At this point some of the more long-term issues can be assessed, such as:

- quality of support;
- ease of package implementation;
- training requirements.

When visiting reference sites, compare the capability of the system users with your existing staff. Although the institutional environment may be comparable, if the sample users are highly technical, it is easy to gain a false impression of the learning curve which the organization has undergone. Valuable feedback may be obtained on the performance of the systems, both peaks and troughs. Remember to discuss seasonal variations in use, for example, year-end reporting or temporary staff administration. From personal experience some of the most useful information comes in reply to the questions 'What went wrong [or less well] in the implementation?'

When a final selection has been made, the reasons should be fully documented and signed off, including the output from the scoring process and notes from site visits. Where the 'least worst' alternative has been selected, it is important to feed back to the staff who helped to create the initial requirements that some may not be met in order to manage their expectations of the new system.

Implementing the software

Project management

After contracts have been agreed, the installation of the software is just one of the tasks to be carried out in order to make the system live. It is likely that there will be some site preparation work, such as hardware, software or communications upgrades. In addition, even packaged software will typically require some customization to fit the institution requirements, which implies a design and development activity.

All the ground rules of formal project management should be applied at this stage. The project manager should be comfortable with the use of planning software tools to help plan and monitor progress against a detailed task list. Regular feedback to the steering committee should be mandatory throughout the project, thus they should have a good understanding of the tasks which need to be accomplished. The revised project plan which is created to control this project phase should encompass the following tasks:

- site preparation;
- software installation;

- design, development and test;
- business process redesign;
- user and technical training;
- data conversion;
- testing and parallel run if required;
- handover;
- end of project review.

The project manager will now face the challenging task of finding sufficient internal resources to support each of these stages in order to meet the timescale set. Where the tasks are specialist, he or she may consider using external resources, possibly from the software supplier. A good example of this would be systems support training for the new software. There is a clear need to ensure user commitment to the new system overall, and this will best be obtained by the user working closely with the third party to ensure that skills are transferred to in-house staff. Again, the benefit of this approach can be seen when training roll-out to all the system users is considered.

Training needs

Very often, software suppliers will deliver standard, system-based training which does not take into account the different roles and responsibilities which exist within the organization. For training to be successful, there should be a clear relationship between the software and the actual task or business process which the user will carry out. For example, the user will be considering all the actions which accompany creating a new starter within the organization, whereas the software supplier may be delivering training on the best use of one particular screen or menu on their system, rather than how this screen or menu might be of use within the institution. Analysis to identify the business processes to be carried out should form the core of any training programme. The software supplier may assist in development of the initial training material, which can then be cascaded to the users, ideally by using in-house staff as trainers. The management of the training track is now seen as a crucial part of the system in order to achieving institutional benefit. Fortunately, the background of the members of an HRIS project management team mean that this factor should be more readily identified and managed than with, for example, financial software.

Development

Where bespoke development forms a significant part of the project, the company can consider a phased approach to system release. For example, initial data load and conversion using the fixed screens and report within the system, followed by a staged release of custom screens and facilities. Again, this will require an associated track of secondary testing, documentation and training which is often neglected. One danger of this phased approach is that users will often see new applications for the software, and try to increase the scope of the project. Although this may ultimately make better use of the system, it will also increase the project length; experienced project managers will guard carefully against 'scope creep' of this type, and point the user firmly back to their original requirements, or suggest that they produce a separate business case.

Post implementation

When the implementation is complete, a final review should be carried out to establish how the final system compares with the original benefits which were anticipated. As a period of time has elapsed, the institution itself may well have changed significantly, so there may be new needs for procedure-based training, support or information. Use of new systems is often retained by a hard core of enthusiasts, who may have to be encouraged to hand their knowledge over to other users in their departments. Fine-tuning of system performance is often required, as the actual usage of a system may vary dramatically from forecast usage. This is often true when management begin to experiment with query tools to interrogate the database, for example, to solve succession planning problems. Such *ad hoc* needs often settle down into a pattern, which can be used to obtain the best system performance possible for all users.

Future trends

The recent dramatic changes in the funding structures within education have forced institutions to reassess the value which information provides to them. Information concerning the human resource of an institution is now seen to be the property of individual departments as well as the whole organization, allowing cost and quality to be monitored on a unit-by-unit basis. Educational institutions are now seen as a service industry, with approximately 75 per cent of operational costs attributable to staff, the control of cash flow and apportionment becomes critical. The concept of HRIS as the tool of a limited few within personnel or finance is being rejected by many major establishments. Again, the additional complexities imposed by multi-site structures create information needs which vary greatly by location. Local authority payroll services may not prove to be an option because of the quality of information or speed of the service offered. Funding Council requirements for information place extra pressures upon the data analysis capabilities of the software.

These business drivers are helping to focus development upon the system interface, as it is recognized that the usability of an HRIS to general management from a wide variety of backgrounds and skills will be critical to their success. Departments will seek to exploit software modelling facilities to achieve the optimal skill mix to support academic needs, and to project this model forward to assess future training needs for succession planning purposes.

Management have been reluctant to gain skills in information technology if this has not been an essential requirement of their role. Often this reluctance has been linked to the fear factor of unfriendly systems, with complex menu structures and incomprehensible error messages. The introduction of systems which can be operated using a mouse to select icons, as in Microsoft Windows or Apple Macintosh, has helped to make computer systems easier to learn. Typically, a manager will first encounter these graphical user interfaces when carrying out a familiar task such as word-processing or using a spreadsheet. The same interfaces are now available in HRIS, encouraging the user to browse and query data according to their needs. The packaged software marketplace will see rapid developments within graphical user interfaces and client-server technology in the 1990s, helping HRIS to deliver the information required to support institutional change. The educational purchaser has become increasingly sophisticated when assessing the true benefit which IT can offer the institution. The solution for the future for many institutions may be to reassess the value which an HRIS can offer and to concentrate their resources upon that area, working with external providers to support non-critical applications. The ability to balance this mix of in-house systems and outsourced solutions will be an essential skill for the next generation of HRIS purchasers.

Bibliography

Ackroyd, S., Hughes, J. A. and Soothill, K. (1989) Public sector services and their management, *Journal of Management Studies*, 26, 6, November: 603–19.

Adams, D. (1991) *Last Chance to See*. London: Heinemann.

Advisory, Conciliation and Arbitration Service (ACAS) (1988) *Discipline at Work*. London: ACAS.

Allison, L. (1990) Academic tenure and conservative philosophy, *Higher Education Quarterly*, 44, 1: 35–9.

Argyris, C. (1990) *Overcoming Organizational Defences: Facilitating Organizational Learning*. Boston MA: Allyn and Bacon.

Argyris, C. and Schön, D. (1978) *Organizational Learning*. London: Addison-Wesley.

Armstrong, M. (1987) *Human Resource Management: A Case of the Emperor's New Clothes?* Personnel Management. 19, 8, August.

Armstrong, M. (1992) *Human Resource Management: Strategy and Action*. London: Kogan Page.

Armstrong, M. and Murlis, H. (1992) *Reward Management*. London: Kogan Page.

Association of University Teachers (AUT) (1990) *Goodwill Under Stress*. London.

Association of University Teachers (AUT) (1991) *AUT Bulletin*. October: 4–5.

Association of University Teachers (AUT) (1993) *Code of Conduct on Personnel Relationships Between Staff and Students in Universities*. London: AUT.

Becher, T. and Kogan, M. (1992) *Process and Structure in Higher Education*. London: Routledge.

Belbin, R. M. (1981) *Management Teams, Why They Succeed or Fail*. London: Heinemann.

Bevan, S. and Thompson, M. (1991) Performance management at the crossroads, *Personnel Management*, November.

Bocock, J. and Watson, D. Common cause: Prospects for renewal in Bocock, J. and Watson, D. (eds) (1994) *Managing the University Curriculum: Making Common Cause*. Milton Keynes, Open University Press.

Bowers, J. S., Brown, D. and Mead, G. (1994) *Industrial Tribunals: Practice and Procedure*. London: Longman.

Bowers, J. S. and Honeyball, S. (1993) *Textbook on Labour Law*. London: Blackstone Press.

Buck, D. (1991) 'The growth of managerialism in universities', unpublished MBA thesis. University of Durham.

Clampitt, P. G. (1991) *Communicating for Managerial Effectiveness*. Newbury Park, CA: Sage Publications.

Clark, I. (1993) HRM: Prescription, description and concept, *Personnel Review*, 22, 4.

College Employers' Forum (CEF) (1993) *Introduction of New Contracts for Existing Staff: The CEF Recommended Implementation Strategy*, Unpublished Report.

Commission of the European Communities (1991) *The Protection of the Dignity of Women and Men at Work*. Brussels: Office for Official Publications of the European Communities.

Commission of the European Communities (1993) *How to Combat Sexual Harassment at Work*. Brussels: Office for Official Publications of the European Communities.

Commission for Racial Equality (1990a) *Words or Deeds?* London: HMSO and Hansard Society Commission.

Commission for Racial Equality (1990b) *Women at the Top*. London: The Hansard Society.

Commission for Racial Equality (1991a) *Annual Report 1990*. London, Commission for Racial Equality.

Commission for Racial Equality (1991b) *A Measure of Equality: Monitoring and Achieving Racial Equality in Employment*. London: CRE.

Committee of Vice-Chancellors and Principals (1993) *Salaries Factfile*. London: CVCP.

Committee of Vice-Chancellors and Principals (1994a) *Equal Opportunities and Recruitment and Selection*. Sheffield: CVCP/USDU.

Committee of Vice-Chancellors and Principals (1994b) *Press Release PR 359*. London: CVCP.

Confederation of British Industry (CBI) (1993) *Too Much Time Out*. London CBI/Percom Survey on absence from work.

Croham, Lord (1987) *A Review of the University Grants Committee*. Cmnd 81. London: HMSO.

Cryer, P. and Elton, L. (1990) Catastrophe theory: A unified model for educational change, *Studies in Higher Education*, 15, 1: 75–86.

Davies, J. L. (1987) The entrepreneurial and adaptive university: Report of the second US study visit, *International Journal of Institutional Management in Higher Education*, 11, 1: 12–104.

Denning, R. W., Hussey, D. E. and Newman, P. G. (1978) *Management Development: What to Look For*. London: Harbridge House.

Department of Education and Science (DES) (1983) *Teaching Quality*. CM 8836 London: HMSO.

Durham University (1990) *Staff Development and Appraisal*.

Elliot, J. (1988) The great appraisal debate: some perspectives for research in Eggins, H. *Restructuring Higher Education: Proceedings of the Annual Conference 1987*. Milton Keynes: Open University Press and the Society for Research into Higher Education.

Enderby v. *Frenchay Health Authority* [1994] ICR 112.

Equal Opportunities Commission (1991) *Training for Women: For the Future Imperative*. London: HMSO.

European Foundation for Living and Working Conditions (1992) *The First European Survey on the Work Environment*. Dublin, Eire.

Farnham, D. (1991) From model employer to private sector model: the PCFC sector. *Higher Education Review*, 23, 2: 7–32.

Farnham, D. and Horton, S. (1993) The new public service managerialism: An assessment, in Farnham, D. and Horton, S. (eds) *Managing the new Public Services*. Basingstoke: Macmillan.

Fender Report: Committee for Vice-Chancellors and Principals (1993) *Promoting People: A Strategic Framework for the Management and Development of Staff in UK Universities.* CVCP: London.

Fletcher, C. (1993) Appraisal: An idea whose time has gone? *Personnel Management*, September.

Fowler, A. (1987) When chief executives discover HRM, *Personnel Management*, January.

Fowler, A. (1991) Performance management; The MBO of the 90s, *Personnel Management*, July.

Fulton, O. (1991) Slouching towards a mass system: Society, government and institutions in the UK, *Higher Education*, 21, 4: 589–605.

Fulton, O. (1993) Institutional strategies for staff renewal, in Barblan, A. (ed.) *Human Resources at University. Journal of the Standing Conference of Rectors, Presidents and Vice-Chancellors.*

Garrett, H. and Taylor, J. (1993) *How to Design and Deliver Equal Opportunities Training.* London: Kogan Page.

Gray, H. L. (1989) Resisting change: Some organizational considerations about university departments, *Educational Management and Administration*, 17, 3: 123–32.

Griffiths, W. (1993) A leaner, fitter future for HR?, *Personnel Management*, October.

Guest, D. (1989) Personnel and HRM: Can you tell the difference? *Personnel Management*, January.

Guest, D. (1991) Personnel management: The end of orthodoxy, *British Journal of Industrial Relations*, 29, 2, June.

Halsey, A. H. (1992) *Decline of Donnish Dominion: The British Academic Professions in the Twentieth Century.* Clarendon Press: Oxford.

Hammond, V. and Holton, V. (1991) *A Balanced Workforce? Achieving Cultural Change for Women: A Comparative Study.* Berkhamsted: Ashridge Management College.

Harrison, R. (1993) *Human Resource Management.* Workingham: Addison-Wesley.

Hay v. Lothian Regional Council [1983] Scottish Industrial Tribunal unreported case 913/83.

Health and Safety Commission (1993) *Annual Report 1992–93.* London: HMSO.

Health and Safety Executive (1992) *Management of Health and Safety Regulations*, S1, No. 3004. London: HMSO.

Health and Safety Executive (1993) *The Costs of Accidents at Work*, HSE, HS(G) 96. London: HMSO.

Heist (1993) *Staff Newsletters in Higher Education.* Leeds. Unpublished Report.

Helm, P. (1989) Bringing in staff appraisal: The experience of one university, *Higher Education Management*, 2, 188–95.

Honey, P. (1989) Building on Learning Styles, in *Learning to Learn Resources.* Bradford: MCB University Press.

Honey, P. and Mumford, A. (1986) *The Manual of Learning Styles.* Maidenhead: Peter Honey.

Industrial Relations Review and Report (1993) *Changing Industrial Relations in Higher Education.* No. 536, May: 7–12.

Institute of Personnel Management Consultative Document (1993) *Managing People – The Changing Frontiers.*

Institute of Personnel Management (1993) *Code on Psychological Testing.*

Jarratt Report: Committee for Vice-Chancellors and Principals (1985) *Report of the Steering Committee for Efficiency Studies in Universities.* CVCP: London.

Jarrell, D. W. (1993) *Human Resource Planning – A Businesses Planning Approach.* New York and London: Prentice-Hall.

Jones, J. E. and Woodcock, M. (1985) *Manual of Management Development*. Aldershot: Gower.

Keep, E. (1992) Corporate training strategies: The vital component?, in Salaman, G. (ed.) *Human Resource Strategies*. London: Sage.

Keep, E. and Sisson, K. (1992) Owning the problem: Personnel issues in higher education policy-making in the 1990s, *Oxford Review of Economic Policy*, 8, 2: 67–78

Kessler, S. (1993) Is there still a future for the unions?, *Personnel Management*, July.

Knell, A. (ed.) (1993) *The Remuneration and Benefits Handbook*. London: Gee.

Levy, M., Matthews, D., Oates, T. and Edmond, N. (1989) *A Guide to Work-based Learning Terms*. Blagdon: Further Education Staff College.

Lindsay, R. (1987) Modular course staff survey, *Teaching News*. Oxford Polytechnic, 17 Spring: 12–15.

Lockwood, G. (1985) Universities as organizations, in Lockwood, G. and Davies, J. (eds) *Universities: The Management Challenge*. Windsor: SRHE/NFER-Nelson.

McCarthy, W. J. (1992) The rise and fall of collective laissez-faire, in McCarthy, W. J. (ed.) *Legal Intervention in Industrial Relations: Gains and Losses*. Oxford: Oxford University Press.

Mackay, L. and Torrington, D. (1986) *The Changing Nature of Personnel Management*. London: Institute of Personnel Management.

Mackie, D. (1990) Personnel's role on campus, *Personnel Management*, May.

Management Charter Initiative (1992) *Middle Management Standards*. London: Management Charter Initiative.

Martinez, P. (1993) *Staff Development: A Business Case Framework*. Blagdon: The Staff College.

Middlehurst, R. (1993) *Leading Academics*. Buckingham: SRHE and Open University Press.

Mumford, A. (1980) *Making Experience Pay*. Maidenhead: McGraw Hill.

Mumford, A. (1989) *Management Development Strategies for Action*. London: IPM.

National Association of Teachers in Further and Higher Education (NATFHE) (1992) *Performance Related Pay*. London.

National Joint Council for Local Authorities' Administrative, Professional, Technical and Clerical Services *Scheme of Conditions of Service* (Purple Book).

National Joint Council for Local Authorities' Services (Manual Workers) *Handbook* (White Book).

National Joint Council for Local Authorities *Salaries and Conditions of Service for Lecturers in Further and Higher Education in England and Wales* (Silver Book).

Nicoll, D. (1994) Heard it through the grapevine, *Intercity*. London: British Rail.

Oxtoby, R. (1979) Problems facing heads of department, *Journal of Further and Higher Education*, 3, 1: 46–59.

Palmer, R. (1989) A career in higher education: Challenge or cul de sac?, *Personnel Management*, April.

Pedler, M., Burgoyne, J. and Boydell, T. (1991) *The Learning Company: A Strategy for Sustainable Development*. New York: McGraw Hill.

Pollitt, C. (1986) Beyond the managerial model: The case for broadening performance assessment in government and the public services, *Financial Accountability and Management*, 2, 3: 155–70.

Polytechnics and Colleges Employers' Forum (PCEF) Bulletin 4: January 1989a.

Polytechnics and Colleges Employers' Forum (PCEF) Bulletin 8: March 1989b.

Polytechnics and Colleges Employers' Forum (PCEF) Bulletin 9: March 1989c.

Polytechnics and Colleges Employers' Forum (PCEF) Bulletin 21: June 1989d.

Polytechnics and Colleges Employers' Forum (PCEF) Bulletin 24: July 1989e.

Polytechnics and Colleges Employers' Forum (PCEF) Bulletin 70: 12 June 1990a.

Polytechnics and Colleges Employers' Forum (PCEF) Bulletin 78: 4 July 1990b.

Polytechnics and Colleges Employers' Forum (PCEF) Bulletin 75: 25 July 1990c.

Price, R. (1989) The decline and fall of the status divide?, in Sisson, K. (ed.) *Personnel Management in Britain*, Oxford: Blackwell.

Randall, G. (1989) Employee appraisal, in Sisson, K. (ed.) *Personnel Management in Britain*, Oxford: Blackwell.

Ridley, T. M. (1992) *Motivating and Rewarding Employees/ Occasional Paper No. 51*. London: ACAS.

Royal Association for Disability and Rehabilitation (1994) *Disability and Discrimination in Employment*. London: RADAR.

Rutherford, D. (1988) Performance appraisal: a survey of academic staff opinion, *Studies in Higher Education*, 13, 1: 89–100.

Rutherford, D. (1992) Appraisal in action: A case study of innovation and leadership, *Studies in Higher Education*, 17, 2: 201–10.

Ryan, J. and Slater, G. (1993) *Equal Opportunities in Appraisal*. Workshop paper for the Higher Education Equal Opportunities Network (June), University of Birmingham.

Schein, E. (1993) *Organizational Culture and Leadership*. San Francisco, CA: Jossey-Bass.

School Teachers' Review Body *Second Report 1993a*, Cm 2151 and *Third Report 1994*, Cm 2466, London: HMSO.

Senge, P. M. (1990) *The Fifth Discipline: The Art and Practice of the Learning Organization*. London: Century Business.

Sheehy Report: *Inquiry into Police Responsibilities and Rewards* (1993b), CM 2280 London: HMSO.

Sisson, K. (1993) In search of HRM, *British Journal of Industrial Relations*, 31: 201–10.

Smith Report: Advisory Conciliation and Arbitration Service (1990) *Report of the ACAS Working Party on Teaching Staff Contracts*. PCEF Bulletin number 78: 4 July 1990.

Smith, D., Scott, P. and Mackay, L. (1993) Mission impossible: Access and the dash to growth, *Higher Education Quarterly* 47, 4: 316–33.

Spurling, A. (1990) *Report of the Women in Higher Education Research Project 1988–90*. Cambridge: King's College Research Centre.

Stevenson, R. L. (1881) El dorado in *Virginibus Puerisque*. London: Chatto and Windus.

Storey, J. (1992a) *Developments in the Management of Human Resources*. Oxford: Blackwell.

Storey, J. (1992b) Human resource management in the public sector in Salaman, G. (ed.) *Human Resource Strategies*. London: Sage.

Swieringa, J. and Wierdsma, A. (1992) *Becoming a Learning Organisation: Beyond the Learning Curve*. Wokingham: Addison-Wesley.

Talbot, C. (1993) Twin Peaks? MBAs and the competence movement – a tale of two courses, *Management Education and Development*, 24(4): 330–46.

Tann, J. (1993) Quality assurance in higher education, some problems and perspectives, in Chan, J. F. L. (ed.) *Quality and its Applications*, Proceedings of International Conference on Quality, Newcastle.

Tann, J. (1994) Managing change in university departments, in Stowey, M. (ed.) *Managing Change in Higher Education*. London: Kogan Page.

Taylor, L. (1992) *Equal opportunities in practice*. Sheffield: CVCP/USDTU.

Teubner, G. (1987) Juridification: Concepts and practices, in Teubner, G. (ed.) *The Juridification of Social Sciences*. New York: De Gruyte.

Thody, A. (1989) University management observed: A method of studying its unique nature? *Studies in Higher Education*, 14, 3: 279–96.

Tight, M. (1988) Institutional typologies, *Higher Education Review*, 20, 3: 27–51.

Toplis, J., Dulewicz, V. and Fletcher, C. (1991) (2nd edition) *Psychological Testing: A Manager's Guide*. London: Institute of Personnel Management.

Torrington, D. (1988) How does human resource management change the personnel function?, *Personnel Review*, 17, 6.

University of Oxford (1993) *Gazette*, 9 December.

Walford, G. (1992) The reform of higher education in Arnot, M. and Barton, L. (eds) *Voicing Concerns: Sociological Perspectives on Contemporary Education Reforms*. Wallingford: Triangle Books.

Warner, D. and Crosthwaite, E. (1992a) Principals and people, *Education*, 3 July.

Warner, D. and Crosthwaite, E. (1992b) People are the first priority, *Education*, 14 August.

Warner, D. and Crosthwaite, E. (1993a) A new university challenge for professionals, *Personnel Management*, January.

Warner, D. and Crosthwaite, E. (1993b) Human resource management in higher education, *Current Business Research*, 1, 3: 48–70.

Williams, G. (1992) *Changing Patterns of Finance in Higher Education*. Buckingham: SRHE and Open University Press.

Willis, L. and Daisley, J. (1990) *Springboard Women's Development Workbook*. Stroud: Hawthorn Press.

Working Mothers Association (1993) *UK Employer Initiatives: Working Examples of Family-friendly and Equal Opportunities Policies*. London: WMA.

Index

accidental management development
  processes, 146
accidents, 120–1, 121–2, 122–3
accreditation of management
  development, 135, 149–50
advertisements, job, 39
  executive recruitment, 89–90, 90–1
advertising agencies, 89
Advisory Conciliation and Arbitration
  Service (ACAS), 12, 14, 164
advisory/service role, 24–5
Allison, L., 10
application forms, 39–40
appraisal, 14–15, 18
  equal opportunities, 40–1
  rewarding performance, 73–6
Argyris, C., 50
assessment centres, 92–3
Assistant Director Human Resources,
  21–2
Associated Newspapers v. *Wilson* and
  Associated British Ports v. *Palmer*
  (1993), 113
association, rights of, 112–13
Association of Polytechnic and College
  Teachers (APCT), 164, 165,
  166–7, 168
Association of Polytechnic Teachers
  (APT), 161
Association of Principals of Colleges
  (APC), 159
Association of University Teachers
  (AUT), 17, 42, 75, 80–1
attitude survey, 63–4

Baker, Kenneth, 154
Barber v. *Guardian Royal Exchange*
  (1990), 101
Becher, T., 71
Belbin, R. M., 53
Berriman v. *Delabole Slate* (1985), 110
Bevan, S., 84
Bilka Kaufhaus v. *Weber von Hartz*
  (1987), 101
Birds Eye Walls v. *Roberts* (1994), 101
Blackpool and Fylde College v. *NATFHE*
  (1994), 115
Bland v. *Stockport MBC* (1992), 126
Blyth v. *Scottish Liberal Club* (1983),
  103
Bocock, J., 19
Bond v. *CAV Ltd* (1983), 98
Boots the Chemist, 36
Boswell, Tim, 169
boundary workers, 45
Bowers, J. S., 97
Boydell, T., 54–5
Brown, D., 97
Buck, D., 74, 78, 85
Burgoyne, J., 54–5
Burnham Committee system, 157, 159
business needs, 176–80
business objectives, 176
business transfers, 109–10

Capper Pass v. *Lawton* (1977), 100
caring responsibilities, 42–3
Carry All Motors v. *Pennington* (1980),
  108

change, 44–5
  management of, 7–19
  process and human resource
    strategy, 25–31
Citizens' Charter, 17
Clampitt, P. G., 56–7
Clarke, Kenneth, 16, 168
College Employers' Forum (CEF), 13,
  169
collegiate culture, 23
Collins v. *Wilkin Chapman* (1994), 100
Commission of the European
  Communities (CEC), 41, 42
Commission for Racial Equality
  (CRE), 36
Commission on University Career
  Opportunity, 37
commitment, 64
Committee of Directors of Polytechnics
  (CDP), 156
Committee of Vice-Chancellors and
  Principals (CVCP), 17, 32–3, 45,
  169
  equal opportunities, 36–7, 40
  Fender Report, 18, 44–5, 46
common law, 95
  industrial action, 114
  termination, 102–3
communication, 56–69
communication audit, 63–4
communication networks, 59–61
communication survey, 64–7
compensation, 106–7
competences, management, 136, 137,
  149–50
Construction (Design and
  Management) Regulations (1994),
  128
consultation, 108–9
contact time, 162
contracting out, 110
contractors, using, 120, 127–8
contracts, employment
  employment law, 97–100
  health and safety, 124–5
  human resource strategy, 24–5,
    26–30
  industrial relations, 153, 155–60,
    161–5, 167
  managing change, 11–14

written statement of terms and
    conditions, 99–100
Contracts of Employment Act (1963), 99
corporate culture, 8–10
corporate-related pay, 77, 79
costs
  accidents and ill-health, 122
  management development, 148–9
Council for National Academic Awards
  (CNAA), 9
Cresswell v. *Board of Inland Revenue*
  (1984), 99
Crosthwaite, E., 2, 4, 83
culture
  collegiate, 23
  corporate, 8–10

Daisley, J., 41
Dawson, Peter, 163
Delaney v. *Staples* (1992), 111
Denning, R. W., 136
Department for Education (DfE), 152,
  155, 165
  powers, 166–9
Department of Education and Science
  (DES), 16–17
  Teaching Quality, 14
Devis (W) and Sons Ltd v. *Atkins* (1977),
  106
dignity at work, 41–2
Dines v. *Initial Cleaning Services* (1994), 110
direct discrimination, 33, 34–5
Disabled Persons (Employment) Acts, 33
discipline, 76, 83
discrimination, 33–6
  see also equal opportunities
dismissal, 102–3
  rights of association, 112–13
  unfair, 104–7
diversity, 19
  managing, 32–43
double loop learning, 49–50
Duffy v. *Yeomans and Partners Ltd*
  (1993), 106
Duport Steel v. *Sirs* (1980), 114
Durham University, 74

education, experience and, 46–7
  see also learning; management
    development

Education Reform Act (1988), 1, 11,
    166
efficiency, communication and, 57–8
Elliot, J., 14
Employee Assistance Programmes
    (EAPs), 133
employee-centred report, 67–8
employee relations, 65
employers
    health and safety law, 130–1
    remedies against industrial action,
        115–16
employment contracts, *see* contracts of
    employment
employment law, 94–117
Employment Protection
    (Consolidation) Act (1978)
    (EPCA), 99–100, 102–3
    redundancy, 107–8
    unfair dismissal, 104, 105–7
empowerment, 80–1
Enderby v. *Frenchay Health Authority*,
    35–6, 101
Enterprise in Higher Education, 47–8
equal opportunities, 32–43
equal opportunities awareness training,
    41
Equal Opportunities Commission, 41
equal pay, 35–6, 100–1
Equal Pay Act (1970), 33, 100
Equal Pay (Amendment) Regulations
    (1983), 33
espoused theory, 50
ethnic minorities, 32
    see also equal opportunities
European Foundation for Living and
    Working Conditions, 121
European Union (formerly European
    Community), 26
    Acquired Rights Directive, 26, 109
    health and safety law, 129–30
    impact of European law on
        employment law, 95–6, 116
    Pregnant Workers Directive, 101
examination boycott, 162, 163–4
executive recruitment, 86–93
experience, education and, 46–7

Fairfield Ltd v. *Skinner* (1992), 111
Fender Report, 18, 44–5, 46

five disciplines model, 51–4
Fletcher, C., 75
flexible contracts, 158, 161–5
flexible working, 43
formal communication networks, 59
Foster v. *British Gas* (1991), 96
Fowler, A., 79
Frankovitch v. *Italian Republic* (1992), 96
Fulton, O., 10
funding, 154–5
    see also holding mechanism
funding councils, 9, 153
further education (FE) colleges, 2, 4–5
Further Education Funding Councils,
    8, 153
Further and Higher Education Act
    (1992), 1–2, 166

Garrett, H., 41
government, central, 155, 166–9
grapevine, 59–61
graphology, 92
Gray, H. L., 10, 13–14, 15
Greater Manchester Police Authority v. *Lea*
    (1990), 34
group learning, 53

Halsey, A. H., 35, 71, 85
Hammond, V., 36, 37
harassment, 37, 41–2
Hay v. *Lothian Regional Council* (1983),
    34–5
Hayward v. *Cammell Laird* (1988), 100
headhunters, 87–8
health and safety, 118–33
Health and Safety Commission (HSC),
    120–1
Health and Safety Executive (HSE),
    122
Health and Safety at Work Act (1974),
    125, 128
Heist, 56
Helm, P., 15
Higher Education Equal Opportunities
    Network, 37
holdback mechanism, 155, 165, 166,
    167–8, 169, 169–70
Holton, V., 36, 37
Honey, P., 146
horizontal communication, 58–9, 65

human resource information systems
  (HRIS), 171–83
human resource strategy, 20–31
Hussey, D. E., 136

Iceland Frozen Foods v. *Jones* (1983), 106
ill-health, 122–3
incorporation, 2, 26
independence, 1–2, 152–5
indirect discrimination, 33–4
individual development plan, 141,
  142–3
industrial action, 154
  deductions from pay, 111–12
  employment contracts, 162–4
  employment law, 113–16
industrial relations, 152–70
Industrial Relations Act (1971), 104
Industrial Relations Review and
  Report (IRRR), 82
industrial tribunals, 97
Industrial Tribunal's Extension of
  Jurisdiction (England and Wales)
  Order (1994), 103
informal communication networks,
  59–61
information technology (IT), 171–83
informing, persuading and, 57
Institute of Personnel Management
  (IPM) *Code on Psychological Testing*,
  92
interfaces, systems, 178, 182–3
interviewing, 40, 91
investment, 23

Jackson, Robert, 72
Jarratt Report, 1, 15, 45, 73, 84
job satisfaction, 80–1
job-sharing, 43
Johnson v. *Notts Combined Police Authority*
  (1974), 108
Johnstone v. *Bloomsbury Health Authority*
  (1991), 98–9, 124–5
Jones, J. E., 136
Judicial Review, 166

Kenny v. *South Manchester College* (1993),
  110
Kessler, S., 3
Knell, A., 77

knowledge, 140, 141, 144
Kogan, M., 71
Kolb's learning cycle, 46–7

learning, 146–8
  see also management development
learning cycle, 46–8, 146
learning organization, 44–55
Lesney Products v. *Nolan* (1977), 108
Leverton v. *Clwyd CC* (1989), 100
Levy, M., 147–8
Lewis v. *Motorworld Garages Ltd* (1985),
  98
lifelong learning, 46
Lindsay, R., 8
Litster v. *Forth Dry Dock Ltd* (1989), 110
local education authorities, 152–4
London Underground Ltd, 36

McCarthy, W. J., 96
MacGregor, John, 165
Mackay, L., 4
McSharry v. *BT* (1993), 126
management activities/responsibilities,
  140, 141, 144
Management Charter Initiative (MCI),
  136, 137, 149–50
management development, 45–6,
  134–51
Management of Health and Safety at
  Work Regulations (1992), 125,
  128, 129
Management Verification Consortium,
  150
Market Investigations Ltd v. *Minister of
  Social Security* (1969), 98
Marleasing v. *ICIA SA* (1992), 96
Marshall v. *Southampton and SWHAHA*
  (1986), 96
Martinez, P., 149
mastery, personal, 52
maternity rights, 101–2
Mead, G., 97
mental models (mindsets), 52
Microsoft Windows, 179
Miles v. *Wakefield Metropolitan District
  Council* (1987), 111
minimal performers, 83–4
mission statement, 22–3
misunderstandings, 62–3, 65

morale, 8–10
Moroni v. *Firma Collo* (1994), 101
motivation, 72–3
Mumford, A., 136, 146–7
Murphy v. *Epsom College* (1984), 108

National Advisory Body for Public
    Sector Higher Education (NAB),
    9, 154
National Association of Teachers in
    Further and Higher Education
    (NATFHE), 155, 156, 159, 168
  appraisal, 75
  contractual change, 27, 28, 158, 161,
    162–5
  European law and incorporation, 26
  industrial action, 12, 154, 162–3,
    163–4
  pay scales, 78
National Joint Council (NJC) system,
    157, 159–60
National Vocational Qualifications
    (NVQs), 135, 150
NB Selection, 89
Neath v. *Hugh Steeper* (1994), 101
negligence, law of, 125–7
Netheremere (St Neots) Ltd v. *Gardiner*
    (1984), 97
new universities, 2, 4–5, 152
Newman, P. G., 136
Nicoll, D., 59–60, 60
Nokes v. *Doncaster Amalgamated Collieries
    Ltd* (1940), 109
NWL Ltd v. *Woods* (1979), 114, 115

observation of teaching, 16
Occupiers' Liability Acts, 126
O'Kelly v. *Trust House Forte* (1983), 98
opportunistic management
    development processes, 146
Opportunity 2000, 37
organization development, 137–40
organization learning, 48–51
  see also learning organization
organizational structure, 3–4
  communication, 58–61
outsourcing, 120
Oxford University, 42

part-time working, 43
Patten, John, 168

pay, 71
  deductions, 111–12
  equal, 35–6, 100–1
  government involvement, 155, 167,
    168
  human resource strategy, 24–5,
    26–31
  industrial relations, 163–5, 169
  managing change, 16–18, 18–19
  PCEF, 156–9
  performance-related, 16–18, 77–9,
    168
Pay Review Board system, 155,
    169–70
Pedler, M., 54–5
pensions, 101
perception, 62–3
performance management, 70–85
performance-related pay (PRP), 16–18,
    77–9, 168
personal computers (PCs), 172–3,
    179
personal development, 80–1
personal mastery, 52
personnel department
  human resource strategy, 24–5
  importance of, 4–5
personnel management, 3–4
persuasion, informing and, 57
Pickstone v. *Freemans* (1988), 100
planned management development
    processes, 146
policing role, 24–5
Polkey v. *A. E. Dayton Services Ltd*
    (1988), 106
polytechnics, 4–5
Polytechnics and Colleges Employers'
    Forum (PCEF), 11, 26, 156–9,
    160, 160–1, 168–9
  contracts, 27, 161–5
Polytechnics and Colleges Funding
    Council (PCFC), 8, 9, 152, 154,
    155
Polytechnics and Colleges National
    Negotiating Committee (PCNNC),
    160–1
Porter v. *Canon Hygiene Ltd* (1993), 96
Post Office, 36
practice, principle and, 54
premises, 126–8

principals
  personnel department's access to, 5
  survey of areas of management, 2
principle, practice and, 54
professionalism, 10
project management, 173–5, 180–1
project sponsorship, 173, 174
Projects IN Controlled Environments
  (PRINCE), 175
promotion, 81–3
psychological testing, 91–2
public sector project management
  methodology (PROMPT), 175
Purple Book, 11, 159, 160

Quality Assessment Committee, 45
questionnaire design, 67

R. v. *Secretary of State for Employment ex
  p. Equal Opportunities Commission*
  (1994), 104
Race Relations Acts, 33
Rainey v. *Greater Glasgow HB* (1987), 100
Randall, G., 73–4
Rank Xerox, 36
Rask v. *ISS Kantineservice* (1993), 110
recruitment, 24
  equal opportunities, 38–40
  executive, 86–93
recruitment agencies, 88–9
redundancy, 107–9
Reid, Sir Bob, 123
repetitive strain injury (RSI), 126
research, 35
resource allocation, 76
response and assessment centres, 92–3
rewards
  managing change, 16–18
  and performance management,
    76–83
  see also pay
Ridley, T. M., 80
Rigby v. *Ferodo* (1987), 103
risk assessments, 132–3
Robb v. *London Borough of Hammersmith
  and Fulham* (1991), 103
Royal Association for Disability and
  Rehabilitation (RADAR), 38
Rutherford, D., 14–15, 15
Ryan, J., 41

safety, health and, 118–33
Scally v. *Southern Health and Social
  Services Board* (1991), 98, 99
Schön, D., 50
School Teachers Review Body,
  17–18
search, 89–90, 91
  see also recruitment
search consultants, 87–8
security, 177
selection, 34–5, 38–40, 89–90
  see also recruitment
selection consultants, 88
selection and implementation of
  information packaged software
  (SiiPS), 175
Senge, P. M., 51–4
service/advisory role, 24–5
Sex Discrimination Acts, 33
sexual harassment, 41–2
shared vision, 52–3
shortlisting, 40
Silver Book, 11, 159, 160, 162, 169
Sim v. *Rotherham Metropolitan Borough
  Council* (1986), 112
Simmons v. *Hoover Ltd* (1977), 103
Sinclair v. *Neighbour* (1967), 103
single loop learning, 49
'skilled incompetence', 50–1
skills, 140, 141, 144
Slater, G., 41
smart cards, 179
Smith Report, 12–13, 14, 164
Social Security Contributions and
  Benefits Act (1992), 102
software, 178–82
  see also human resource information
    systems
Spijkers v. *Gebroeders* (1986), 110
Spurling, A., 37
St John of God (Care Services) Ltd v.
  Brooks (1992), 106
staff appraisal, *see* appraisal
staff development, 40–1, 45–6
  see also learning organization;
    mangement development
Standing Conference of Principals
  (SCOP), 156
statute law, 95
  health and safety, 128

Stevens v. *Bexley Health Authority* (1989), 96
Storey, J., 3
strategic management, 137–40
stress, 81
strike ballots, 114–15
strikes, 113–16, 164
  see also industrial action
student participation rates, 153, 162
sub-contracting, 120, 127–8
support for carers, 42–3
Swieringa, J., 49, 50
System Floors (UK) v. *Daniel* (1982), 99
systems thinking, 53–4

Talbot, C., 150
Tann, J., 45, 54
Taylor, J., 41
Taylor, L., 37
teaching, observation of, 16
teaching quality assessment, 47
team learning, 53
team performance, 77, 79
technical environment, 178–9
Ten Oever v. *Stichting* (1993), 101
termination, 102–3
  see also dismissal
theory in use, 50
Thomas v. *NCB* (1981), 100
Thompson, M., 84
Tight, M., 19
Times Education Supplement, 90
Times Higher Education Supplement, 90, 165
Torrington, D., 4
Trade Union and Labour Relations (Consolidation) Act (1992) (TULRCA), 105, 109, 112–13, 114–15, 115–16
Trade Union Reform and Employment Rights Act (1993) (TURERA), 99, 101–2, 109, 113, 114, 125
trade unions, 26, 96–7, 169
  consultation and redundancies, 108–9
  contracts, 12–13, 27
  industrial relations, 156–7, 159, 161
  rights of association, 112–13
  see also under individual names

training
  courses, 143–5
  equal opportunities, 40–1
  needs and HRIS, 181
  see also management development
Transfer of Undertaking (Protection of Employment) Regulations (1981) (TUPE), 105, 109–10
transfers, business, 109–10
Treasury, 155
tribunals, industrial, 97
triple loop learning, 50
two per cent holdback mechanism, 155, 165, 166, 167–8, 169, 169–70

unconscious learning, 146–7
under-performers, 83–4
understanding, 140, 141, 144
unfair dismissal, 104–7
unions, *see* trade unions
United States of America (USA), 155
universities, 2, 4–5, 152
Universities Funding Council (UFC), 9
University Grants Committee (UGC), 9
user requirements, 175–6

vertical communication, 58–9
vision, shared, 52–3

Wages Act (1986), 111
Warner, D., 2, 4, 83
Watson, D., 19
Western Excavating v. *Sharp* (1978), 105
White Book, 11
Whitley Council system, 159
Wierdsma, A., 49, 50
Wiggins, A. J., 165
Willis, L., 41
Wiluszynski v. *London Borough of Tower Hamlets* (1989), 112
women, 32–3, 35, 38
  see also equal opportunities
Women in Higher Education Network (WHEN), 37
Woodcock, M., 136
Woolf, Geoff, 163
work-based learning model, 147–8
worker status, 97–8
Working Mothers Association, 43
written communication, 57

The Society for Research into Higher Education

The Society for Research into Higher Education exists to stimulate and coordinate research into all aspects of higher education. It aims to improve the quality of higher education through the encouragement of debate and publication on issues of policy, on the organization and management of higher education institutions, and on the curriculum and teaching methods.

The Society's income is derived from subscriptions, sales of its books and journals, conference fees and grants. It receives no subsidies, and is wholly independent. Its individual members include teachers, researchers, managers and students. Its corporate members are institutions of higher education, research institutes, professional, industrial and governmental bodies. Members are not only from the UK, but from elsewhere in Europe, from America, Canada and Australasia, and it regards its international work as amongst its most important activities.

Under the imprint *SRHE & Open University Press*, the Society is a specialist publisher of research, having some 55 titles in print. The Editorial Board of the Society's Imprint seeks authoritative research or study in the above fields. It offers competitive royalties, a highly recognizable format in both hardback and paperback and the worldwide reputation of the Open University Press.

The Society also publishes *Studies in Higher Education* (three times a year), which is mainly concerned with academic issues, *Higher Education Quarterly* (formerly *Universities Quarterly*), mainly concerned with policy issues, *Research into Higher Education Abstracts* (three times a year), and *SRHE News* (four times a year).

The Society holds a major annual conference in December, jointly with an institution of higher education. In 1992, the topic was 'Learning to Effect' with Nottingham Trent University. In 1993, it was 'Governments and the Higher Education Curriculum: Evolving Partnerships' at the University of Sussex in Brighton, and in 1994, 'The Student Experience' at the University of York. Future conferences include in 1995, 'The Changing University' at Heriot-Watt University in Edinburgh.

The Society's committees, study groups and branches are run by the members. The groups at present include:
Teacher Education Study Group
Continuing Education Group
Staff Development Group
Excellence in Teaching and Learning

Benefits to members

Individual

Individual members receive:

- *SRHE News*, the Society's publications list, conference details and other material included in mailings.
- Greatly reduced rates for *Studies in Higher Education* and *Higher Education Quarterly*.
- A 35 per cent discount on all Open University Press & SRHE publications.
- Free copies of the Precedings – commissioned papers on the theme of the Annual Conference.
- Free copies of *Research into Higher Education Abstracts*.
- Reduced rates for conferences.
- Extensive contacts and scope for facilitating initiatives.
- Reduced reciprocal memberships.

Corporate

Corporate members receive:

- All benefits of individual members, plus
- Free copies of *Studies in Higher Education*.
- Unlimited copies of the Society's publications at reduced rates.
- Special rates for its members e.g. to the Annual Conference.

Membership details: SRHE, 3 Devonshire Street,
London, W1N 2BA, UK. Tel: 0171 637 2766
Catalogue: SRHE & Open University Press, Celtic Court,
22 Ballmoor, Buckingham MK18 1XW.
Tel: (01280) 823388

MANAGING CULTURE

Peter Anthony

The management of culture currently dominates the attention of the controllers of both private and public institutions. Culture is believed to provide the key to a commitment to excellence from which will follow success, survival and profit. Some of the extensive literature implies that effective management depends upon cultural management, that nothing else needs to be done.

Managing Culture examines these claims and explains why they have been made. It describes some examples of cultural change as a preliminary to the main purpose which is to present some critical questions about the case for cultural management and about the confusions that lie behind it. The book argues that there are likely to be severe practical difficulties about the control and prediction of the outcome of change in the field of culture. It goes on to suggest that there is a real danger of cultural management causing considerable organizational damage when the instigators of change programmes are easily led to believe that the changes have worked when they have not. In these circumstances, the managers of organizational culture may find that their organizations are no longer under their control: there is a divorce between their perception and reality.

The book ends positively by asserting the advantages of understanding the culture of organizations in order to have some real hope of influencing, rather than controlling, their development.

Contents

Introduction – New cultures and how to grow them – Goals and aspirations – Definitions – Methods – Which culture? – The threat to management: schizophrenia – The threat to leadership: isolation – Culture versus reason – Culture in perspective – References – Index.

128pp   0 335 09788 X (Paperback)   0 335 09789 8 (Hardback)

TOTAL QUALITY MANAGEMENT IN THE PUBLIC SECTOR
AN INTERNATIONAL PERSPECTIVE

Colin Morgan and Stephen Murgatroyd

TQM is a set of concepts, tools and applications which has been so successful in manufacturing industry that we are now witnessing experimentation in the transference of Total Quality Management to the public sector provision of government, health and education in North America, Europe and elsewhere. TQM is starting to set a new paradigm for management approaches in the public sector and 'not for profit' enterprises. All key public service managers will at least need to know the basics of TQM, its possibilities and limitations for the public sector, and particularly the types of applications which could work for them.

For all public sector managers this book provides: a clear understanding of the key concepts of TQM; a critical understanding of their fit and relevance to the public sector; empirical evidence of TQM applications in government, health and education; and exploration of the public sector TQM possibilities yet to be realized. It draws throughout on case examples from Britain, Canada, the USA and continental Europe which illustrate the application of TQM to the public sector.

Contents
Part 1: The nature of TQM in the public sector – Total Quality Management – Leading thinkers for Total Quality Management – Applying Total Quality Management in the public sector – Part 2: Applications of TQM to public sector organizations – TQM and health care – TQM and education – TQM and social services – TQM developments in government service – Issues and problems in adopting TQM in the public sector – Appendix – References – Index.

224pp   0 335 19102 9 (Paperback)   0 335 19103 7 (Hardback)